Informatica® PowerCenter™

The Complete Reference

High Cost

No BI features

This book discusses the usage of software from Informatica and other corporations. Purchase of this book does not entitle the readers to use this software without obtaining a license from the respective corporation first. Examples and code samples in this book are provided on an as is basis with no warranty, implied or otherwise. The author and publisher are not responsible for any data loss or unauthorized data usage that may have resulted in use of the software discussed in this book. Despite of our sincere efforts to keep this book error free, some may have crept in. We would really love to hear back from the readers on any feedback, comments and compliants.

ISBN: 1499766734   ISBN (13): 978-1499766738

Supplemental material of this book is available at:
http://www.powercenterbook.com. Author can be reached at
author@powercenterbook.com

Acknowledgements

When I started writing this book, I seriously underestimated the effort. Without the support and encouragement from many, this book would have never seen the light.

I owe my first and largest debt to my wife, Divya, who supported my efforts way beyond what was fair to expect. Thank you. Your name belongs on the cover of this book every bit as mine does.

Next, a big thank you to my parents, Smt Lakshmi and Sri Gopala Krishna for continously believing in me even when you had no reason to. Thanks are due to my brother Kiran and his wife Geetha. You taught me to think broader and aspire higher. A final thank you to my grandfather Sri Suryanarayana Murthy. His every breath was an inspiration.

I would also like to thank Wilshire Software Technologies, India for introducing me to the Informatica's technologies. I never expected I would love Informatica's products so much so that I will write a book on them.

Table of Contents

Before you begin

An introduction to Informatica PowerCenter

PowerCenter is industry's leading Data Integration software that enables its users to integrate various data stores (such as databases, flat files...) and transform their data in multiple ways. Data Integration software such as PowerCenter provides out of the box integration with many databases and applications, thus allowing the developers to focus on their data transformation requirements. Designer (a PowerCenter client tool) is a graphical user interface based integrated development editor used to develop mappings (unit of code) in PowerCenter. When a mapping is developed, it points to a source (from where data is read) and a target (where data is written). This mapping can then be executed to read data, transform it and then finally load the transformed data into the target. When a database changes, for example, a customer moved his database from Microsoft SQL Server to Oracle, he can simply change the mapping to point to the new source and target without having to worry about any integration challenges. Assuming the connectivity between the PowerCenter and oracle database is established, developers need not worry if their code will properly integrate with the new database. If it's supported, it works. It is that simple. The mapping would run the same regardless of the database to which it is pointing. Developers do not have to bind any drivers or jar files (java archive files) to the code. As long as the Informatica Administrator established a connection between PowerCenter and the database, developers just have to point their mappings to pre-defined connections. This keeps the business logic separate from its integration aspects, thereby, making data integration a lot simpler.

PowerCenter vs. custom coding

The most obvious question, of course, is why PowerCenter? There are so many programming languages out there. A developer can pick any language of his/her choice and build a code that pretty much does the same as a PowerCenter mapping. This section of the book compares PowerCenter with Custom Coding to set a perspective for the reader.

To understand this better, let's look at some steps that need to be performed in a typical java program to write a class file that will read a table and write the contents into another table in a different schema/database.

1. Import proper packages to interact with databases
2. Create a JDBC URL to connect to the source database
3. Setup the username, password and other properties for source
4. Create a JDBC URL to connect to the target database
5. Setup the username, password and other properties for target
6. Create a source connection with the source JDBC URL and source properties
7. Create a target connection with the target JDBC URL and target properties
8. Build a SQL statement to read from the source
9. Execute the source SQL query and fetch a result set
10. Create a statement from the target connection
11. For every record in the source:
    a. Execute an Insert SQL on the target statement
12. Close the target statement
13. Close the source statement
14. Close the target connection
15. Close the source connection
16. Compile the java program

17. Run the program
18. Validate the results

Now, let's look at the steps that need to be performed in the PowerCenter clients:

1. Import the Source table definitions into the PowerCenter designer
2. Import the target table definitions into the PowerCenter designer
3. Create a mapping (PowerCenter unit of code) and map the data flow to indicate which columns of source flow into the target table
4. Create connections to point to the source and the targets
5. Create a session in a workflow – provide the connections to source and target databases
6. Run the workflow
7. Validate the results

Now, without getting into the technical details of how both java program and PowerCenter mapping are developed, if we compare the time spent on each step in both the approaches, it is evident that while writing a java program, a developer will have to spend enough time on every step from properly importing the packages to creating a connection, statement and result set. Contrarily, a PowerCenter developer focuses his/her entire energy on defining the data flow and connecting to the source/target databases. In the simplest example above, we have not even considered many aspects such as the program's ability to log debug information to a log file, which is a very important requirement while building enterprise applications. All such additional features require additional coding and, hence, extra effort in testing, while in PowerCenter, a session log is, by default, available for every session that is built and developers can choose the level of information at which they expect PowerCenter to log.

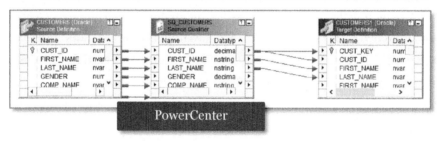

It is also important to understand that a DI tool such as PowerCenter is not intended to replace programming languages. It is intended only to perform Data Integration in a smart way. For example, a simple "Hello World" program which is extremely easy to write in Java cannot be built in PowerCenter because PowerCenter needs a source of information and a target to write to and is not a tool to build GUIs.

As we proceed further in the book, we will learn more of such differences and see how DI tools such as PowerCenter not only have smaller learning curves but also have a more productive output in lesser time, as far as data integration is concerned.

Who is this book for?

The PowerCenter developer community widely refers to the PowerCenter help manuals and knowledgebase. This book does not intent to replace these resources. This book only serves as a starting point to new developers and as an additional reference to the experienced developers. While the help manuals are apt for a quick reference, they do not have a structured approach to teach PowerCenter. This book aims to deliver exactly that: a structured way of learning PowerCenter. This book also attempts to equip its readers with adequate skills to be an Informatica Certified Developer. While the certification is not the sole agenda of the book, the book attempts to teach PowerCenter in a way that supplements the reader's preparation for the certification.

How is this book organized?

For easy reference, the book is divided into parts and each part is divided into chapters. The first part of this book introduces the readers to PowerCenter. It talks about the PowerCenter architecture and some underlying concepts that form the foundation of the knowledge shared in the rest of the book. This part purely focuses on familiarizing the user with the PowerCenter IDE, different windows, tabs and dialog boxes that reader will use in the due course of the development. We write our first program here. The second part (Core DI) introduces the readers to the core development aspects of PowerCenter. During this part, we focus primarily on learning different types of transformations. A transformation is a logic unit that can transform the data given to it in a specific way. Transformations are to PowerCenter mappings what functions are to traditional programs. The third part (Advanced DI) teaches advanced concepts such as flat files, XMLs, change detection, etc. In this part, we go beyond transformations and start looking at the bigger picture that paves way into the next part. The fourth part is Enterprise Data Integration. Here we learn about advanced topics such as High Availability, Partitioning and Pushdown optimization. Towards the end of this part, we learn about governance and best practices. The final part of this book is an addendum that introduces the readers to next generation Informatica tools such as DQ platform: Informatica Developer.

PowerCenter version

At the time of writing this book, the latest PowerCenter version is 9.6.0. Therefore, this book refers to all PowerCenter objects with regard to the same version. If you are on an older version (8.5 or above), the concepts pretty much remain the same – with few exceptions. If you are using a later version than the one used in this book, we hope that the concepts still remain the same but we strongly advise you to read the release notes to account for any differences.

Labs and resources

Labs in this book are available online at www.powercenterbook.com

Legend

The book uses several icons to represent different kinds of text. They are detailed as below.

 This is information

 This is a best practice. Try to follow it as much as you can

 This is a tip. It is good to know some tips. Isn't it?

 This is very important. Please pay attention

 This icon indicates that to perform activities in current section, you may need administrative privileges

This icon is used to represent the labs. Labs help you understand steps involved in specific tasks

This icon represents internal or external reference. This book has references to PowerCenter manuals, Support Knowledgebase and other resources or other sections within this book itself

This icon is used to indicate that developers need to contact their PowerCenter Administrators/DBAs to get some of the information discussed in this section

PART 1

INTRODUCTION TO

POWERCENTER

1

PowerCenter Architecture

1.1   Introduction to PowerCenter

PowerCenter is a Data Integration engine that can perform high speed data extraction, transformation and loading. Its rich GUI based Integrated Development Environment allows rapid development with minimal code. PowerCenter has an extensive transformation language and its code does not need to be compiled. Using vibe virtual data machine underneath, PowerCenter allows universal data access. In other words, a mapping can be written to access one data store and can be modified to access another data store without affecting rest of the logic.

1.2   Informatica Vibe virtual data machine

Informatica's Vibe Virtual data machine allows the users to "map (code) once and deploy anywhere". Powered by Vibe, Informatica PowerCenter mappings are deployed on premise for enterprise data integration. They can be deployed to

Informatica Cloud, Informatica Data Quality (developer tool) or even to cutting edge Hadoop platform, with few exceptions

 This chapter of the book introduces the PowerCenter concepts and architecture; however it does not delve into the details. As we go through the subsequent chapters in this book and our understanding of PowerCenter evolves, we will revisit some of these concepts in detail.

1.3   PowerCenter components

PowerCenter architecture is based on client-server model. It consists of PowerCenter server and PowerCenter client tools. Below is a list of all of the components that are part of the PowerCenter architecture

1.3.1   PowerCenter Domain

In its simple terms, Domain can be defined as an environment. You will have a PowerCenter domain for each environment. For example, if you have Development, Test and Production environments, you essentially create 3 different domains – one for each environment. Domain information is stored in a set of tables, which are created and configured as part of PowerCenter server installation. These domain tables store metadata related to services within the PowerCenter, users, groups, etc...

1.3.2   Informatica Node

A node is a machine participating in the Informatica Domain. Typically, a node consists of CPU, Memory and Disk. A node can be active or passive depending on the services it is hosting. Informatica domain can consist of more than one node. These nodes can host a wide variety of operating systems such Windows, Linux, HP-UX, etc. Informatica server software is installed on each node participating in a domain.

1.3.3   PowerCenter Services

A domain consists of several services, such as license service, PowerCenter Repository Service and PowerCenter Integration Service. Each of this service provides a unique functionality to clients.

1.3.4   PowerCenter Repository Service (PCRS)

A PowerCenter Repository is a set of tables created when your Informatica Administrator creates a PowerCenter Repository Service during post installation process. The entire code that a developer builds is stored inside the repository. Repository contains hundreds of tables, whereas PowerCenter stores the developer's code within these tables very intelligently. It is hard to manually look at these tables and comprehend and hence, they should be left alone unless there is a dire need to look at them. Along with developer's code, repository also contains metadata like definitions of the tables used by the mappings, source and target connections, etc...

When the developer runs a Workflow (a job in PowerCenter), its information is fetched from the repository. Thereafter, the runtime statistics are stored back in the repository again. Hence the repository is a key and live element in PowerCenter architecture

1.3.5   PowerCenter Integration Service (PCIS)

An integration service is the engine that actually runs PowerCenter workflows (jobs). Integration services continuously interact with PowerCenter Repository to fetch the information of the job it is about to start and keeps the repository up-to-date regarding the status of the job, including the processed row counts. Each workflow is assigned to an integration service. Each integration service can run one or more workflows at the same time. Workflows can also be scheduled to run on Integration Service at specific date/time.

1.3.6   Grid

A grid is a collection of nodes. A PowerCenter Integration Service can run upon an individual node or on a grid. When an Integration Service runs on a grid, it automatically load balances the workflows that it is executing, such that the resources (nodes) are optimally utilized. When a node in the domain fails, integration service can be configured to failover the workflows running on that node to another node(s) to provide a seamless failover of the jobs.

1.3.7   Putting it all together

Now that we have a basic understanding of each component, let's take a look at it all together. See the picture below.

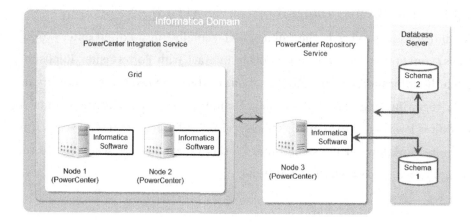

The above picture represents a single Informatica domain, containing 3 nodes. Out of these, two nodes (node 1 and node 2) are participating together to form a grid. An integration service is running atop of this grid. Node 3 is hosting a PowerCenter repository service, whose repository tables lie in the schema 1 of the database server. The schema 2 of the same database server hosts the domain metadata tables. Informatica server software is installed on all the 3 nodes.

While there are many possible configurations for the given nodes, the one above is an example for understanding how the components fit together in the Informatica PowerCenter architecture.

1.4   Repository objects

As mentioned before, PowerCenter Repository consists of several tables that hold the different objects created using PowerCenter client tools. In this section of the book, we look at different types of objects that can be created in a PowerCenter repository using various client tools. With a few exceptions, objects in repository are hierarchical in nature as discussed below.

1.4.1 Folders

Folders are the top level objects that can be created within a repository. A folder consists of several objects that form PowerCenter code. Most of the objects created by a developer during the lifecycle of development are stored within a folder. This includes mappings, sessions and workflows. It is typical to have a folder for each project being developed in the repository. It is not uncommon for customers to have hundreds of folders in the same repository, even though the performance of such a repository depends on the amount of objects within each folder and the number of users connected to it at any given time. Examples of folder names are:

→ DataWarehouse

→ DataMart

→ ProjectX

→ CustomerInfoDB

1.4.2 Sources

Sources are table definitions imported from a database into the PowerCenter repository. These table definitions are used while developing mappings to define the attributes to read from. Once imported, the table definitions remain independent of the underlying database. Hence, if a table definition in the source database changes, it needs to be re-imported again. Sources are stored within folders. Thus, a source can be imported into multiple folders. In which case, each definition is unique and must be maintained separately. Sources can be grouped into data sources. They must be unique within a data source. So, within a given data source in a given folder, there can be only one source having a certain name. Developers can organize the sources into different data sources as they see fit. However, each source definition can be associated with only one data source. The same data source can be imported into PowerCenter repository under different data sources. For example, a source table "employees" can exist in data sources "Data Warehouse" and "Data Mart". These two table definitions need not be identical. But "Data Warehouse" data source itself cannot have two tables of the name "employee".

1.4.3   Targets

Conceptually similar to sources, targets are table definitions imported into PowerCenter repository to define what attributes are being written to. Targets are also stored within folders, although they do not have any grouping (such as data sources). Hence, every target definition within a folder must be unique, where uniqueness is defined by the table name.

1.4.4   Transformations

Transformations are not only the most fundamental objects in PowerCenter repository but are also the most important. Fundamentally, a transformation processes the data. This includes modifying data, reordering it, transposing it and, in some cases, generating it as well. There are several built-in transformations such as sorter, rank and aggregator. But developers can also build custom transformations and embed java code into PowerCenter. Each transformation is built to perform one unique operation on data. Developer can combine any permissible combinations of these transformations to meet their data processing needs

1.4.5   Ports

Columns in transformations are known as ports. Data once read from a data source is converted into PowerCenter's universal data format. All the transformations exchange information through the ports. While writing the data to the target, PowerCenter Integration Service converts the data from universal format to native format of the target databases. Therefore, the source and targets contain columns, whereas the transformations contain ports.

1.4.6   Mappings

Mappings are units of code that read data off one or more sources, optionally transform it and write it to one or more targets. A mapping, in its simplest form, is a data flow that defines how the data moves from a given source to a given target and how it is to be transformed in between. In a simple pass through mapping, the data is written as-it-is to the target without any changes. In a more complex mapping, data may perform change detection, then sort, aggregate and finally calculate summary of transactions and load them to the target.

1.4.7   Session Task

When a mapping is created, the developer defines the data flow from a source to a target with or without transformations in between. These source and target definitions might have been imported previously using the source analyzer and the target designer. It is important to note that while doing so, PowerCenter only imports the table definition and does not retain the connectivity information such as the database name, user name, password. This is ideal because when a developer imports table definitions, he/she might have done so with their individual logins which usually have read only access to data. However, when the job runs, we would like it to use an application having write access to it. This keeps the application independent of any individual credentials. So the connectivity to the source and the target needs to be specified to be able to execute the mapping. This is exactly where the session fits in. A session contains connectivity and runtime information for a mapping. The session itself does not have any code but it is linked to a mapping and associates the runtime configuration to it. While a mapping defines "how" the data flows, session defines "where" the data comes from and where it goes. A session also defines other runtime metadata such as commit interval, schema/owner name overrides, etc.

1.4.8 Workflows

 A workflow defines the logical order of execution of tasks such as sessions. While a session itself is linked to a mapping and hence indirectly defines the data flow between a source and target, most data integration applications are usually more complex than interacting with a single source/target. When there are multiple sessions involved, there usually is an order in which they need to be executed. For example, before loading transactions data, one has to ensure that the customers' and products' data for the corresponding transactions is up-to-date. This ensures the data integrity and avoids any key violations. Hence, a workflow is created where the order in which the sessions need to be executed can be defined. Sessions can be configured to run in sequence or in parallel or a combination of both.

 Workflow is the only runnable unit. So, even if there is a single session, the session is added to a workflow and the workflow is executed.

1.5 What happens when you run a workflow?

When a PowerCenter workflow is ran, it initializes itself and then it initializes the session(s) within it in the order defined. When a session initializes, it establishes connectivity to its source and target database(s). If the mapping is built to read from file(s), it will verify that the source file indeed exists. If the mapping is built to write to a file, it will attempt to create the file/overwrite it/append to it depending on the session configuration. Then it will start reading the source data – one block at a time. Once a block of data is read, it is transformed and then written to the target. Each block of data is independently read, transformed and written in parallel. Look at the picture below

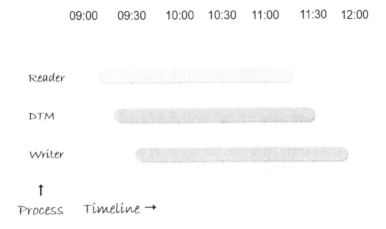

While a session is physically a single component, it depends on several processes to perform its tasks at runtime. The 3 most important processes are shown in the picture above. Reader is a process that reads data from the sources defined in the mapping. DTM is the Data Transformation Manager (engine), powered by vibe the Informatica's data virtual machine, which transforms the data as per the mapping specification. Writer is the process that writes the data to the target. In the above picture, the processes are shown against a timeline. In the sample timeline above, it can be noticed that the reader process starts at about 09:05 and starts buffering blocks of data. Once it has enough blocks to transform, the DTM kicks in at about 09:20 and starts transforming the data that is already buffered by the reader. Once the DTM has transformed enough blocks, the writer process is triggered (at about 09:35), which starts writing the transformed data into the target. From about

09:35, all the three processes run in parallel. Writer is writing the transformed data provided by DTM, while DTM is transforming the data buffered by reader and the reader is buffering the next set of blocks. At 11:15, reader has completed buffering the last set of blocks from the source, while DTM completes transforming at 11:30 and the writer finally completes writing its last block at about 11:50.

 Timeline referenced above is not an accurate representation of the time taken by reader, DTM and writer processes. It just conveys the general sense of their interaction with each other.

1.6   PowerCenter clients

PowerCenter has more than one client. In this section, we take a look at them and understand their functionality and usage.

1.6.1   Informatica Administrator

Informatica Administrator is a thin client. It is a web based application that can be accessed from a browser by pointing to its URL. Administrator is used to administer the PowerCenter environment including:

→ Creating and managing services (like repository service, integration service, etc...)

→ Authentication and authorization

→ Create and manager users

→ Create and manage groups

→ Establish and maintain AD authentication

→ Manage privileges and roles

→ Manage connection objects

→ Manage domain logs

→ Start, shutdown, restart services

→ Backup, restore repositories and domain

1.6.2   Repository Manager

As the name suggests, Repository Manager is used to manage the repository. Typically, it is used to perform the following:

→ Create and manage folders

→ Manage folder permissions

→ Query the repository objects

→ Deployments: Copy folders and objects from one repository to another

1.6.3   Designer

Designer is one of the tools where PowerCenter developers spend most of their time. This is where they define the data flows called mappings, import source and target table definitions to use into the mappings. This is where they debug their mappings, build reusable transformations, etc. In short, this is where the development of the data integration processes happens.

1.6.4   Workflow Manager

Workflow manager is where sessions and workflows are developed and managed. Workflow manager is also used to develop and manage:

→ Relational connections

→ Application and other connections

→ Session tasks, command tasks and other tasks

→ Reusable tasks as such as command tasks

→ Reusable sessions

→ Worklets

→ Assign workflows to run on Integration services and grids

→ Start, stop, recover workflows

1.6.5   Workflow Monitor

Workflow monitor is a read-only client where developers can monitor and keep track of their workflows and sessions. One can view the current status of a running or completed sessions, row counts for each source and target, error messages and detailed session and workflow logs. Developers can also restart and recover their workflows from the workflow monitor.

  All PowerCenter clients can connect to more than one domain/repository at the same time.

2

Installing PowerCenter clients

2.1 How to get the software?

Getting the PowerCenter software is a very straight forward process. Raise a shipping SR in the Informatica Support. Support will provide a download link to download the software along with a username and password.

 Usually you receive the links to download PowerCenter server, client and documentation together. It is recommended to install the Informatica Documentation as well for easy reference of product manuals.

Navigate to the URL provided to you in the email to download the software. You will be prompted to login.

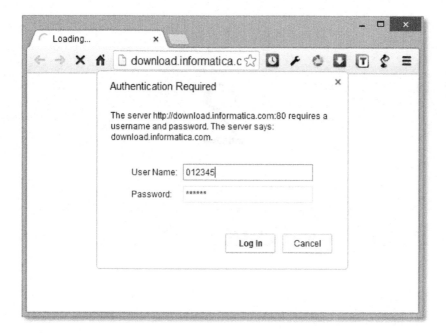

Type in the username and password provided to you by Informatica along with the download links. Your username is usually a number.

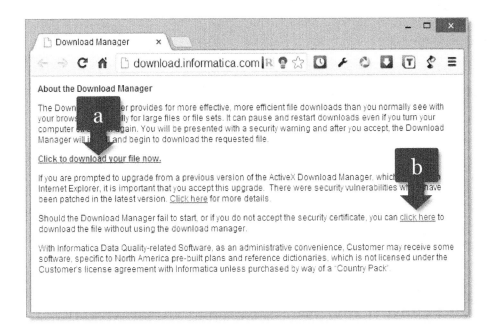

Once you login, you will see a page similar to above picture. You will be presented with two options: (a) to download using a download manager or (b) to download directly. Downloading via the download manager gives you the option to restart/resume downloads in case of network failures.

 Informatica uses a JAVA based download manager to download the software. Ensure that you have an updated JAVA on your machines to avoid issues during the download.

Once you click on the download manager link (a), a JAVA prompt may appear asking for your permission to run. If it does, click on the Run button. A Save dialog box will appear. Choose a location where you would like to save the installer and then click Save. The download manager will start the download as shown below:

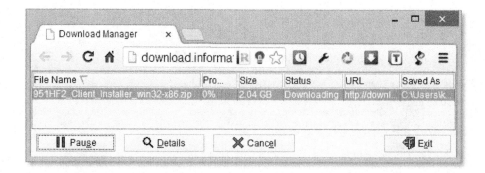

Wait for the download to finish. Once the download is complete, extract the zip file.

2.2 Installing Informatica clients

 Informatica client installer is a consolidated installation that is used to install more than just PowerCenter. At the time of writing this book, Informatica client installer is used to install:

→   PowerCenter clients

→   Developer client

→   B2B Data Transformation client

While the scope of this book is just PowerCenter, due to its relative simplicity, this part of book will also discuss installation of the other 2 clients as well.

2.2.1 Step 1: Start the installer

Go to the directory where you extracted the zip file downloaded from Informatica. Right click the installer (install.bat) and "Run as Administrator".

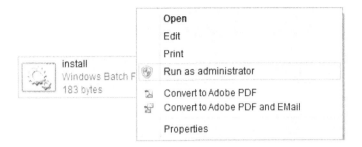

Windows will prompt you to allow the program to make changes to the computer, click "Yes". The installer will take few minutes to initialize.

2.2.2 Step 2: Choose to install or upgrade

The installer will provide you two options:

→ Install clients

→ Upgrade existing clients to the latest version

For a fresh install, choose Install clients. If you already have one or more clients, select the ones you need to additionally install.

2.2.3 Step 3: Verify and accept requirements

The installer will display the minimum requirements for the installation to be successful. This includes the operating system version and the 4 GB disk space requirement. Simply click "Next".

2.2.4 Step 4: Choose clients to install

The installer will present you option to choose among the clients you want to install. The Informatica client installer is a consolidated installer used to install clients for more than one product. Here are the three options the installer will present

→ PowerCenter client: for PowerCenter

→ Informatica Developer: for Data Quality, Data Services and other products

→ Data Transformation Studio: for B2B Data Transformation

Based on what you are licensed for, choose the clients you want to install on your machine.

2.2.5 Step 5: Specify Installation directory

The recommended location will be C:\Informatica\96. You can choose any location of your choice.

 It is recommended not to use any spaces in the install location

2.2.6 Step 6: Eclipse setup (optional)

If you only chose PowerCenter in Step 4, skip this step. You will not see this screen. This step will appear only if you choose B2B Data Transformation studio to be installed. Installer will prompt you to specify Eclipse installation. You will be provided with two options:

→ Install Data Transformation Studio and a standalone copy of eclipse

→ Install Data Transformation Studio on an existing Eclipse installation

Eclipse is an IDE that is also used by several other programming languages such as Java. If you are a Java programmer, or have any Java IDEs, you probably already have eclipse installed on your machine. You can then, choose the option to select an existing eclipse installation. In such a case, remember that if you ever uninstall the other Java IDE environment, it might affect your B2B client installation. Make your selection and click "Next".

If you are not sure, if you already have eclipse installed on your machine, go ahead and select 'install a standalone copy of eclipse'. You can have more than one copy of eclipse on a PC.

2.2.7 Step 7: Review and start the installation

Installer will show you the choices you made so far one last time, before it starts setting up the clients. Review them and click "Install".

2.2.8 Step 8: Installation progress

Installer will start copying files to your machine and configuring them. This process takes about 15 minutes to complete.

2.2.9 Step 9: Installation summary

The installer will show a summary of the installation and the path to the install log. Click "Done" to close the installer.

Once the installation is complete you must logout and login again to complete additional system configurations.

Post installation, the client installation log is available at
<Installation path>\Informatica_xxx_Client.log
Where xxx is the version of Informatica Clients you installed.

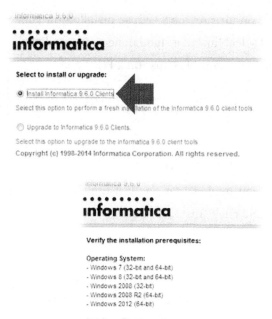

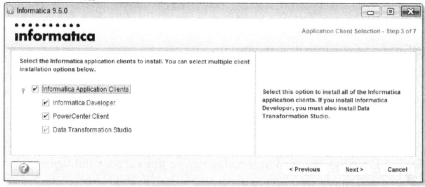

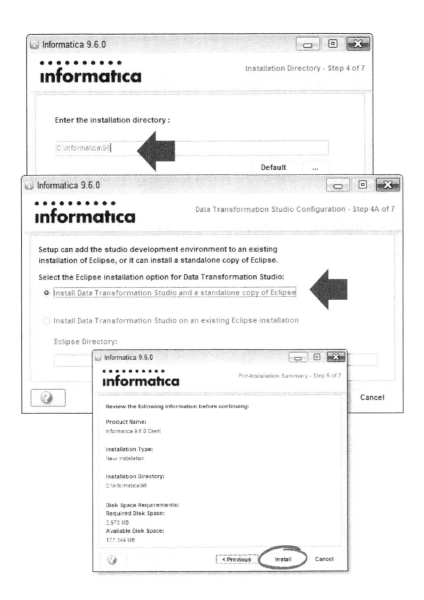

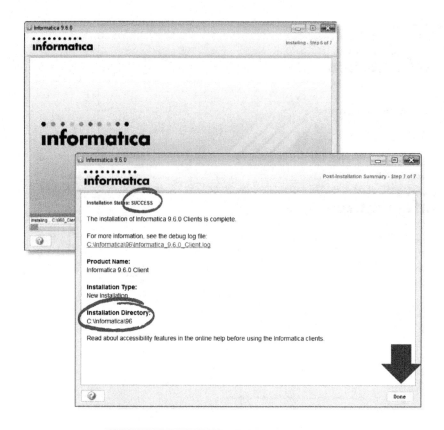

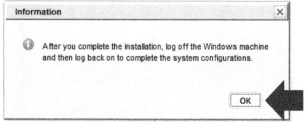

2.3   First time configuration

Once you have installed the PowerCenter clients, you need to perform a first-time configuration. You need to let the PowerCenter client know the details of the PowerCenter server so that it can communicate with it. Note that even though this is a first time configuration, it is not necessarily a one-time configuration. You will have to repeat these steps for each domain you wish to access from this client. If you have 3 domains, say Development, Test and Production, you would need to repeat these steps 3 times.

2.3.1 Step 1: Open PowerCenter client

Go to the Start menu → `Informatica` → `PowerCenter` client to launch the `PowerCenter Designer`. If a tip shows up, click "`OK`" to close it.

2.3.2 Step 2: Configure domains

Click on the Repositories in the left hand side navigator. Then go to `Repository` menu → `Configure domains`

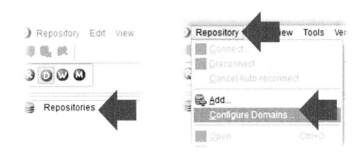

2.3.3 Step 3: Add a domain

Click on the new icon to add a domain

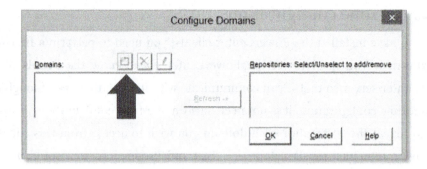

Add domain dialog box will appear. Provide the domain name, the master gateway node and the port number on which Informatica services are running. This information should be provided to you by your Informatica Administrator.

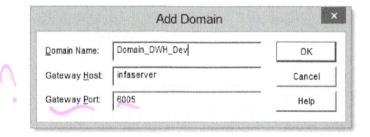

Click OK to save the domain. PowerCenter will automatically refresh the Configure Domains to display all available repositories in the domain.

2.3.4 Step 4: Select the repositories in the domain

Check the repositories you would like to add. Then click OK. The repositories will now be available in the designer

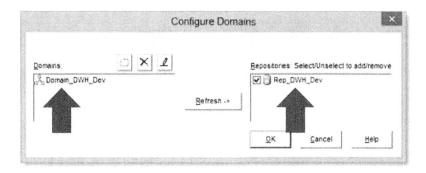

2.3.5 Step 5: Login to the designer

Double click on the repository you just added or right click on the repository and click "Connect". A login dialog box appears. Provide your username, password and the security domain. If you do not have AD authentication setup, your security domain will be Native and the option to change it will be greyed out.

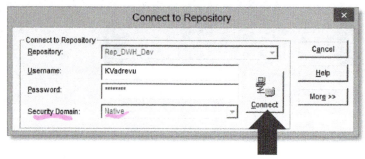

3

The PowerCenter client UI

3.1   What about the clients?

PowerCenter has more than one client. So, it could get really confusing for the beginners if they are not understood correctly. There is a good reason behind different clients' tools – they serve different purposes. In this chapter, we introduce the workspace of the clients. This chapter will introduce you to the UI of the clients so that it is easy for you when we go to the next chapter – to build your first PowerCenter application.

3.2   Designer

PowerCenter Designer has a unique interface that allows developers to rapidly develop data integration applications. A developer builds and manages several kinds of objects in Designer, primarily:

→ Source definitions

→ Target definitions

→ Reusable transformations

→ Mapplets

→ Mappings

Although we have not discussed some of these objects yet, we will include them in chapters ahead. For now, to get started, it is enough to know that such objects exist.

Take a look at the snapshot of the PowerCenter Designer. Some of the highlighted components are:

a. Menus and toolbar: Menus contain various commands that allow you to do different activities based on your current operations. Toolbars provide quick way to access some of the popular commands that allow you rapid data flow development.

b. Repository navigator: Navigator lists all the mapping related objects in the repository in a tree fashion for quick access. To open any object, right click on the object and click open.

c. Workspace: This is where developers perform most of their activities. This is where you import table definitions, develop reusable transformations and mappings.

d. Output window: It is a small dock able window at the bottom of the screen. It contains several tabs such as save, validate, etc. Each of these tabs display messages from PowerCenter server. For example, when you save a mapping, the response from Repository Service is displayed in the "Save" window. Apart from the general UI elements, the following elements are of special interest for developers. Some of them are highlighted in the next picture.

e. Client tools: Quickly open/jump between PowerCenter client tools with a single click. These can also be accessed from the Tools menu.

f. Transformations toolbar: This toolbar can be used to quickly add different kinds of transformations into a mapping with one-click. These transformations can also be created by accessing the menu Transformations→Create.

g. Tools: There are 5 tools that can be accessed by this toolbar:

   → Source Analyzer: Switch to this layout to import source table definitions

   → Target Designer: Switch to this layout to import target table definitions

   → Transformation Developer: Switch to this layout to create reusable transformations. Non-reusable transformations are created within the mapping itself

   → Mapplet designer: Switch to this layout to create mapplets (reusable mappings)

   → Mapping designer: Switch to this layout to create mappings (unit of code in PowerCenter)

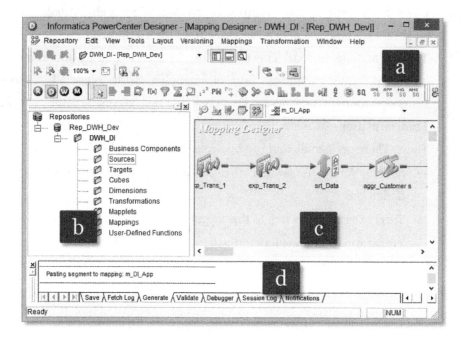

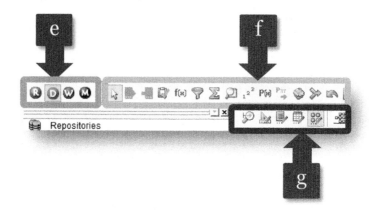

3.3 Workflow Manager

Workflow manager is the PowerCenter client used to define session tasks and workflows. In some ways, its user interface is quite similar to that of the PowerCenter Designer. Additionally, it has several unique features of its own. First, let's look at the layout of workflow manager:

a. Menus and Toolbar: Menus contain various commands that allow you to perform different activities based on your current operations. Toolbars provide a quick way to access some of the popular commands that allow rapid development of workflows.

b. Repository navigator: Navigator lists all the workflow related objects in the repository in a tree fashion for quick access. To open any object, right click on the object and click open.

c. Workspace: This is where developers perform most of their activities, while in workflow manager. This is where workflows, session tasks and email tasks are created/edited.

d. Output window: It is a small dock able window at the bottom of the screen, and contains several tabs such as save, validate, etc. Each of these tabs display messages from PowerCenter server. For example, the "Notifications" tab will display any notifications from the Integration Service, like workflow start notice.

e. Connections: Access relational, FTP, queue, application connections in a single click. Each of these buttons open a corresponding connection editor that lets you manages connections. These can also be accessed from Connections menu.

f. Tasks toolbar: This toolbar can be used to quickly add different kinds of tasks (such as sessions, emails and commands) into a workflow with one-click. These can also be created by accessing the menu Tasks → Create.

g. Tools: There are 3 tools that can be accessed by this toolbar:
   → Task developer: Go to this layout to create reusable tasks
   → Worklet designer: Go to this layout to create worklets (reusable workflows). Although we have not discussed the concept of worklets yet, we will discuss it in subsequent chapters.

→ Workflow designer: Go to this layout to create and manage workflows. Workflows are logical order of execution of the tasks and are the executable code units in PowerCenter.

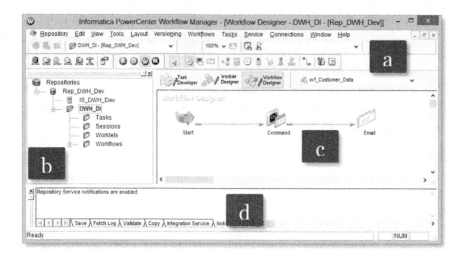

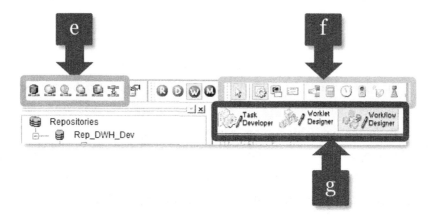

3.4   Workflow Monitor

M   Workflow monitor is where you monitor your currently running jobs and history of the job executions. You can also use this UI to fetch session and workflow logs. Session logs contain detailed information about every step of the session execution. Workflow monitors present a Gantt chart (timeline) view and a Task (list) view in which developers can browse through the scheduled, running and complete workflows, sessions and other tasks and access their status and logs.

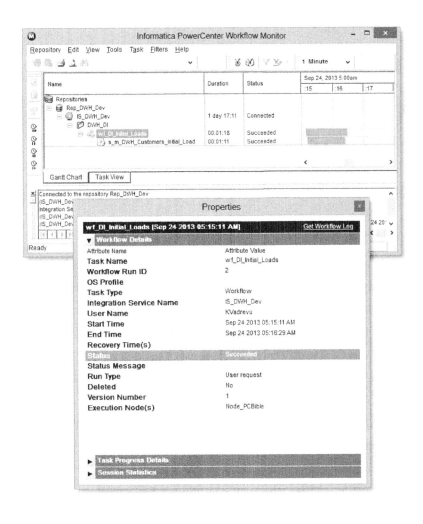

4

Lab 1 – Your first PowerCenter Application

4.1   As we begin lab 1...

Now you are ready to develop your first Data Integration application in PowerCenter. But before we begin, here's what you need to know first. In this chapter, we will build an application that will read the customers table from CustDB schema (Customers Database) and load them to DWH schema (Data Warehouse) in an Oracle database. While most of the demos and exercises in this chapter use an Oracle database, you can perform the same steps, with few exceptions, on almost any database supported by PowerCenter. This application will perform a straight load from this source table to the data warehouse schema. There will be no transformation of the data at this point. As we go further into the book, we will evolve our case study and application to a full-fledged data integration application by adding more sources, targets and transformations. But for now, we keep things simple.

4.1.1 Prerequisites

This is a list of what you need to have ready to start building this application

a. A source database/schema with the customers table

b. Any relational database/schema with the customers dimension

c. Username, password, connectivity details to both source and the warehouse

d. A complete PowerCenter server setup

    1. A PowerCenter repository service configured and ready to use

    2. A PowerCenter Integration service configured and ready to use

    3. A username and password (native authentication or AD authentication) setup for you

    4. The user should have the following permissions and privileges:

        a. At least 1 folder with write access

        b. Ability to import table definitions in to PowerCenter client

        c. Ability to work with the client tools: Designer, Workflow Manager, Workflow Monitor

e. PowerCenter clients installed on your local desktop

f. PowerCenter domain configured in the PowerCenter client

4.1.2 Steps to be executed

Here is a comprehensive list of all the steps we will perform as part of building this application. Each of these steps is explained in detail in the subsequent sections of the book:

a. Define the data mapping

    1. Open the PowerCenter Designer

    2. Login to the PowerCenter repository

  3. Open the repository folder

  4. Import the source definitions

  5. Import the target definitions

  6. Create a mapping

 b. Setup Runtime information

  1. Login to the PowerCenter Workflow Manager

  2. Open the repository folder

  3. Create a new workflow

  4. Create a new session

  5. Create a new source connection

  6. Create a new target connection

  7. Edit the session, assign the connections

 c. Execute and Monitor

  1. Run the workflow

  2. Monitor the workflow for its completion in Workflow Monitor

  3. Login to the database to verify the data load results

4.2   Define data mapping

Any data mapping begins with a data definition. To be able to map the data flow from a source to a target, we should first define them. Fortunately, we do not have to define the tables in PowerCenter from scratch. PowerCenter provides a way to import the definitions from databases, files and applications. In this section, we will learn to import the definitions from source and target databases to PowerCenter. PowerCenter uses ODBC connectivity to import these definitions. Hence, we need to create ODBC connections first. We will create 2 ODBC connections – one for the Source and one for the Target

4.2.1   Creating an ODBC connection

Go to `Control Panel` → `All Control Panel Items` → `Administrative tools` → `ODBC Data Sources (32-bit)`. Note that the PowerCenter clients are 32-bit software and do not have access to 64-bit ODBC drivers. Go to `System DSN` tab, click on the `Add` button. Choose a database driver based on the database from which the tables need to be imported.

> It is important to use the native drivers or Data Direct drivers (installed along with PowerCenter client) for the database you are trying to import to avoid any unexpected issues during the execution.

4.2.2   Import tables into PowerCenter Designer

Now open PowerCenter Designer and login to the Repository. In the Repository Navigator, double click on the PowerCenter folder to open it (or right click on the folder and select `Open`). The workspace will open to the right. Switch to the Source Analyzer (). Go to the `Sources`→`Import from the database` (). In the `ODBC data source` drop down, select the ODBC connection you created in the previous section. Provide a username, owner name (owner of the tables you are attempting to import), and the corresponding password. Then click `connect`. PowerCenter will display all the tables present in that schema in the "`select tables`" tree. Click on the Customers table and then click `OK` to import the table definitions.

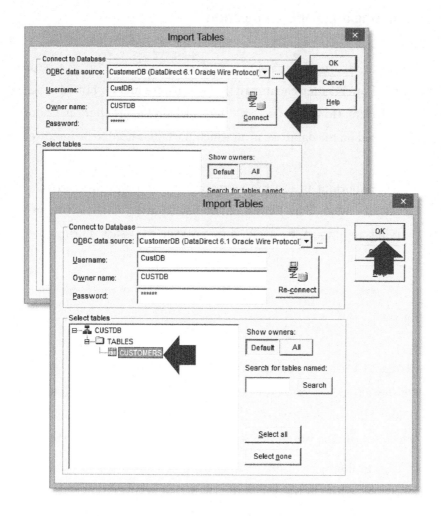

Selected tables will now be imported into the Source Analyzer as shown in the picture. Also, notice the way the tables are grouped in to the ODBC name (CustomerDB in this case) in the source section within the repository navigator.

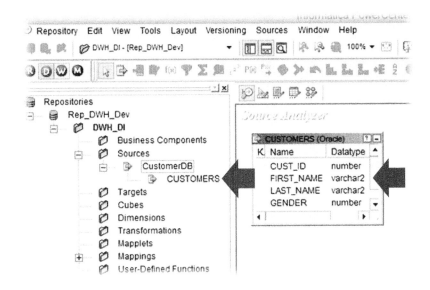

Now repeat the same steps to import target definitions:

a. Switch to target designer (⬇️)

b. Go to the Targets → Import from database (📇)

c. Import Tables dialog box is displayed

d. Provide a username, owner name and password to connect to the database
    (a data warehouse in this example) and then click connect

e. Select the Customers table and then click OK

f. Customers table is now imported into the Target Designer and can be seen
    in the Repository Navigator. Note that unlike the sources; target tables are
    not grouped based on their ODBC name.

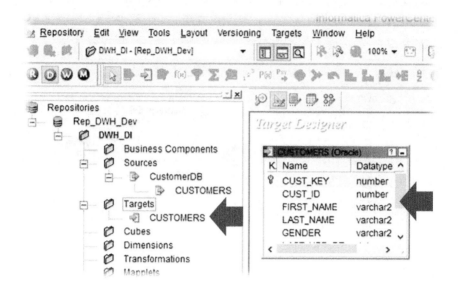

4.2.3   Save the changes

Yes, this is important. The tables we imported are not yet saved to the repository. To save them, go to the Repository menu and click Save (🖫).

 Changes to the repository are not automatically saved. Remember to save your work frequently.

4.2.4   Define the mapping

Now that we have table definitions within PowerCenter, it is time to create the mapping. We begin by switching to mapping designer (🖧). Then go to the Mappings menu →Create (⊢⊩). Provide the mapping name as `m_DWH_Customers_Initial_Load`. This will create a blank mapping in the workspace. Now, drag the source object (CUSTOMERS) from the repository navigator into the workspace. You will notice that two objects will appear in the workspace.

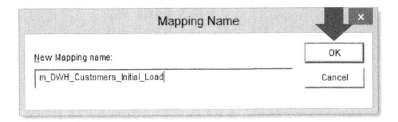

The object with the green title bar is the source definition, which appears with another object known as Source Qualifier. The columns in your source definition are linked (blue arrows) to the source qualifier automatically. We will learn more about Source Qualifier later on.

Similarly, drag the target (CUSTOMERS) from repository navigator into workspace. You will notice that the target will appear in the workspace alone with no links to any other object in the workspace. Your mapping will look similar to this:

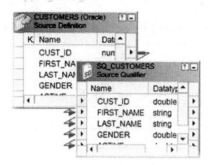

Now, we have to establish links from the source qualifier to target. To do so, we will drag one column at a time from the Source Qualifier and drop it on the target transformation's appropriate column. While doing so, you will notice that the cursor changes to . This indicates that when you drop it, a link will be established between the column you dragged and the column you dragged it on to.

> When using drag-n-drop to link ports you must drop the port on the column name and not on the transformation's title bar.

Here is a table showing how to establish the links:

Source Object	Source Column	Target Object	Target Column
sq_customers	cust_id	customers1	cust_key
sq_customers	cust_id	customers1	cust_id
sq_customers	first_name	customers1	first_name
sq_customers	last_name	customers1	last_name

Notice that we have the same `CUST_ID` column populating in both `CUST_ID` and `CUST_KEY` in the target. Now, your mapping should look like this:

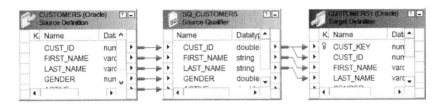

Lab 1 mapping

We have intentionally left the other fields. We will populate them in the subsequent chapters. Now, we save the mapping to complete the designer.

4.2.5   Summary

Let us try to understand what we just did. Everything we did so far can be summarized as:

> "Read `Customers` table data (from `CustomerDB` schema) into a Source Qualifier and then load the first name and last name fields in the target table. Populate the Customer ID column value from the source qualifier into the Customer Key and Customer ID columns in the Data Warehouse `Customers` table".

While we just defined the data map, we still have some work to do before we can load the data. Read on to the next section.

4.3   Setup runtime connections

The connections we used in the designer to import tables are not stored in the repository. Typically, a developer has access to only non-production environments. Thus, he/she uses connections to these environments to import table metadata and design mappings. Once the mapping design is complete, we have to configure the mapping to run (by creating a workflow and session). During this process, we have to setup runtime connections. These runtime connections point to development environment during design/development phase and to production during production execution. Since runtime connections reside out of mapping logic, the code is not impacted when connections are updated during deployments.

4.3.1   Creating connections

Login to workflow manager, if you do not have it open already.

Click the Workflow Manager icon ( ) in the designer to open the workflow manager and automatically log in to the repository. All currently opened folders in Designer will also be opened in Workflow Manager.

Now, go to the `Connections` menu → `Relational` ( ). This will open the `Relational connection Browser`. Click `New`. In this example, we will select `Oracle`. If you have setup your source and DWH in a different database, choose accordingly.

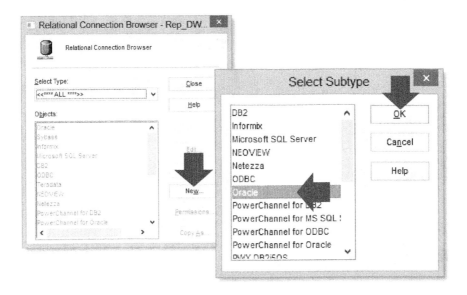

A `Connection Object Definition` dialog box will appear. Fill in the details such as connect string, username and password so that it points to the `CustomerDB`, which is our source database. Name the connection as `DI_Ora_CustomerDB`. Now repeat the steps to create a connection to Data Warehouse called `DI_Ora_DWH`. Your connections should look similar to the image given below

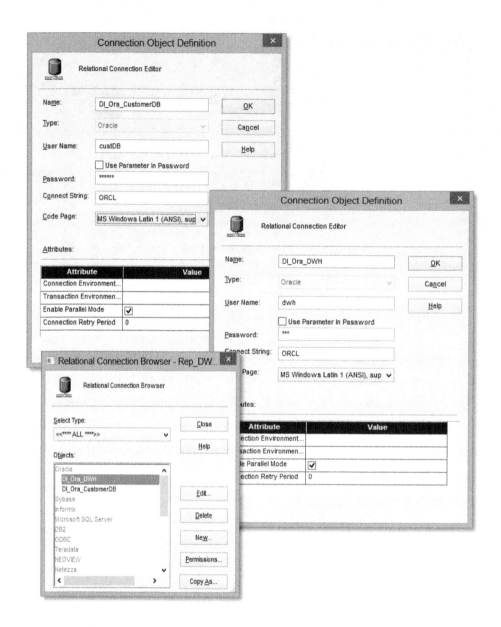

Now, click close to close the Relational Connection Browser.

4.4   Create a workflow

Now that we have defined a data map, it is time to setup runtime information and run it.

4.4.1   Creating workflow

In the workspace, click the `Workflows` menu → `Create` (). Create Workflow dialog box appears. Name the workflow as `wf_DI_Initial_Loads`. Ensure that the integration service is assigned to one allocated to you by your Informatica Administrator. Click `OK` to close the dialog box.

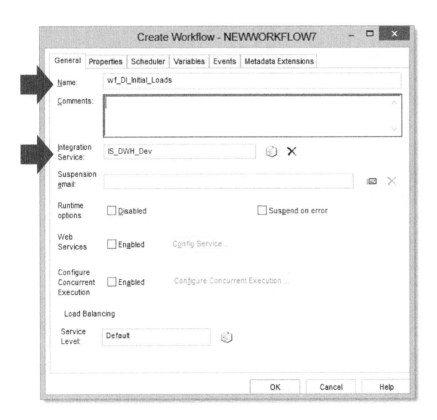

A blank workflow is created in the workspace as shown in the snapshot.

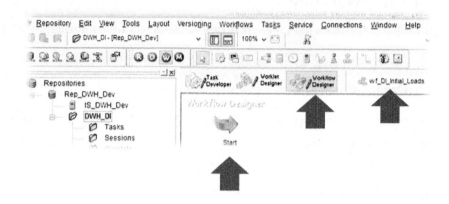

4.4.2   Creating session

Now create a new session by clicking the session icon ( ) in the tasks toolbar and then in the workspace. A new mappings dialog box will appear with a list of mappings in the current folder in the repository. Select the mapping m_DWH_Customers_Initial_Load and click OK.

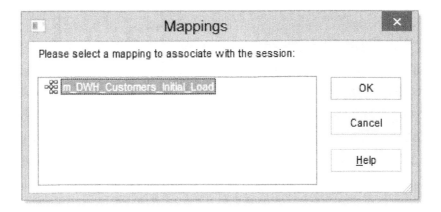

A new session will be created. Click on the create link ( ) button in the tasks toolbar and drag a link from the Start to the session task you just created. Your workspace will now look like the image given here.

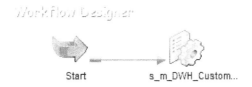

Notice the way an ellipsis is shown when a session name is too long. To always see the full session name, Go to `Tools` menu → `Options` → `General` tab → check the `Always show full name of tasks` and click `OK`.

4.4.3   Configure the session

Now that we have created a session, we need to configure it to be able to run it successfully. This primarily involves associating connections to the mappings' source and targets. Double click on the session to open it. You can also alternatively right click on the session and click `Edit`. In the `Mapping` tab, on the left hand side, under the `Sources` category, click `SQ_CUSTOMERS`. On the right hand side, 3 horizontal panes are displayed. Minimize the first pane called `Readers` by clicking the expand/collapse icon (⬆) next to it. In the `Connections` pane, click the select arrow (⬇). When the `Relational Connection Browser` dialog box appears, click the `Use Object` and then select the `DI_Ora_CustomerDB` connection and then click `OK`. In the `Properties` pane, set the Owner name as `CustDB` or to any owner/schema, where you have setup your source tables. Similarly, in the left hand side, under `Targets` category, select `CUSTOMERS1`. In the `Connections` pane on the right, click the select icon (⬇) and select the `DI_Ora_DWH` as the connection. In the `Properties` pane, change the `Target load type` to `Normal` (default is `Bulk`). We will learn about the target load types in Chapter 23 – External (bulk) loaders. Set the `Table name prefix` to `DWH` or the username/schema where you have setup the Data Warehouse tables. Your source and target properties will now look like the snapshot here.

To set the Target load type as `Normal` instead of `BULK` for all subsequent sessions you create, Open Workflow Manager → `Tools` menu → `Options`→ `Miscellaneous` tab → set the `Target Load Type` as `Normal`.

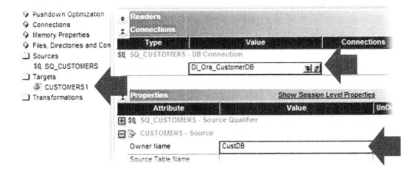

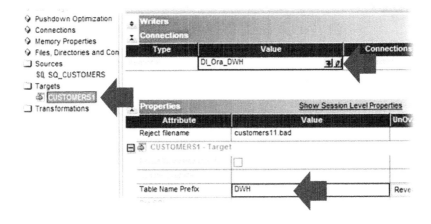

4.5 Run the workflow

Changes can be saved by clicking on the save toolbar button (▦). Before we execute the workflow, it is always a good practice to ensure that the workflow monitor is open so that we can track the workflow progress. Therefore, we start by opening the workflow monitor. To do so, right click on the integration service in the repository navigator and click `Run Monitor`. This will open the workflow monitor, log you in and then automatically connect to the Integration Service for active status and alerts.

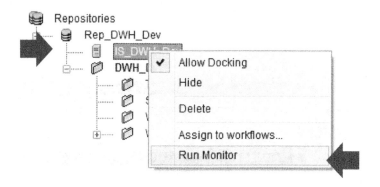

Now, to execute the workflow, go to `Workflows` menu →`Start Workflow` command or right click on blank workspace (not on the session or any object) and click `Start Workflow` (✦). A start workflow window is displayed while the workflow manager communicates with the integration service to start the workflow. Some users may receive a windows firewall alert while trying to execute the workflows. If prompted, click `Allow access`.

In the Workflow Monitor, notice the status of the workflow. It should succeed with Source Success Rows and Target Success Rows as 10,000 each. Log into your DWH schema now to verify that the data load is complete and accurate.

4.6   Understanding workflow monitor

Workflow monitor provides a wide variety of useful information about the session. Ranging from basic information as the workflow/session start time, end time and status, it also provides a great insight into the number of records that were successfully read, loaded, number of records with any issues and so forth. The Get Session Log link displays the session log which contains detailed information about every step of the session.

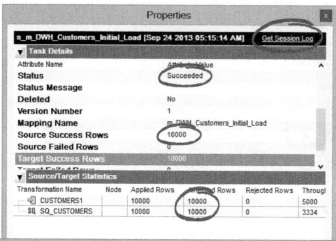

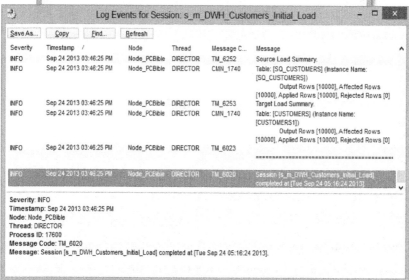

5

Understanding the
Client User Interface

Now that we have built a running application, it is time to understand the client UI in detail. PowerCenter client has a very intuitive interface and is designed to develop data integration applications at rapid speed. By understanding certain UI aspects, you will be able to adapt to the product which will help you in executing the upcoming exercises. In this chapter, we will go back and look at the application we just developed. However, our focus will be on understanding the client and it's UI.

5.1 Browsing vs. opening a folder

In PowerCenter Designer and Workflow Manager, you can browse the repository objects without having to open the repository folder. However, to open an object within a folder, you must open the folder first. To browse the objects, click on the plus sign (⊞) in the repository navigator. To open the folder, right click on the folder and click `Open`, or simply double click on the folder name when it is collapsed (not open for browsing).

Folder that is currently open is displayed in the dropdown in the standard toolbar and is also highlighted in bold letters in the repository navigator.

5.2   Designer workspace

Let's start looking at some of the aspects of PowerCenter Designer.

5.2.1   Understanding the ports

A transformation may contain input ports, output ports and/or input-output ports (pass through ports). This can be easily identified without having to open/edit the transformation. As shown in the picture below, a data flow triangle (▶) is displayed to represent the same. If the triangle is displayed before the port name, it represents that the port can accept data from other transformations. If the triangle is displayed after the port name, it represents that the port can provide data to other transformations. If a port has both, it means that the port value is passed through. A pass through or I/O (input-output) port means that the port value remained unchanged in the transformation. But this port can be used in expressions within the transformation to derive or calculate values for other ports.

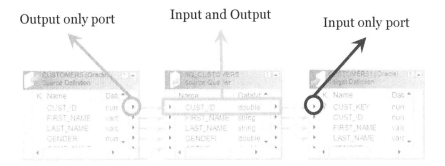

5.2.2 Working with the links

A link represents a data flow between ports. To create a link between two ports, just drag and drop the port from the source transformation on to the target transformation. Note that dropping the port on a port within the transformation and dropping it elsewhere <u>do not</u> yield same results. Dropping it on a port of another transformation *links* the ports, whereas dropping it elsewhere *copies* the port i.e. creates a new port in the target transformation and then links them. To delete a link, just click on the blue arrow (selection is highlighted in red) and press the delete key.

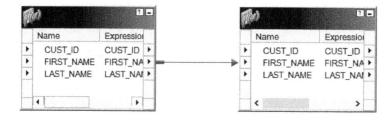

Dropped on the port name

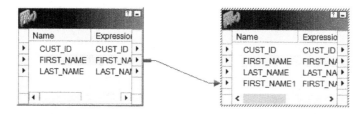

Dropped elsewhere on the transformation

Regular link   Selected link

5.2.3   Transformation properties

Viewing or editing transformation properties is really simple. Just double click on the title bar of the transformation or right click on the transformation title bar and click Edit.

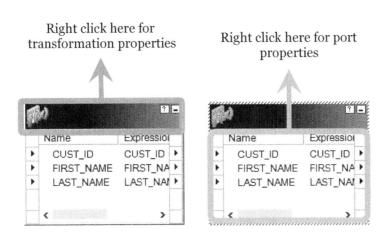

Right click here for transformation properties

Right click here for port properties

Regular transformation

Selected transformation (notice the border)

5.2.4 Arranging icons in the workspace

While working with complex mappings, the transformations we built in the workspace start appearing extremely disorganized. The `Arrange All` and `Arrange All Iconic` features of designer can help us clean up the workspace. Just right click anywhere in the blank workspace and choose one of these options

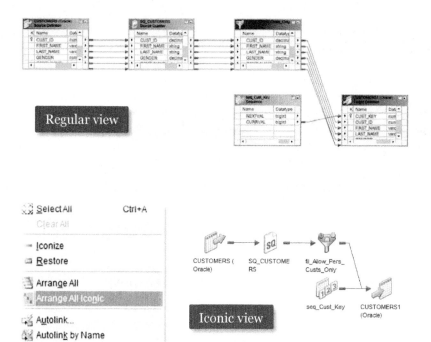

PART 2

CORE

DATA INTEGRATION

6

A simple case study

Now that we have understood the basics and developed a (sort of) hello world application, it is time for us to get on to the core development aspects. To get there and to understand them better, we will take help of a case study. In fact, we already did. In Lab 1 – Your first PowerCenter application, we loaded customers table from a `CustomerDB` to a Data Warehouse. We will use this case study as a guideline to understand and relate several features and functionality of the PowerCenter. With PowerCenter, Data Integration is simple and so will be this case study.

 If you are not planning on using the examples and case study used in this book and rather prefer examples of your own, you can skip this chapter. But it is highly recommended to read through it as the rest of the book will refer to this case study extensively.

This case study is about a fictional bank named Bharani that is building its first Data Warehouse. Like any other bank, Bharani offers different kinds of checking, savings and credit card accounts to its customers. Each customer may have one or more accounts with the bank and each account can have more than one customer to facilitate joint accounts. Bharani also has a rewards program where transactions that are eligible for rewards are accumulated and rewards' money is credited to the account at the end of each month. Bharani has several legacy systems that maintain the data and also deliver it to other applications within the company. Bharani is now venturing into Data Warehousing and Business Intelligence to improve its operational efficiency and provide customers better services by building a Data Warehouse. Since they do not have enough in-house expertise on the Data Warehousing, the requirements are not set in stone and are mostly figured as they go. So, as Phase 1, Bharani would like their DWH to be simply a Data Integration application where they accumulate data from several different applications. Below is a high level requirement list for Phase 1 of DWH:

a. Perform a one-time initial load of customer data from `CustomerDB` into the Data Warehouse. `CustomerDB` is an in-house built application that holds master customer data. `CustomerDB` uses Oracle as its database.

b. Build a delta detection process to identify changes in `CustomerDB` and apply them in the `DWH`.

c. `CustomerDB` keeps a track of all contact information for the customer. All current and previous addresses, phone numbers and emails are maintained. Receive active contact information and store them in the `DWH`. `CustomerDB` has existing extracts (built for other systems previously), where address data is extracted into a flat file and telephone, email information is extracted as an XML file. Both of these are to be consumed and loaded to `DWH`.

d. `ActivCustomer` system contains information about active and inactive customers. Receive a feed from this system and ensure that the `DWH` is up-to-date.

e. Fetch active accounts information from `OnlineDB` and load them to Data Warehouse.

f. Transactions are to be loaded from several source systems. Each source system provides transactions that occurred through various channels. For example, online transactions are routed through a different system than in-store transactions. Each of these systems has a different interface – some real time (MQ Series, JMS) and some batch (oracle). Load all these transactions into the Data Warehouse.

7

Core Transformations

7.1   Introduction

This chapter introduces you to several core transformations. Each section of this chapter introduces you to one core transformation and discuses, to a certain detail, different uses and use-cases for that particular transformation. Each section starts with discussing a transformation and ends with an example/exercise based on the Bharani Bank case study.

 For reading convenience, this book deviates from Informatica's classification of core and advanced transformations.

7.2   Transformations

A transformation is an object that processes and transforms the data within the PowerCenter memory base. A transformation is not responsible for reading or writing the data from and to a data store. It processes the data that is already into PowerCenter memory and is not yet written to the target. The kind of transformation determines how it transforms the data. For example, a sorter transformation reorders the rows, whereas a filter transformation will determine if a record is eligible to continue in the data flow or needs to be dropped. A mapping may contain more than one transformation. With certain exceptions, the output of a transformation can be connected as input to one or more transformations and vice-versa. The order and the flow are defined by the developer in the mapping. As demonstrated in the picture, the data is read by reader in blocks. These blocks of data are then transformed as per the mapping. Each transformation reads the data block, applies its transformation and hands over the transformed data block to the subsequent transformation(s) for further processing. The output of the last transformation(s) is then handed over to the writer. For ease of understanding, the picture here represents the transformations to be sequential. In a true run time scenario, these transformations can be sequential, parallel or any combination thereof. It is also important to understand that the data blocks may not be physically copied over repeatedly. The picture is only a logical representation of what happens underneath and need not necessarily represent its physical implementation.

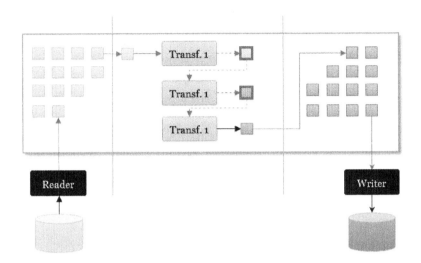

7.3   Transformation categories

Transformation can be categorized in two ways.

Based on their effect on rows:

- → Active transformations
- → Passive transformations

Based on connectivity:

- → Connected transformations
- → Unconnected transformations

7.3.1   Active transformations

Active transformations change one or more from the following:

a. The transaction boundaries: Usually all data in a block gets committed together. However, some transformations may perform actions that may cause some data in the block to commit at a different time than the rest. This may be intentional and needed. For example, if we are grouping the data by a certain field such as employee department and if a data block contains data related to two departments, they will be committed whenever the last record for that group is received and processed. This changes the transaction boundaries.

b. The order of rows: Transformations like sorter change the order in which rows pass through them, thus affecting the transaction boundaries.

c. The row type: A row that is originally supposed to be an insert may just have been flagged as update after evaluating its data.

When passing the data through active transformations, all ports that are needed by subsequent transformations must go through it. Data from two active transformations cannot be merged without a join. Since data coming out of two active transformations do not have the same transaction boundaries, integration service cannot identify how to merge the data without specifying a join condition.

7.3.2   Passive transformations

Passive transformations are in contrast to active transformations and usually operate at column level rather than at row level. Examples are expression transformation that can perform calculations or modify strings. Passive transformations can be connected in parallel and the data from them can be merged without a join.

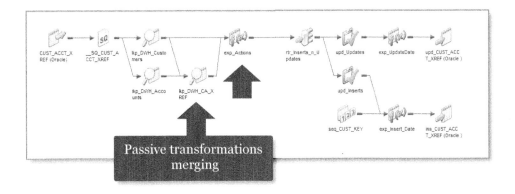

(i) Some transformations are active or passive based on their functionality. For example, a sorter is always an active transformation. However, some transformations are active or passive based on their usage. For example, a lookup transformation returning one row is passive, but if it returns multiple rows, it is considered active.

7.3.3   Connected transformations

A mapping usually consists of transformations connected / linked to each other. The inputs and outputs of the transformation are connected to other transformations or to inputs/outputs. Such transformations are called as connected transformations. Connected transformations require at least one input port and one output port connected to other objects.

7.3.4   Unconnected transformations

Some special transformations can remain in the mapping without being connected to any objects at all. Some examples are stored procedure transformations. If used only once, it can be used as a connected transformation, but if the stored procedure needs to be invoked more than once, it can be created as an unconnected transformation and called via an expression transformation.

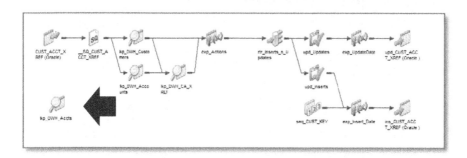

7.4   Filter transformation

Filter is an active transformation used to decide whether or not to allow certain records to continue in the data flow. This decision is made by evaluating a condition against every input row. If the condition evaluates to TRUE, the row is passed on to the next transformation. If the condition evaluates to FALSE, the row is ignored. The condition can be as simple as comparing an input value to a static value or as complex as comparing calculated expressions. Filter transformation is comparable to WHERE clause at the database level.

Property	Description
Filter condition	An expression/condition that will evaluate to TRUE or FALSE. You can use the port names in the filter transformation and most functions in the transformation language to build this expression.

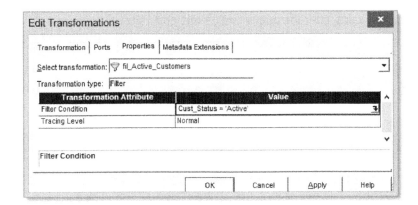

7.5   Sequence Generator transformation

Sequence generator is analogous to the sequences in databases. It provides unique incremental values that can be used for primary and surrogate keys or any column that requires unique numbers. In Sequence generator, you can configure:

Property	Description
Start value	The number from which you want to start the sequence. Default: 0 Maximum: 9,223,372,036,854,775,806
Increment by	Step number. Increment is added to the current value to derive the next value. Default: 1 Maximum: 2,147,483,647

Property	Description
End value	Maximum value till which integration service will continue to generate values. Default, Maximum: 9,223,372,036,854,775,807
Current value	Shows the current value of the sequence generator.
Cycle?	If you check this box, integration service will go back to start value after the current value hits end value.
Reset?	If you check this box, integration service will always start with the same start value for every session run. In the default mode (unchecked), at the end of the session, the current value of the session is stored as a current value so that next session run continues this value.

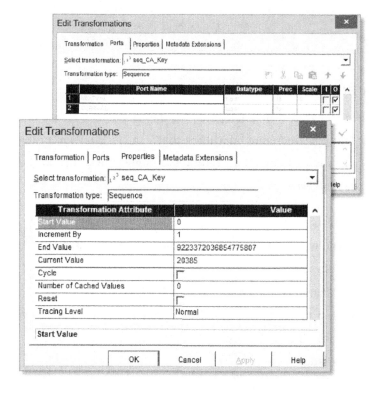

7.6   Lab 2 – Using filter, sequence generator

Business requirement:

Business users of Bharani bank have looked at the initial data we loaded for the customers table and they have the following thoughts. Bharani bank has two types of customers: personal (individual) customers and business customers. As part of Phase 1 of their data warehouse project, Bharani bank wishes to have only personal customers in their DWH. Bharani bank also wishes to have all their data warehouse tables to maintain data using an independent surrogate key that is not generated based on the input or on the data.

Challenges:

→   Not all data needs to be loaded. Some data should be filtered out.

→   Surrogate key (unique numbers) needs to be generated for both customers and accounts.

Technical solution:

Earlier, we had loaded all the customer data available in the `CustomerDB.Customer` table. For personal customers, `first_name` and `last_name` are populated and for business customers, `comp_name` (company name) is populated. Now, we will add a filter to this mapping to load only personal customers into the data warehouse. We will skip the company name column from being loaded to Data Warehouse. We will also leverage Sequence Generator transformation to generate unique keys for customers and accounts.

Steps for solution:

a.   Open the Designer

b.   Connect to the repository, by double clicking it and then provide your username and password

c.   Double click the DWH folder. Workspace will open

d. Drag the mapping into the workspace or right click on the mapping and click open. Mapping will open in the workspace

e. Now, select all the links between source qualifier and the target. You can click on the link (arrows) and press DEL key to delete the link. When you select the link, the link color changes to red to indicate the selection. You can drag your mouse around the links to select multiple links simultaneously. When you try to delete the links, PowerCenter will prompt for confirmation. Click Yes.

f. Filter the data

   1. Create a filter transformation by clicking the filter icon ( ) in the transformations toolbar and then click in the workspace. A new filter transformation is created in the workspace. This filter transformation will have a name called FILTRANS. We will change the name later.

   2. Now, drag ALL the columns from source qualifier into the filter transformation.

   3. Double click on the title bar of the filter transformation (you can also right click and go to Edit). The filter transformation dialog box appears. In the Transformation tab, click the Rename button. Name the filter as fil_Allow_Pers_Custs_Only and click OK. Go to Properties tab. Click the down arrow ( ) next to Filter Condition. This will open an expression editor. Remove the default value of TRUE. Type CUST_TYPE=1 and then click OK to close the expression editor. Click OK again to close the filter properties.

   4. Connect the ports CUST_ID, FIRST_NAME, LAST_NAME from filter to the target.

g. Create a sequence generator

   1. Create a sequence generator transformation ( ) by clicking the sequence generator icon in the transformations toolbar and then click in the workspace. A new sequence generator transformation is created in the workspace. The sequence generator will have only 2 output ports and no

input ports. The sequence generator is named SEQTRANS. We will change the name later.

2. Double click the sequence generator title bar to open its properties. In the Transformation tab, click Rename. Name the transformation as seq_Cust_Key and click OK to close the dialog. Click OK again to close the transformation properties.

3. Now drag the next value (NEXTVAL) from sequence generator on to the cust_key column in the target.

h. Save the mapping

i. Create a workflow

1. To run this mapping, open the workflow manager, double click on the DWH folder to open it in the workspace and drag the workflow into the workspace. This will open the workflow. If you already had the workflow open, you need to refresh the session so that it can download the changes you saved to the mapping. To do so, right click on the session and click Refresh Mapping.

2. Double click the session or right click the session and click Edit. Session properties will open. Go to Mapping tab. In the left hand navigator, select the target and in the 3rd pane to the right, check the box Truncate Target Table. If the DWH user in your environment does not have enough permission to truncate a table, skip this step and truncate the table manually.

3. Click OK to close the session properties. Save the workflow (Repository menu → Save) and start the workflow by right clicking the blank workspace and clicking on the Start Workflow command.

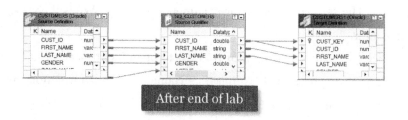

After end of lab

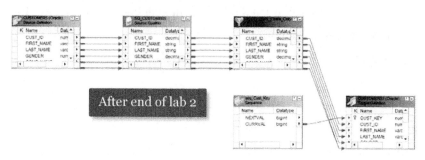

After end of lab 2

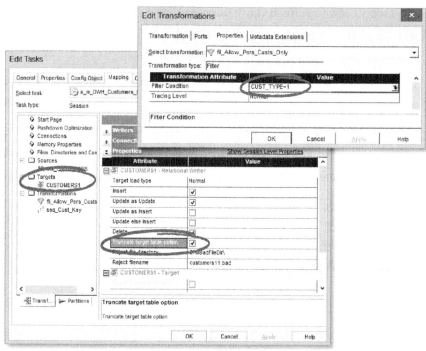

7.7   Source qualifier transformation

Source qualifier transformation represents the data read from source(s) into the integration service. You will notice however, that there is no transformation representing the data that is about to be written to the target(s). If you are a hard core database developer, you probably already guessed why. In simple terms, INSERT clause in SQL is much simpler than SELECT. A simple SELECT will read data of a table. But SELECT gets more complicated when you introduce WHERE clause, ORDER BY, joins, IN clause, EXIST clause etc, to read data from more than a single data object. Same applies to the data in PowerCenter as well. PowerCenter allows you to do tasks like this via the Source Qualifier transformation. Since source qualifier is allowing us to control/manage source data, its properties vary drastically based on the type of the source. For example, a relational source qualifier (source qualifier connected to a source that is pointing to a relational database such as oracle) allows you to define a WHERE clause, whereas a flat file source qualifier does not. In this section, we will see different ways of using Source Qualifier to control and manage the source data. Let us take a quick glance at Relational Source Qualifier properties:

Property	Description
SQL Query	Use this property to customize the SQL generated by PowerCenter. Use case: Add hints or perform complex joins
User Defined Join	When more than one source is linked to the Source qualifier, use this property to define how they need to be joined.
Number of sorted ports	If more than zero, PowerCenter will generate an ORDER BY clause to its default query to sort the data based on those fields. Columns included in the 'order by' will be based on the order of columns in source qualifier.
Select distinct	Check this if you want PowerCenter to automatically add DISTINCT clause in the select query it is generating.

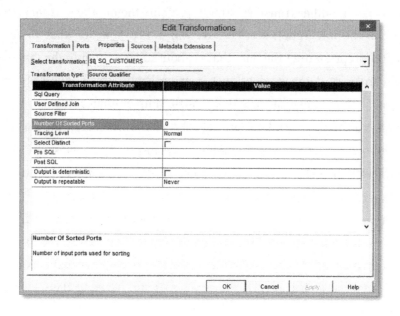

7.7.1   Pipeline

A data flow derived from a source qualifier is known as Pipeline. A pipeline consists of all sources connected to a source qualifier, all transformations and other objects that receive its data all the way till the targets.

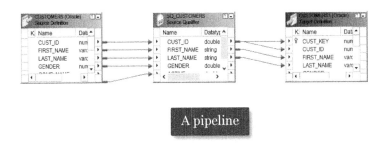

A pipeline

7.7.2   Source qualifier data reads

At run time, PowerCenter will generate a SELECT statement based on the columns that are linked from source qualifier to the next transformation(s). If a source qualifier has 5 columns but only 3 of them are connected to the next transformation, PowerCenter will generate a query selecting only 3 columns from the source table.

<u>Generates</u>: SELECT ACCT_NRFROM ACCOUNTS

<u>Generates</u>: SELECT ACCT_NR, ACCT_TYPE FROM ACCOUNTS

 To preview the SQL query PowerCenter generates for a source qualifier, open the source qualifier properties, go to Properties tab, open the value SQL query and then click Generate SQL. This will generate the SQL that PowerCenter will use at runtime.

7.7.3 Filtering source data

Source qualifier can be used to filter source data. Applying a source filter is real easy. Just type the expression in the Source Filter property. This expression needs to be a valid SQL expression as it will be evaluated by the database to which the source will connect. If the source connected to this source qualifier is an oracle database, this expression must be a valid oracle expression. If the source is Microsoft SQL Server, the expression must be a valid SQL Server expression and so on. At run time, PowerCenter will append value provided in the `Source Filter` to the generated SQL after the `WHERE` clause.

 For relational source qualifiers, When you provide a `Source Filter`, do not add the `WHERE` keyword as PowerCenter will automatically add it.

Some examples of Source Filter:

Source Filter	Query generated
create_date > sysdate – 10	SELECT … From … WHERE CREATE_DATE > SYSDATE – 10
active is not null	SELECT … From … WHERE active IS NOT NULL
dept_no in(select dept_no from dept)	SELECT … From … WHERE dept_no in(select dept_no from dept)

7.7.4   Sorting the data at database level

Many computations require sorted data and most of them run faster with sorted data. But if we have indexes in the databases on the same columns that we would like to sort on, it makes more sense to sort it at the database level and just read the results into PowerCenter rather than trying to sort it all over again. This is precisely the use of Number of Sorted Ports property of source qualifier. When provided with a value greater than zero, PowerCenter will select that many columns from the source qualifier and generate an ORDER BY clause in its SELECT statement. While generating the columns list for ORDER BY, PowerCenter will refer to the order of ports in the source qualifier (Ports tab). To redefine a new sort order, simply switch to Ports tab and use the move up (⬆) and move down (⬇) buttons to rearrange the ports.

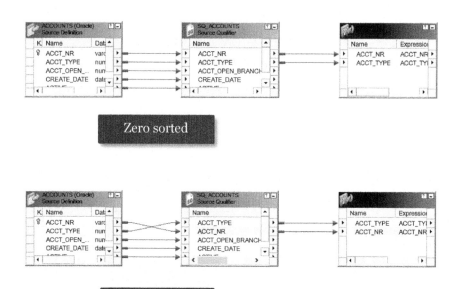

7.7.5   Customize/add hints to SQL

The SQL query generated by PowerCenter can be customized using Source Qualifier's SQL query property. Developers can take the default query generated by PowerCenter and customize it instead of trying to build the query from scratch. To generate the default query, open the source qualifier properties and go to the `Properties` tab, SQL query and then click on the `Generate SQL` button.

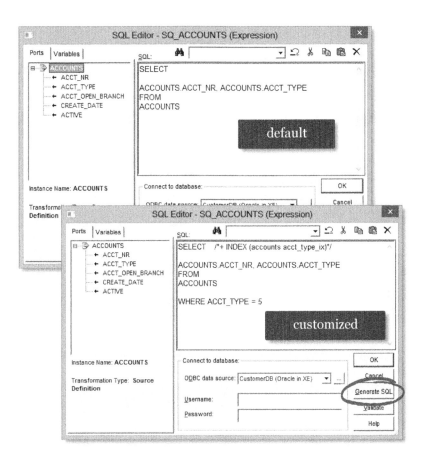

7.7.6   Database level joins

A source qualifier is representing a set of data that is being fetched from a data source. So, if we are reading from a single table, we have a single source qualifier in the mapping. If we have two tables, well, it depends. If we have two tables from the same database or schema, we can have the data from both of them read into the PowerCenter and then join them using joiner transformation (we haven't covered joiner transformation yet. Just know it exists, details will come soon). But if these tables are huge and have relationships at the database level, it might make more sense to join them at the database and only fetch the joined data into PowerCenter for further processing. In this scenario, we create two source objects in our mapping, and attach them to a source qualifier. This allows us to join the data at the database level and read the results into PowerCenter. To setup database level joins using source qualifier, perform the following steps:

a. Login to designer.

b. Connect to the repository, open a folder and create a new mapping.

c. In the repository navigator, select more than one source (use CTRL key or SHIFT key to make multi-selection) and drag them in to the mapping.

d. Each source will be added along with a corresponding source qualifier.

e. One by one, delete all the source qualifiers. You will only have sources in your mapping now. When PowerCenter prompts, click Yes to confirm.

f. Click the source qualifier icon (or Transformation→Create menu item) to create a new source qualifier.

g. When select sources dialog box appears, select two or more sources (use CTRL key or SHIFT key to make multi-selection) and click OK.

h. A source qualifier is added with links to all the sources. Edit the source qualifier. Go to Properties tab and edit the User defined join. In the SQL window, type the join condition. You can also use the Ports tree on the left to populate actual column names. Click OK to close the SQL and OK to close the source qualifier properties.

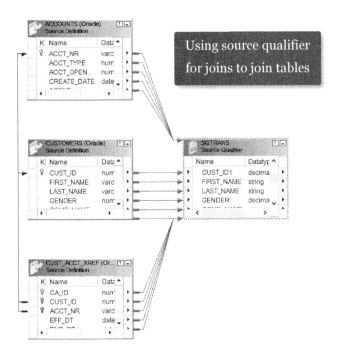

Using source qualifier for joins to join tables

7.8   Lab 3 – Using source qualifier

Business requirement:

The customers table in the source contains both personal (individual) and business customers. The accounts table contains accounts held by both kinds of customers. Bharani bank would like to load only personal customers and their associated information into the Data Warehouse as part of their Phase 1 implementation. Hence, we need to load accounts associated to only personal customers to the data warehouse. A customer may hold more than one account at Bharani Bank. Customers can also have shared savings accounts – meaning each account can belong to more than one customer. This complex many to many relationship is maintained in a customer-account cross reference table. The process that loads accounts table must take this cross reference table into account to ensure that only accounts associated with personal customers are loaded.

Challenges:

a. A many to many relationship exists between customers and accounts. Thus, accounts table needs to be joined to cross reference table, which again needs to be joined with customers to get the proper association.
b. Only personal accounts need to be processed. If possible, we should try not to load the business accounts.

Technical solution:

Source qualifier can be used to perform homogenous joins. Since the customers, accounts and the cross reference table are all in the same database and can be accessed from the same database connection, we will leverage source qualifier to do this join, thus pushing the join operation to database instead of performing it at PowerCenter level.

Steps for solution:

a. Login to the designer, open the DWH folder
b. Import source
    1. Switch to the Source Analyzer
    2. Go to Sources→Import from Database menu. Connect to the CustomerDB and import the ACCOUNTS and CUST_ACCT_XREF tables, if you have not already done so
c. Import target
    1. Switch to Target Designer
    2. Go to Targets→Import from Database menu. Connect to DWH and import ACCOUNTS and CUST_ACCT_XREF tables, if you have not already done so
d. Switch to Mapping Designer

e. Create a new mapping m_DWH_Init_Load_Accounts

f. Add sources and source qualifier:

1. From the Repository Navigator, select CUSTOMERS, ACCOUNTS and CUST_ACCT_XREF tables and drag them all into the mapping.

2. 3 sources will be created with 3 corresponding source qualifiers.

3. Delete all the source qualifiers, by selecting each of them and pressing the DEL key. When prompted, click Yes to confirm the delete.

4. Add a new source qualifier by clicking the source qualifier icon (SQ) in the toolbar and then on the blank workspace.

5. When Select Sources… dialog appears, select all 3 sources and click OK.

6. Edit the source qualifier. In the Transformation tab, click Rename and change the source qualifier name to _sq_cust_acct_n_xref.

7. In the Properties tab, update the following properties

Property	Value
User defined join	accounts.acct_nr = cust_acct_xref.acct_nr and customers.cust_id = cust_acct_xref.cust_id
Source filter	customers.cust_type = 1
Select distinct	Checked (✓)

8. Click OK to save

g. Create a sequence generator transformation and rename it as seq_Acct_Key

h. Drag the accounts target table (DWH) into the mapping

i. Join the columns between the source qualifier and target as given below

Source object	Source qualifier column	Target column
seq_acct_key	Nextval	acct_key
accounts	acct_nr	acct_nr
accounts	acct_type	acct_type
accounts	acct_open_branch	acct_open_branch
accounts	create_date	create_date
accounts	Active	Active

j. Save the mapping

k. Login to the workflow manager

l. Open the existing workflow of name `wf_DWH_Initial_Loads`

   1. Create a new session for the mapping we just created

   2. Assign connections in the session properties →`Mapping` tab such that source is `DI_Ora_CustomerDB` and target is `DI_Ora_DWH`

   3. Change the `Target Load Type` from `Bulk` to `Normal`

   4. Create a link from the session `s_m_DWH_Init_Load_Customers` to the session we just created (`s_m_DWH_Init_Load_Accounts`)

m. Save the workflow

n. Select the new session and right click on the session and click on `Start Task`

o. Accounts load will complete. Verify the data loaded

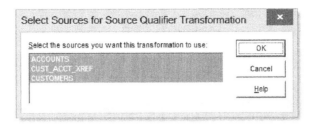

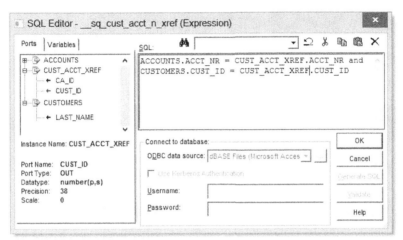

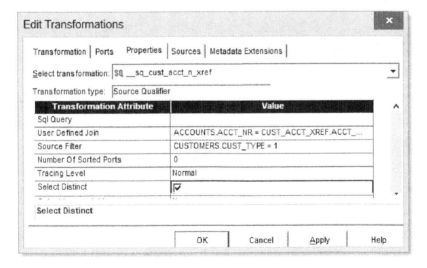

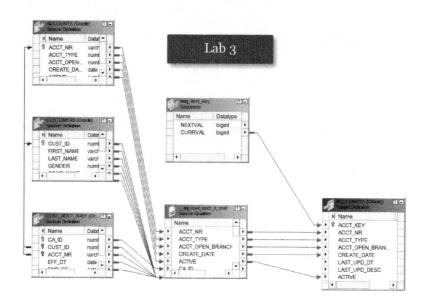

7.9 Expression transformation

fx Expression transformation is probably the most widely used transformation within the PowerCenter. It provides great flexibility in performing column level operations. A huge collection of transformation language can be used to perform column level operations within this transformation. From simple tasks like concatenating first name and last name to forming a full name and more complex tasks like transposing rows into columns, expression transformation comes in handy everywhere. It is difficult to understand the power of expression transformation without understanding the transformation language itself. However, in this chapter, we will try to learn the usage of this transformation rather than focusing on the functions of the transformation language. That will be a discussion for another chapter.

7.9.1   Ports

Creation of an expression transformation is really simple and is just like any other transformation. However, expression transformation has a unique ability that several other transformations do not: support for variable ports. A port is simply a data attribute. A row is made up of ports. For example, an employee row is made of 3 ports: emp_id, emp_name and emp_salary. In a transformation, ports represent the data that is flowing into the transformation, out of the transformation and any temporary data that the transformation is using as part of its processing. Based on the type of value it is storing, ports can be classified as:

→ Input port: Brings data into the transformation.

→ Output port: Flows data out of this transformation. An output port may receive its data from an input port or a variable port.

→ Input-Output port: A pass through port. The value that is brought into the transformation is passed as-it-is to the subsequent transformation(s).

→ Variable port: Holds temporary data during the transformation processing. A variable port may receive its data from an input port, input-output port or another variable port.

In addition to the above classification, there are several special ports that are available in certain transformations. For example, sort key ports available in sorter transformation are used to define the data attributes upon which, rows need to be sorted. An expression transformation can have any number of input, output, input-output and variable ports.

Once a value is assigned to a variable port, it will retain its values until it is changed again. For example, if a data set has 3 rows and the data is flowing in, now, when the 1st record reaches the expression, variable port is empty because it is not evaluated yet. Once the transformation processes row 1, the value evaluated for the variable port is stored. Now row 1 is handed over to the next transformation and row 2 is picked up by the expression. However, now all input ports and input-output ports will contain the values from row 2, whereas all variables will contain values from row1 processing. Integration service will then start evaluating the variables in the order they are defined in the transformation. Finally, output ports are evaluated and output data for row 2 is generated and handed over to the next transformation.

The order of evaluation ports is always:

a.   Input ports

b.   Input-output ports

c.   Variable ports (in the order they are defined in the transformation)

d.   Output ports

7.9.2   UI to manage ports

The designer UI allows you to create, modify and delete ports in an expression (and many other transformations). To do so, you have to open the transformation and go to the ports tab.

Icon	Description
	Create a new port
	Delete current port – no confirmation prompted
	Copy the current port into clipboard
	Paste the copied content as a new port
	Move the current port one up
	Move the current port one down

7.9.3 Evaluation

It is important to understand how variable and output ports are evaluated. Each port is evaluated and processed independent of others and in the order defined in the transformation.

7.9.3.1 Data types

Each port's value must evaluate to a value which matches the port data type. If the data types mismatch, PowerCenter will throw an error. If the data types are mismatch but compatible, PowerCenter will throw a warning but will continue. For example, if the port is defined as a string and the expression evaluates to a number, PowerCenter will throw a warning (both at design and run time) and will perform an *implicit conversion* to convert the number into a string. However, if the port is defined as a number and the expression evaluates to a string, PowerCenter will throw an error at the design time. If you continue to save your mapping, it will be marked as invalid (a red exclamation next to the mapping icon) and the corresponding session will be marked as impacted and invalid. Invalid sessions cannot be executed.

7.9.3.2 *Assignments*

In addition to data types, the result of an expression must always be a value and cannot be another expression. For example, let's say we have a port called Gender of type string with length of 1 character. Now consider the expressions below:

	Expression	Description
✓	IIF(GenderCode = 1, 'M', 'F')	Valid expression. If Gender code is 1, value 'M' is stored in Gender field. Otherwise, value 'F' is stored in Gender field.
✗	IIF(GenderCode = 1, Gender = 'M', Gender= 'F')	Logically Invalid expression. Value to a port cannot be assigned from another port. Result of each port is assigned to that port itself.

The problem with the second statement above is that it contains 3 individual statements (2 assignments and one condition). When PowerCenter looks at his expression, it will evaluate it as:

a. Is gender code 1?
   a. If yes, Is Gender value M?
      i. If yes, return TRUE
      ii. If no, return FALSE
   b. If no, Is Gender value F?
      i. If yes, return TRUE
         1. If no, return FALSE

End result is that if gender code is 1, the value will either evaluate to TRUE or FALSE because both Gender = 'M' and Gender = 'F' are treated as conditions, not assignments.

 In PowerCenter transformation language, there is no way to assign a value to a port from within another port. The only way to assign a value to a port is to write that value/expression in that port itself.

7.9.3.3　*Order*

The order in which ports are defined in a transformation is the exact order in which the ports get evaluated. So, if you have variable ports depending on other variable ports, it is important to define them in the order of their dependency. The order can be changed anytime using the move up (⬆) and move down (⬇) buttons.

7.9.4　Expression editor

Expression editor is the dialog box that allows you to rapidly build expressions. To open the expression editor, open the transformation; go to Ports tab. Click on the port you would like to edit. Once the port is highlighted, click the edit icon (🔽) at the end of it. This will open the expression editor. The expression editor consists of the following parts:

a. Expression tree: Lists all the available functions in the PowerCenter's transformation language reference. When you click on the function, the bottom part of the tree shows the syntax for the function along with some quick help on using it.

b. Expression: To insert a function or keyword from the expression tree, simply double click on the function/keyword in the expression tree. It will be automatically inserted at the cursor location.

c. Operators: A list of supported operators are displayed here as buttons. To insert them into the expression, simply click on the button. It will be inserted at the cursor location.

d. Validation and save: The `Validate` button will validate the expression for any syntax errors, data type errors and other design level errors. The `OK` button will close the expression editor and assign this expression to the current port.

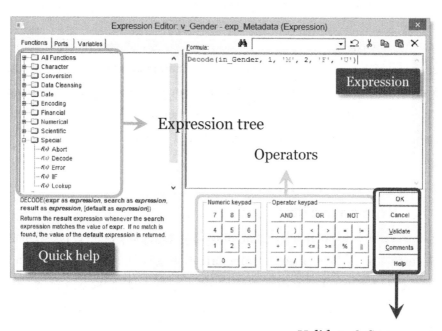

Validate & Save

7.9.5   Operators

In this section, we look at some basic expressions and how to use them. Let's start by looking at operators. Operators are special symbols that perform specific operations on one or two or three operands and then return a result. Based on their usage, operators are classified as:

a.   Arithmetic operators
b.   String operators
c.   Comparison operators
d.   Logical operators

When more than one operator is used in a given expression, Integration Service will evaluate them in the order mentioned above.

7.9.5.1   Arithmetic Operators

Operator	Description	Usage Example
+	Add	Port1 + Port2
-	Subtract	Port1 – Port 2
*	Multiply	Port1 * Port2
/	Division	Port1 / Port2
%	Remainder of the division	Port1 % Port2

 Any operator or function in PowerCenter transformation language returns NULLs, if one or more parameters in its input is NULL.

7.9.5.2 *String Operators*

There is only one string operator: Concatenation. Concatenation appends string 2 immediately after string 1.

Operator	Description	Usage Example
||	Concatenate	Port1 || Port2 Port 1 || ' ' || Port2

7.9.5.3 *Comparison Operators*

Comparison operators compare two values and return a TRUE or FALSE.

Operator	Description	Usage Example
=	Equal to	IIF(Port1 = Port2, 'Same')
>	Greater than	IIF(Port1 > Port2, More')
>=	Greater than or equal to	IIF(Port1 >= Port2, 'More or same')
<	Less than	IIF(Port1 < Port2, 'Less')
<=	Less than or equal to	IIF(Port1 <= Port2, 'Less or same')
<> or != or ^=	Not equal to	IIF(Port1 != Port2, Not equal')

7.9.5.4   *Logical Operators*

Logical operators are extensions of comparison operators as they operate on one or two Boolean expressions and return a TRUE or FALSE.

Operator	Description	Usage Example
AND	Return TRUE if both the join conditions are TRUE	IIF(Port1 = Port2 AND Port3=Port4, TRUE)
OR	Return TRUE if any one of the conditions evaluates to TRUE	IIF(Port1 = Port2 OR Port3 = Port4, TRUE)
NOT	Negates the Boolean expression value. True becomes false and vice-versa	IIF(Port1 is not null, TRUE)

> (i)   Any operation involving a NULL always evaluates to NULL.

7.10 Lab 4 – Simple expressions

<u>Business requirement</u>:

  Bharani Bank has reviewed the data we have loaded for them so far. They like the core data that we loaded, but have suggested some metadata changes to some of the columns. We are required to perform these changes and reload some of these tables. These changes are listed below.

Customers table:

Column	Data in source is	Transformation requirement
Gender	Numeric	Convert 0 to U (Unknown) Convert 1 to M (Male) Convert 2 to F (Female)
Customer type	Numeric	Convert 1 to P (Personal) Convert 2 to B (Business)
Last update date	N/A	Date when the mapping runs
Last update desc	N/A	Set to default value of 'Initial Load'
Active	Numeric	Convert 1 to Y (Active) Convert 0 to N (Inactive)

Accounts table:

Column	Data in source is	Transformation requirement
Account type	Numeric	Convert 1 to SAV (Savings) Convert 2 to CHK (Checking) Convert 3 to CRD (Credit Card)
Last update date	N/A	Date when the mapping runs
Last update desc	N/A	Set to default value of 'Initial Load'
Active	Numeric	Convert 1 to Y (Active) Convert 0 to N (Inactive)

Steps for solution:

a. Login to the designer, open the DWH folder

b. Switch to the Mapping Designer

c. Open the customer initial load mapping (m_DWH_Initial_Load_Customers)

d. Create a new expression transformation by clicking on the expression icon (f(x)) in the toolbar and then click in the workspace

   1. Drag and drop the gender, cust_type, active ports from the filter transformation into the expression

   2. Edit the transformation and rename it to exp_Metadata

   3. Go to the Ports tab

   4. Rename the 3 ports to add a prefix of 'in_'. Now your ports should be in_GENDER, in_CUST_TYPE, in_ACTIVE

      i. Uncheck the checkbox in the 'O' column (Output). Now all these three ports become input-only ports. You will also notice that the expression column becomes blank for all these ports.

   5. Click the create port button (⋮⋯⋮)

      i. Edit the new port created. Rename it to v_Gender. Set its data type as string and its precision to 1.

      ii. Check the V column to make it a variable port. The I and O columns will be automatically unchecked for you and a default text of v_Gender will appear in its expression. Edit the expression by clicking on the edit icon (📝)

      iii. Set the expression to Decode(in_Gender, 1, 'M', 2, 'F', 'U') Validate the expression and Expression parsed successfully message will appear. Click OK to close it.

   6. Similarly create the following variable ports:

Port name	Type	Precision	Expression
v_Cust_Type	String	1	IIF(in_Cust_Type = 1, 'P', 'B')
v_Last_Upd_Date	Date/time		SYSDATE
v_Last_Upd_Desc	String	255	'Initial Load'
v_Active	String	1	IIF(in_Active = 1, 'Y', 'N')

7. Variable ports are used to only compute values and hence variables cannot be directly linked to next transformations. To do so, we need output ports. Let's create output ports as shown below:

Port name	Type	Precision	Expression
o_Gender	String	1	v_Gender
o_Cust_Type	String	1	v_Cust_Type
o_Last_Upd_Date	Date/time		v_Last_Upd_Date
o_Last_Upd_Desc	String	255	v_Last_Upd_Desc
o_Active	String	1	v_Active

8. Your expression transformation will now look like this:

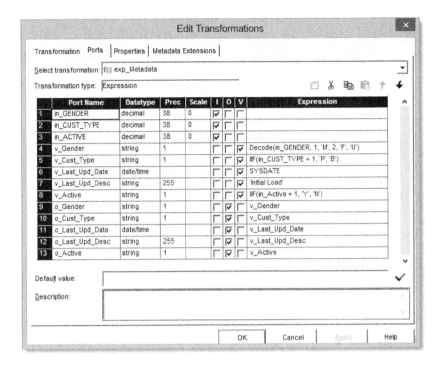

9. Close the expression

e. Now drag the 5 output ports (gender, customer type, last update date, last update description, active) one by one on to the corresponding ports in the target. Drop these output ports exactly on the name of the port you want to link.

1. Since you already have ports linked to the same target columns, PowerCenter will prompt so and ask for your confirmation to remove the existing link and establish the new one. Click `Yes`.

f. Save the mapping

g. Your customers mapping will now look like this:

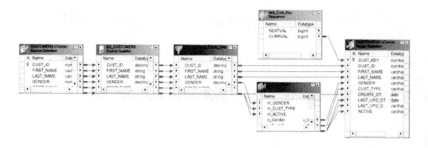

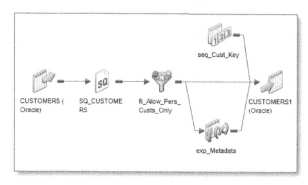

h.   Now open the accounts mapping

　　1.   We will again follow the similar steps.

　　2.   Create a new expression called `exp_Metadata`

　　　　i.   Drag the account type and active ports into it

　　　　ii.   Rename the input ports to have a prefix of "`in_`" and convert them to input only ports by unchecking the checkmark in 'O' column

　　　　iii.   Create the following variable ports

Port name	Type	Precision	Expression
v_Acct_Type	String	1	Decode(in_Acct_Type, 1, 'SAV', 2, 'CHK', 3, 'CRD', 'UNK')

Port name	Type	Precision	Expression
v_Last_Upd_Date	Date/time		SYSDATE
v_Last_Upd_Desc	String	255	'Initial Load'
v_Active	String	5	IIF(in_Active = 1, 'Y', 'N')

iv. Create corresponding output ports

Port name	Type	Precision	Expression
o_Acct_Type	String	5	v_Acct_Type
o_Last_Upd_Date	Date/time		v_Last_Upd_Date
o_Last_Upd_Desc	String	255	v_Last_Upd_Desc
o_Active	String	1	v_Active

v. Connect the output ports to the target

3. Your expression and final mapping should look like shown in the picture

i. Now open workflow manager and the workflow we built. If you already have the workflow open, you MUST refresh the sessions (right click the session →Refresh Mapping).

1. Ensure that the Truncate Target Table option is set in both the sessions. If you do not have permissions to truncate the tables via PowerCenter session, truncate them manually.

2. Save the workflow

j. Run the workflow

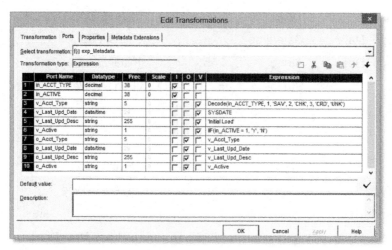

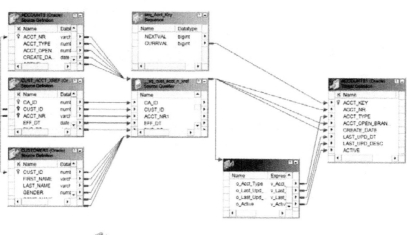

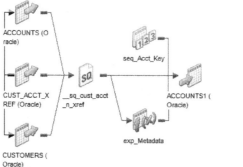

7.11   Union transformation

Sometimes similar data is stored in different physical objects for storage and performance reasons. For example, it is not uncommon to distribute transactions into a table partitioned by year or actually physically separate transactions by year into different tables. However, when there is a need to read and process both current and history data, we need the ability to read more than one source of data and append them together. Appending is very different from a joining even though both operations use more than one data source. A join merges two data sets based on one or more common columns. As a result, the joined dataset typically contains distinct columns from both the datasets. Append, on the other hand, merges the datasets that have the same structure. As a result, the appended data set contains the same number of columns but the total record count will be a sum of records from both the datasets.

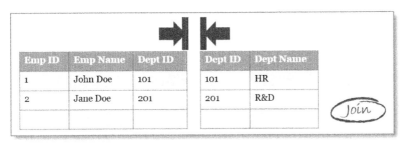

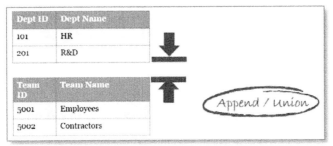

Append is most commonly known as union. A union transformation has many input groups (set of ports) and one output group. Ports and their data types must be exactly the same between all the input groups. PowerCenter integration service processes data belonging to all input groups in parallel. Hence, the output of the union is not guaranteed to be in the same order as input.

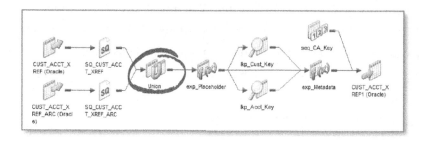

7.12   Router transformation

If Filter transformation can be compared to an IF condition, router transformation can be compared to a switch statement. A router is simply multiple 'if conditions' or multiple 'filter transformations'. When data needs to be diverted, based on multiple conditions, instead of adding multiple filters, we can add a single router transformation and define several groups in it. A router takes one input group (set of ports) and provides several output groups – each group qualified by a filter condition. If the data meets the condition of an output group, data is routed to it. If data does not match any group, it will be automatically directed to the "default" group.

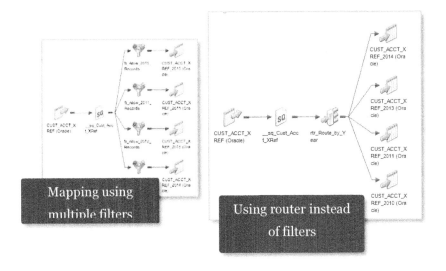

Mapping using multiple filters

Using router instead of filters

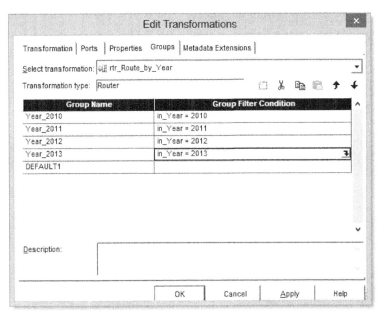

7.13   Lookup transformation

As the name itself suggests, lookup transformation looks up a value in a table/file and returns a corresponding value. Lookup transformation is also capable of returning more than one value, in fact a full row for the corresponding value. One of the most common use cases for a lookup is to identify the presence of a record. For example, before you load data into a table, you would like to know if a copy of this record already exists in the target table. Hence, lookup is widely used in change detection / delta detection processes. Lookup is also extensively used to resolve reference data. For example, while loading customers' dimension, you might want to resolve the customer type Id (a numeric value) to its description. So 1 becomes personal customer, 2 becomes business customers and so on.

Here's a quick glance on the lookup properties:

Lookup property	Description
SQL override	Provide a SQL here to replace the default SQL PowerCenter generates
Table name	If SQL is not overridden, PowerCenter generates SQL statement for the table name provided here
Source filter	An optional WHERE clause that PowerCenter will append to its SQL when fetching lookup data
Caching enabled?	If checked, PowerCenter Integration Service will cache all the table data for faster processing. If caching is disabled, PowerCenter will directly query the table for every match to be performed

Lookup property	Description
Policy on multiple match	What needs to be done when there is more than 1 matching record for the given lookup input? Available options are: - Use first value: select the first matching record in the set - Use last value: select the last matching record in the set - Use any value: selects the first record based on its index - Report error: log error and skip the record

7.13.1   Lookup creation

Every lookup transformation is associated with a data object. If the data object is already imported into PowerCenter, you can choose from the list or you can choose to import a new table or file while creating the lookup transformation. The link between the lookup and the data object itself is not a hard one. Meaning, once the lookup transformation is created, the only reference lookup will have to its data object is its name (table name or the file name – not the object name). PowerCenter designer copies all the ports in the selected data object into the lookup. This makes it easy for developer to define lookups without having to create all the ports again.

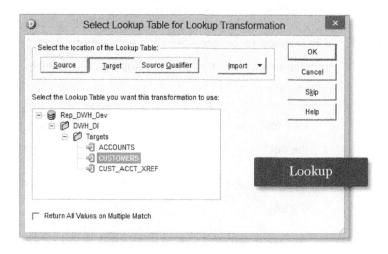

7.13.2   Lookup ports

A lookup transformation typically contains input ports (data to be matched), lookup ports (data to be matched against) and the output/return ports (data to be retrieved for the matches). Input ports are typically copied from transformations before the lookup and can be named in any fashion. The lookup and output ports must exactly match the column names of the lookup table. PowerCenter uses these port names to generate the SQL that will be executed on the lookup table.

7.13.3   Lookup caches

When a relational lookup transformation is used in a mapping, Integration Service will execute its SQL query and load the entire result set into memory. For Flat file lookups, the entire file content is loaded into the memory. This memory data structure, known as lookup cache, is built during session initialization and will be discarded at the end of the session by default. Having the lookup data in a cache helps PowerCenter perform matches faster.

7.14   Lab 5 – Union and lookup

Business requirement:

The customers at Bharani Bank can have more than one account. Some accounts can have more than one customer associated with them. Examples are family accounts and joint accounts. So Bharani Bank maintains a cross reference table to resolve the many to many relationships between these entities. If a customer has 3 accounts, this cross reference table will contain the customer id 3 times, each with a different account number. If one of these accounts is a joint account, that account number will repeat again with the second customer id. If a customer closes an account and opens a different account, the current cross reference will be end-dated and a new entry will be created with the corresponding account number. However, if the status of the customer-account relationship is changed, same record will be updated. All end-dated records are moved to an archive table once a year to improve the performance of the core table.

Bharani Bank also wishes to load this cross reference table into the Data Warehouse. However, they would like to have both active and inactive associations loaded to same table instead of keeping them separate. Having a consolidated table for associations helps them drill down the customer's historical transactions with ease.

Challenges:

a. The cross reference table contains customer ID and Account Number to identify the relationships. However, Data Warehouse uses surrogate keys (Customer Key and Account Key), which need to resolved before loading.

b. The cross reference data is stored in two tables: Active table and Archive table. Data from both these tables need to be merged and loaded to Data Warehouse.

Technical Solution:

To merge the data from both the cross reference tables (active and archive), we will use a union transformation. The output of the union transformation is then passed into two lookups – one for customer key resolution and another for account key resolution. Their inputs will be customer id and account id. The output will be customer key and account key. This data is then loaded into a data warehouse.

Steps for solution:

    a.   Go to mapping designer

    b.   Create a new mapping called "`m_DWH_Init_Load_CustAcctXref`"

    c.   Drag the `CUST_ACCT_XREF` and `CUST_ACCT_XREF_ARC` source tables into the mapping. Import the tables, if needed

    d.   Drag the `CUST_ACCT_XREF` target into the mapping. Import it if needed

    e.   Create a new union transformation by clicking the icon (⊌) in the transformation toolbar

        1.   Drag all the columns from `SQ_CUST_ACCT_XREF` into it. All ports are created in the union and are linked to the source qualifier

        2.   Open the union properties and go to `Groups` tab

        3.   A new input group called `NEWGROUP` is already created for you

        4.   Rename it to `Active`

        5.   Create a new group by clicking the new icon (⬚) and rename it as `Archive`

        6.   Go to the `Group Ports` tab and ensure that all the ports from the `CUST_ACCT_XREF` tables can be seen.

7. Now connect the ports from the other source qualifier to the union (to the `Archive` group)

f. Create a new expression (ℱ⁽ˣ⁾)

1. Drag the output of the union into the expression

2. Open the expression and rename it as `exp_Placeholder`. There will be no logic in this expression but it will help make the mapping more readable. Do not worry, there is no performance impact due to this

g. Create a new lookup transformation (🔍)

1. In the select lookup table dialog box, click the `Target` button at the top and then select `Customers` table. Click `OK`

2. A lookup transformation of name `LKPTRANS` is created

3. Drag the `Cust_ID` field from `exp_Placeholder` into the lookup. It is copied as `CUST_ID1` at the bottom

4. Edit the lookup transformation

   i. Rename the transformation as `lkp_Cust_Key`

   ii. In the ports tab, rename the `CUST_ID1` as `in_CUST_ID` and make it an input only port by unchecking the output column (`O`). Do not rename the `CUST_ID` port. Its name should be left as it is

   iii. Remove all the ports except `in_CUST_ID`, `CUST_KEY`, `CUST_ID` fields using the delete icon (✂)

   iv. Make `CUST_ID` as lookup only port by unchecking the output column (`O`)

   v. Go to the `Condition` tab and click a new condition icon (🗋)

   vi. In the new condition row created, make sure `CUST_ID` is in the lookup column and `in_Cust_ID` is selected in the transformation port

   vii. Click `OK` to close the lookup properties

h. Create a new lookup transformation. Select `Target`→`Accounts`

1. From `exp_Placeholder`, drag the `ACCT_NR` column into the lookup. It will be created as `ACCT_NR1`

2. Edit the lookup

    i. Rename the lookup as `lkp_Acct_Key`

    ii. Rename the `ACCT_NR1` as `in_Acct_NR` and make it as input only port

    iii. Delete all ports except `in_Acct_NR`, `ACCT_KEY` and `ACCT_NR`

    iv. Make the `ACCT_NR` as lookup only port

    v. In the `Condition` tab, create a new condition row with `ACCT_NR` as lookup table column and `in_Acct_NR` as transformation port

    vi. Save the lookup

i. Create a new expression and rename it as `exp_Metadata`

    1. Drag the `CUST_KEY` from `lkp_Cust_Key` into the `exp_Metadata`

    2. Drag the `ACCT_KEY` from `lkp_Acct_Key` into the `exp_Metadata`

    3. Drag the `EFF_DT` and `END_DT` from `exp_Placeholder_1` into `exp_Metadata`

    4. Edit the `exp_Metadata` and create 3 output only ports:

        i. `LAST_UPD_DT` as `date` data type with expression value as `SYSDATE`

        ii. `LAST_UPD_DESC` as `string` data type with `255` precision and value as `'Initial Load'` (with the quotes)

        iii. `ACTIVE` as `string` data type with 1 precision and value as `IIF(IsNull(END_DT), 'Y', 'N')`

    5. Create a new sequence generator and rename it as `seq_CA_Key`

j. Connect the `seq_CA_Key.NEXT_VAL` to the `CA_Key` in the target

    1. Connect all other attributes from `exp_Metadata` to the target

k. Save the mapping

l. Your mapping should now look similar to the picture shown (wrapped for detailed view)

m. Go to workflow manager, create a new session in
`wf_DWH_Initial_Loads`

1. Link this session such that it runs AFTER both the customers and accounts sessions

2. In the session properties, set the source and target connections. Since we created target based lookups, also assign Data Warehouse connection to `$Target` in the `Properties` tab →`$Target` connection value

3. If the target is oracle, change the `Target Load type` from `Bulk` to `Normal`

n. Save the workflow and start the session

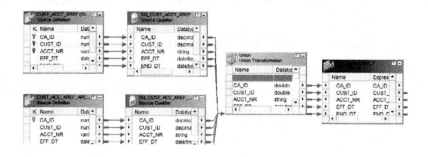

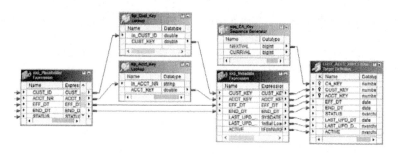

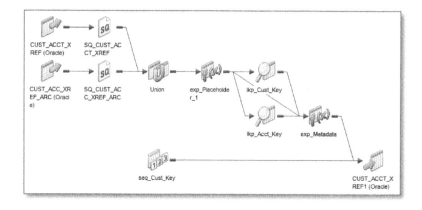

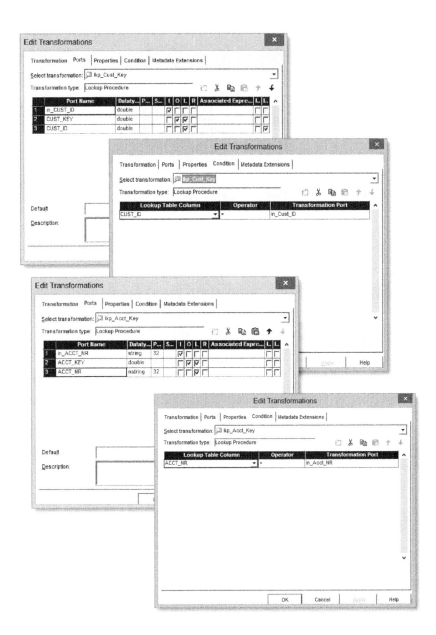

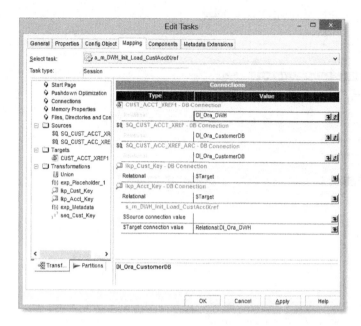

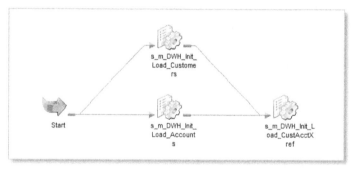

7.15   Joiner transformation

Earlier we have seen how to use source qualifier to perform joins on database tables, so the first question that comes to one's mind is why another transformation to perform joins? Well, there's a catch with source qualifier that we did not talk about earlier. Source qualifier represents the data from one or more sources that are being fed into the PowerCenter Integration Service. However, a source qualifier uses a single connection for all the sources it represents. So source qualifier makes perfect sense to join tables that are in same schema or in the same database. But when multiple sources are in different databases or of different database types, source qualifier cannot be used. Imagine a table in Oracle and a table in Microsoft SQL Server that needs to be joined. This join cannot be performed at the database level, at least with the way most databases are setup. This is exactly where a joiner comes into play. A joiner allows us to join heterogeneous datasets. A joiner can be used to join relational tables, flat files and any other data stream that can be added to PowerCenter. Unlike source qualifier, joiner does not depend on the underlying database engines. A join operation happens completely in the PowerCenter Integration Service memory and operates on PowerCenter's universal data format.

7.15.1   Master and detail

A joiner involves two data streams: a Master and a Detail. A master is the parent data set, while a detail is the child data set. A joiner can receive only two inputs. Multiple joiners can be used to join more than 2 data sets. To perform n number of joins, you will require n-1 joiner transformations.

In the designer UI, the first set of ports that you drag into a joiner transformation is considered detail. You can always change this in the ports tab of joiner by checking/unchecking the "M" for Master and "D" for Detail columns.

7.15.2   Types of joins

Joiner supports different kinds of joins. These types of joins are very similar and analogous to the joins performed at the database level. You can change the join type in `Properties` tab of Joiner.

Normal join

This is the default join type. In this join, Integration service retains all the matching records from both master and the detail. If a matching record is not found on either side, it will be discarded. At the database level, this is also known as an inner join.

Master outer join

In a master outer join, integration service will keep all the matching records and also the unmatched *detail* records. Any master record that does not have a match will be discarded. For the records where there is no matching in the master, NULL is populated for the ports connected from the master.

Detail outer join

It is an exact opposite to master outer join and keeps all records from the master regardless of a match along with any matching detail records. Unmatched detail records are discarded. NULL is populated where the detail records are missing a match.

Full outer join

A full outer join is a combination of Master outer join and Detail outer join and keeps all records from both the sources. When a matching record is not found on either side, corresponding ports will contain a NULL value.

> By default, Joiner is *not* case sensitive but is space sensitive. Since CHAR fields contain padded space, they may not match to their VARCHAR counterparts unless the spaces are trimmed explicitly.

7.16   Lab 6 – Joiner

Business requirement:

 The customer address information stored in the CustomerDB is to be loaded to the Data Warehouse. To do so, the geographical information referred to by these addresses must be loaded to the data warehouse. A geography dimension is already created which needs to be populated first. The geography data in source (geography database) is a normalized structure while dimension in the data warehouse is a de-normalized table. The records need to be flattened out to be loaded into this dimension.

Challenges:

a.   Data from multiple tables need to be flattened out without losing any data attributes.

b.   City information is mandatory but states' information is available only for United States at this time. If the state for a given city is not available, the record should still be retained.

Technical solution:

A joiner transformation is used to join the tables from geography database and then load to the geography database. An outer join will be used to join the states master data so that all the cities' information, whether or not a state is available will be loaded to the data warehouse.

Steps for solution:

a. Open the designer, connect to the DWH_DI folder

   1. If not already done so, import the GEO_CITIES, GEO_STATES, GEO_COUNTRIES tables from the GEO schema

   2. Go to the target designer, import the GEO_DIM table from the DWH schema

b. Switch to the mapping designer

c. Create a new mapping called m_DWH_Init_Load_GEO_Data

d. Drag the GEO_CITIES, GEO_STATES, GEO_COUNTRIES source tables into the mapping

e. Drag the GEO_DIM target table into the mapping

f. Add a joiner transformation

   1. Drag the SQ_GEO_CITIES columns (except the ACTIVE port) into the joiner

   2. Then drag all the ports (except ACTIVE port) from SQ_GEO_COUNTRIES into the joiner

   3. Edit the joiner

   4. Rename the joiner as jnr_Cities_n_Cntrys

   5. In the Properties tab, verify the join type is Normal join

   6. In the condition tab, add a new condition by clicking new icon

   7. Set the condition as CNTRY_ID1 = CNTRY_ID

   8. Close the joiner properties by clicking OK

g. Add another joiner

1. Drag all ports from the `jnr_Cities_n_Cntrys` except `CNTRY_ID1` into the new joiner

2. Drag `STATE_ID`, `STATE_NAME` and `STATE_CD` from the `SQ_GEO_STATES` into the new joiner

3. Edit the new joiner

4. Rename it as `jnr_Cities_n_States`

5. In the properties tab, set the `Join type` as `Master Outer join`

6. In the condition tab, add a new condition by clicking the new icon

7. Set the condition as `STATE_ID1 = STATE_ID`

8. Click `OK` to close the joiner properties

h. Add a new expression transformation as a placeholder. Call it as `exp_Placeholder`

1. From the joiner `jnr_Cities_n_States`, drag the following columns in this order: `CITY_NAME`, `STATE_NAME`, `STATE_CODE`, `CNTRY_NAME`, `CNTRY_CD`, `CURR_CD` into the expression

i. Create a new sequence generator transformation and name it as `seq_Geo_ID`

1. Connect the ports from sequence generator next value and all ports in expression to the target

j. Save the mapping

k. Go to workflow manager

l. Create a new relational connection in `Connections` menu →`Relational` to point to the database/schema where you have setup the `GEO` tables. Name this connection appropriately (For ex: `DI_Ora_GEO`)

m. Edit the workflow `wf_DWH_Initial_Loads`

1. Create a new session for this mapping we just created.

2. Connect the start task to this session so that it runs in parallel to everything else.

3. Edit the session. Go to the `Mapping` tab. Select the `GEO_DIM` target.

4. Set the `Target Load Type` to `Normal`

5. Check the `Truncate Target Table` option.

6. Set appropriate connections for the source (`DI_Ora_GEO`) and the target (`DI_Ora_DWH`)

n. Run the start task command to run the task and verify the target data.

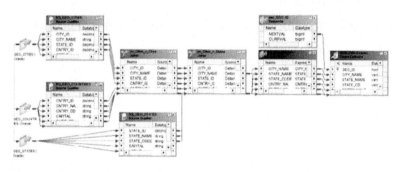

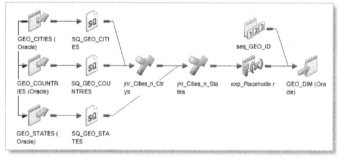

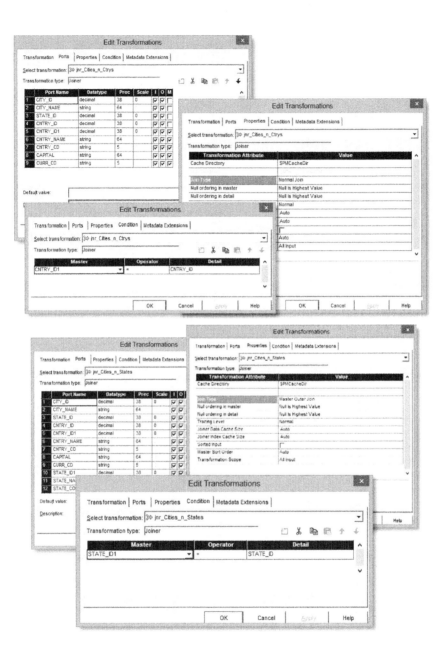

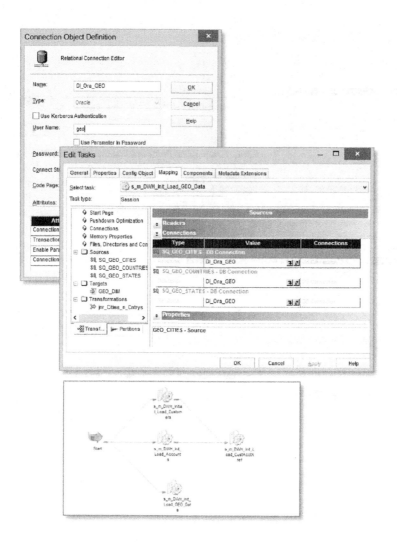

7.17   Sorter transformation

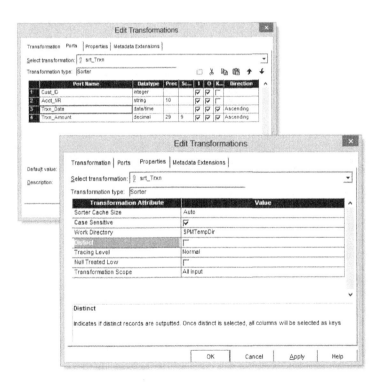Sorter transformation is used to sort in stream data within the PowerCenter. While sorter is, at times, used to generate sorted output, it is most widely used in conjunction with joiners and aggregators to improve their efficiency. Sorter functionality is actually quite simple. It reorders the data based on the keys specified in the transformation. The sorter transformation also allows the option to output distinct rows after the sort operation. More than one port can be configured as the sort key. When multiple ports are configured as sort keys, PowerCenter will depend on the order of ports to define the order of the sort. When a port is selected as a sort key, direction is enabled so that developers can define the sort key as ascending or descending.

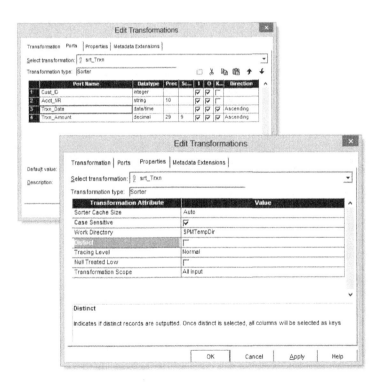

7.18   Aggregator transformation

 Aggregator transformation can group input data into groups so that aggregations such as min, max, sum can be computed. When PowerCenter reads data into the aggregator, its starts grouping them based on the group by ports defined within the aggregator transformation. Variable ports and output ports are allowed within an aggregator. These ports can contain expressions with aggregate and non-aggregate functions. The following aggregate functions are available with aggregator transformation:

a. AVG

b. COUNT

c. FIRST

d. LAST

e. MAX

f. MEDIAN

g. MIN

h. PERCENTILE

i. STDDEV

j. SUM

k. VARIANCE

Refer to the transformation language reference in PowerCenter help for more details on these functions.

7.19   Lab 7 – Sorter and aggregator

Business requirement:

As part of the Data Warehouse being built, Bharani Bank is interested in summary tables for gathering quick facts. One of these summary tables includes the number of transactions per transaction type for every month and year. A reporting tool is used to generate a report as shown below. The bank doesn't want the reporting tool to compute any information. All data must be pre-computed including the totals. Only cleared transactions (Status 4) should be a part of this report. Some of the important columns and their data are as shown below:

Year	Month	No. of Transactions
2000	JAN	95,978
2000	FEB	88,568
...	...	...
2000	ALL	78,434,720
2001	JAN	3,68,521
...	...	...

Challenges:

    a.   Data must be aggregated at two levels: years and month

    b.   An additional row must be inserted that represents the whole year

    c.   Process only cleared transactions

Technical Solution:

A sorter is used to sort the data by year and month and then two aggregators are used – one to calculate the sum per year and one to calculate per month in the year. This data will then be union'ed and loaded to a single table. Expressions are used to get year and month values out of the transaction date.

Steps for Solution:

a. Open the designer and DWH_DI folder

b. If not already imported, import transactions and its related tables from TRXN into the Source Analyzer

c. Import the summary table SUM_YEARMON_TRXN from the data warehouse into the target designer

d. Create a new mapping m_DWH_Sum_YearMonthTrxn

e. Drag the TRXN and TRXN_TYPE sources into the mapping

    1. Delete the default source qualifiers

    2. Create a single source qualifier for both the tables

    3. Rename the source qualifier as __sq_TRXN_n_TYPE

    4. Set the user defined join in the new source qualifier as TRXN.TRXN_TYPE = TRXN_TYPE.TRXN_TYPE_ID

    5. Set the Source Filter as TRXN.TRXN_STATUS = 4

f. Create a new expression transformation

    1. Drag TRXN_DATE, TRXN_AMOUNT, TRXN_TYPE_NAME into the expression

    2. Rename the expression as exp_Date_Values

    3. Create the following output ports:

Port	I	O	V	Type	Expression
o_Year		✓		Integer	To_Integer(To_Char(TRXN_DATE, 'YYYY'))
o_Month		✓		Integer	To_Integer(To_Char(TRXN_DATE, MM'))
o_MonthName		✓		String(3)	To_Integer(To_Char(TRXN_DATE, 'MON'))

g. Create a new sorter transformation

    1. Drag o_Year, o_Month, o_MonthName, TRXN_AMOUNT, TRXN_TYPE_NAME into the sorter

  2. Rename the sorter as `srt_Yr_Mon_Typ`

  3. Set the sort keys as `o_Year`, `o_Month`, `TRXN_TYPE_NAME` in that order

h. Create a new aggregator

  1. Drag all ports from sorter into it

  2. Rename it as `aggr_Yr_Mon`

  3. Set the `o_Year`, `o_Month`, `TRXN_TYPE_NAME` as group keys

  4. Create a new output only port called `o_Mon_Amount` as `double` and set its expression as `sum(TRXN_AMOUNT)`

i. Create another aggregator

  1. Drag `o_Year`, `TRXN_AMOUNT`, `TRXN_TYPE_NAME` from sorter into it

  2. Rename it as `aggr_Yr`

  3. Set the `o_Year` and `TRXN_TYPE_NAME` as group keys

  4. Create a new output only port called `o_MonthName` as `string(3)` and set its expression as `'ALL'` (with the quotes)

  5. Create a new output only port called `o_Yr_Amount` as `double` and set its expression as `sum(TRXN_AMOUNT)`

j. Create a new union transformation

  1. Drag the `o_Year`, `o_MonthName`, `TRXN_TYPE_NAME`, `o_Mon_Amount` from `aggr_Yr_Mon` into the Union

k. Edit the union transformation

  1. In the `groups` tab, rename the `NEWGROUP` to `ALL_MONTHS`

  2. Create a new group called `YEAR`

  3. Close the dialog box

  4. Link the `o_Year`, `o_MonthName`, `TRXN_TYPE_NAME` and amount (`o_Yr_Amount`) between the `aggr_Yr` and the union transformation into the group (`YEAR`)

l. Create a new expression

  1. Drag all the output ports from the union into the expression

2. Rename it as `exp_UpdateDate`

3. Create a new output only port called as `o_Last_Update_Date` of `date` data type and set its expression to `SYSDATE`

m. Drag the target `SUM_YEARMON_TRXN`

1. Link all the ports from the `exp_UpdateDate` to the target. Leave the update description unconnected

n. Save the mapping

o. Go to workflow manager

p. Create a new relational connection `DI_Ora_TRXN` with values to connect to the transaction database

q. Create a new workflow called `wf_DWH_Summary_Tables`

r. Create a new session for this mapping

1. Set the `DI_Ora_TRXN` as the source connection for this session

2. Set the `DI_Ora_DWH` as the target connection

3. Set the target load type to `Normal` and select the `Truncate Target Table` option

s. Save the session and run the workflow

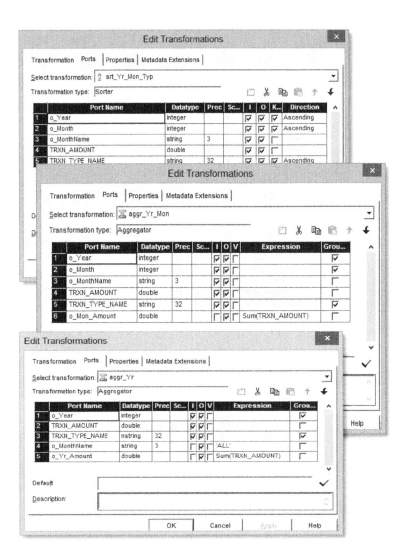

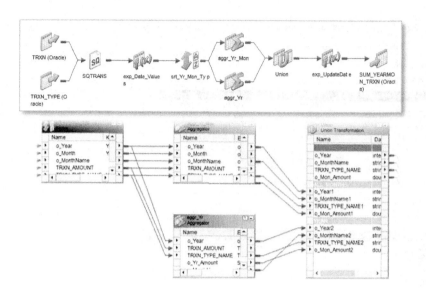

7.20 Rank transformation

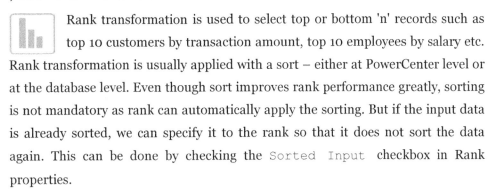

Rank transformation is used to select top or bottom 'n' records such as top 10 customers by transaction amount, top 10 employees by salary etc. Rank transformation is usually applied with a sort – either at PowerCenter level or at the database level. Even though sort improves rank performance greatly, sorting is not mandatory as rank can automatically apply the sorting. But if the input data is already sorted, we can specify it to the rank so that it does not sort the data again. This can be done by checking the `Sorted Input` checkbox in Rank properties.

7.21 Update strategy transformation

Update strategy transformation is used to mark the rows in a pipeline as Insert, Update, Delete or Reject. By default, PowerCenter Integration Service treats all input rows as inserts. Update strategy allows the users to mark the rows otherwise. It is most commonly used in conjunction with a lookup transformation. A lookup is used to identify whether or not a record exists in the target table. Update strategy is then used to mark if the record is Insert (if it didn't exist in the target), Update (if it already exists in the target) or Reject (if the record already exists but hasn't changed).

PART 3

ADVANCED

DATA INTEGRATION

8

Flat file processing

8.1   Introduction

Flat files are one of the most fundamental data stores. They are directly stored on the operating system's file system. There are two types of flat files that are widely used for data storage and exchange:

    a.   Delimited Files

    b.   Fixed width files

In both the file formats, each row is typically represented by a line. Each line is separated by a line separator (CRLF – Carriage Return Line Feed in Windows and Line Feed in UNIX platforms). These line separators are invisible characters and can be added into a file by simply pressing the enter key (↵).

Delimited files:

In delimited files, each row is divided into columns with a column separator in between. Most commonly used separators are comma (CSV file), tab (TSV file) and pipe.

A sample CSV (Comma Separated Values) file is shown below:

```
CUST_ID,CITY,ZIP

1,Whitehall,18052

2,Redwood City,94065
```

Fixed width files:

Fixed width files do not use a delimiter but instead, use fixed positions to represent start of each column. Data within the column is usually left aligned, but can also be right aligned in some cases. A sample fixed width file is shown below with margins

```
1          10          20          25    30
|--------- |--------- |--------- |----- |
CUST_ID    CITY                   ZIP
1          Whitehall              18052
2          Redwood City           94065
```

PowerCenter supports both the file formats. In terms of development, operating with flat files is very similar to operating with the databases. We follow the same steps as with the databases:

a. Import the flat file structure into PowerCenter
b. Develop a mapping
c. Create a workflow
d. Create a session
e. Run the workflow

Some notable differences while operating with flat files as compared to operating with databases:

a. A relational connection is not needed since no database engine is required. However, the file name and its location must be specified. The location specified must be relative to the Integration Service.

b. Relational tables have truncate target table option, which allows us to empty the table before load. Files, similarly, have overwrite and append modes. In overwrite mode, the whole file is replaced with every session run. In append mode, the data is appended to the existing contents of the file.

c. Relational tables accept insert, update and delete operations. Files do not support these. Hence, to perform these operations, we should read the file as an input, compare the changes and write the resultant to a new file.

d. Data integrity can be maintained in the tables with the help of referential integrity. With files, such integrity has to be explicitly maintained. PowerCenter will not perform any integrity checks when reading from / writing to files.

8.2   Working with delimited files

To import delimited files into PowerCenter as a source or target, we operate in source analyzer or target designer. In this section, we will look at everything you need to know about operating with delimited files. To be able to import a flat file into the designer, you need a copy of the file (just a few sample records with same structure will do).

8.2.1   Importing delimited file definitions

To import file, choose `Sources` (or `Targets`) menu →`Import from file`. 'Open flat file' dialog box appears. By default, only `.dat` files are displayed. Select `All files (*.*)` option from `Files of type` drop down. Flat File Import Wizard appears.

Choose `Delimited` as the file type and provide a name for the source. Designer will, by default, provide the file name as the name of the source. If you have a list of field names in the first row, check the `Import field names from the first line.` `Start Import at Row` will be automatically updated to 2. If you want to skip more lines, you can increase the counter.

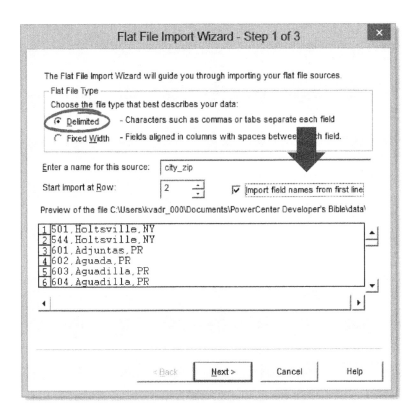

Select the delimiter checkbox. If your file delimiter is not present in the check boxes, check `Other` and provide a character. If you provide more than 1 character in the other, Designer will treat all the characters as delimiters. To change this behavior, you can check the `Treat multiple delimiters as AND`. If your text fields have quotes around them, select single quotes or double quotes in the

`Text Qualifier`. If you have too many fields and defining length fields is very time consuming, you can start with a default, by checking the `Use default text length`. All text fields will then, by default, will have this length. Note that if your file has field names in the first line, they are not yet shown on this screen.

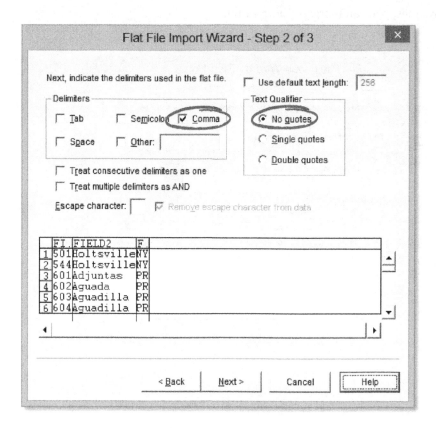

In the last step (step 3) of the wizard, your field names are displayed on the right hand side of the screen with sample data in the bottom screen. You can select each column on the right and update their definitions on the left and finally click finish to import the definitions. You will notice that all the flat files are organized under `FlatFile` category in the repository navigator. The flat file properties can always be changed by double clicking on the source or target to get its properties and then clicking on the `Advanced` button.

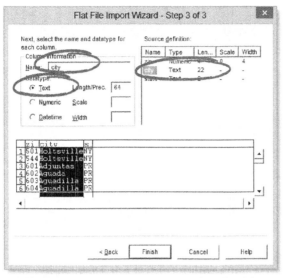

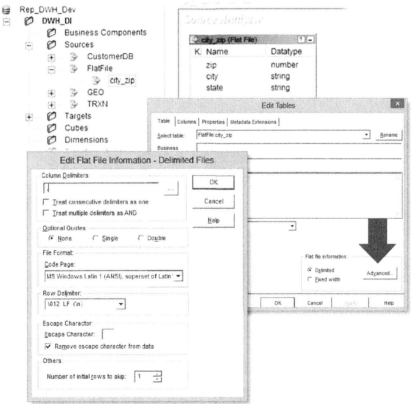

8.3   Working with fixed-width files

In fixed width files, each column starts at a specific position and spans for a pre-defined length. If the data of an attribute is less than the length allocated to it, it is padded with spaces, usually to the right.

8.3.1   Importing fixed-width file definitions

To import fixed-width files, we follow the same steps as with the delimited files. Go to the `Source Analyzer` or `Target Designer` and choose `Sources` (or `Targets`) menu → `Import from flat file.` `Flat File Import Wizard` starts. Choose `Fixed Width` in the flat file type. In step 2 of the wizard, sample contents of the file are displayed along with a rule on top. Click on the rule to add markers to define the start position of each field. When you click on the rule or on the data at a position, a black vertical line will appear indicating the position. In the next screen, define the column names and click Finish to complete the wizard.

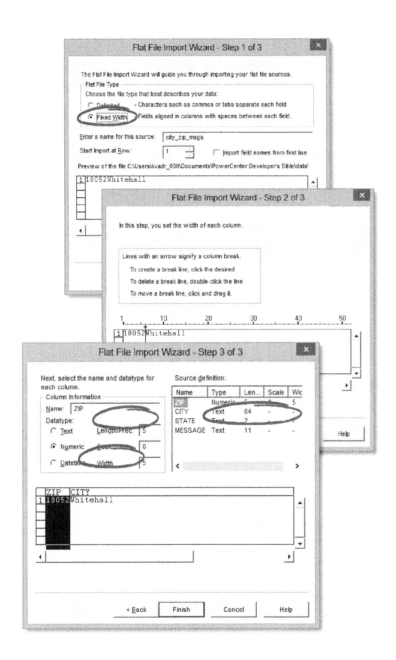

8.4   Session properties for flat files

Several delimited file properties can also be overridden at the session level. When a mapping is created with a flat file source or target, appropriate properties appear in the session's mapping tab. In addition to what we typically see in the designer, several run time properties also appear in the sessions.

 File's design time properties such as column data types cannot be edited in the session. Likewise, file's run time properties such as file location and file name can be edited only at the session level.

When a flat file source is present in a mapping, a File Reader appears in the session properties (a). No connections will be displayed by default (b) and file specific properties are displayed in the properties section (c). For flat file targets, a writer appears in place of reader and target specific properties appear in (c).

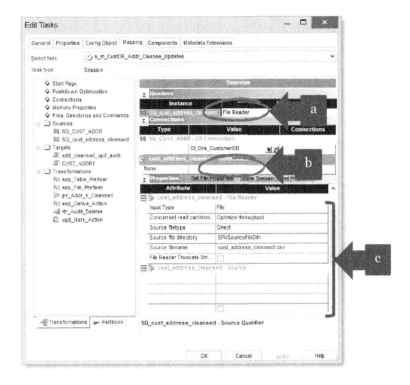

Following properties appear in the sessions when a flat file source is used in a mapping:

Source file directory	This directory/location is accessed by Integration Service. Integration service expects the source files to be present here during session initialization.
Source filename	Name of the file that is being read.

You can use either windows slash (\) or UNIX style slash (/) in the directory paths. PowerCenter will automatically convert this based on the underlying operating system on which Integration Service is running.

 Windows is not case sensitive but UNIX, Linux based operating systems are case sensitive. Use caution when keying in the file names and paths. PowerCenter will pass the file names and paths as-is to the underlying operating system.

When a flat file target is used in the mapping, following properties are available:

Append if exists	By default Integration service will overwrite the target file if it already exists, check this box to append the content to it.
Create target directory	By default integration service expects the target directory to be available and writeable. If not, integration service fails the session with appropriate error code. If this box is checked, PowerCenter will automatically create the target directory structure, if it is not present already.
Header options	There are three possible values for this option: → No header : Default; no header content is written to the file → Output field names: Field names, as present in the target definition, are written at the top of the file → Use header command output: The header command

	is executed at the OS level and its output is added as a header to the file
Header command	If provided, and the header options are set to use header command, output of this command is added at the top of the file
Footer command	If provided, output of this command is added at the bottom of the file after all the contents are written from the current session
Output type	There are two options for this property: → File: Default. Content is written to a file → Command: output of the current session is redirected as input to the command specified in the "command" property

8.5   Direct and indirect files

When flat files are used as a source in the mapping, the Source File Type session property is available for the source. This property can be set either to Direct file (default) or Indirect file. A direct file contains the data that belongs to the file. An indirect file contains a list of file names that contain the data. In data integration, it is a common aspect to receive several files from the same source on a given day. In such cases, an indirect file containing all the files received can be created so that PowerCenter can consume them without any modifications to the sessions. The flat file definition in designer consists of a file name port that allows the developers to access the file name (when using indirect files) within the mapping itself. This property helps in building logic that is applicable to certain files and not to others, even though they are received as part of the same indirect file list.

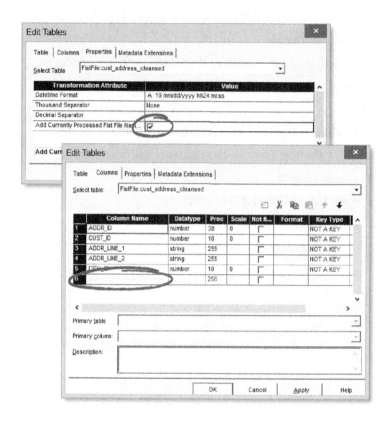

8.6   Lab 8 – Flat files

Business requirement:

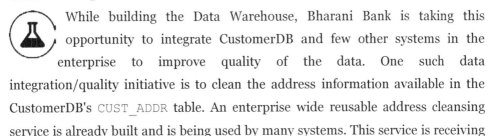 While building the Data Warehouse, Bharani Bank is taking this opportunity to integrate CustomerDB and few other systems in the enterprise to improve quality of the data. One such data integration/quality initiative is to clean the address information available in the CustomerDB's CUST_ADDR table. An enterprise wide reusable address cleansing service is already built and is being used by many systems. This service is receiving customer address information from the same system that is loading the address data into the CustomerDB. Due to some technical reasons, these updates are not being pushed to CustomerDB. Bharani Bank would now like us to integrate CustomerDB with this address cleansing system. The address cleansing service will send the cleansed output once a day in a delimited file. This file is to be processed and loaded to CUST_ADDR table in the CustomerDB. Since the input to the address cleansing service is not CustomerDB, it is possible that there is a discrepancy between what the CustomerDB has and what the address services sends back. The delimited file contains the following structure:

Column	Data type	Description
Addr_ID	Integer	Unique ID to identify each address entry in the Customer Address table
Cust_ID	Integer	Customer ID from the CustomerDB
Addr_Line_1	Varchar2(255)	Address line 1
Addr_Line_2	Varchar2(255)	Address line 2
City_ID	Integer	Refers to a city in the GEO_CITIES table in the GEO database.
Active	Integer	An integer indicative active(1) or inactive(0) status of the address

Bharani Bank expects the following data scenarios to occur and have provided corresponding resolutions:

Data scenario	Action to be taken
The Address ID provided by address cleansing service is not present in the CUST_ADDR table	Insert this record into the CUST_ADDR table
The Address ID provided by address cleansing service is present in the CUST_ADDR table	If the address line 1 or line 2 or City ID is different from the one in the CUST_ADDR table, then update the record. Otherwise, reject/ignore the record
If the CITY_ID, ADDR_LINE_1 and ADDR_LINE_2 are all blank	The record cannot be cleansed and should be deleted from the system. Any deleted record must be logged into a file

Challenges:

a. Read data from a file and a table and join them
b. Based on the joined data, determine for each record whether the record is to be inserted, updated, rejected or deleted
c. Write the deleted records into a flat file for audit

Technical solution:

We read the CUST_ADDR table and the cleansed data we received from the address service. Since one is a table and the other is a flat file, we need to use Joiner transformation to join this data. This will be a normal join, since we only need the matches. By looking at the attributes on either side, we will determine the action to be taken in an expression. Based on the action, we will use update strategy to change the record type. We will then use a router to route a copy of the deleted records in to an audit log.

Steps for solution:

a. Open the designer and import the CUST_ADDR table, if it's not already imported. Import this table as both source and target.

b. Import the CSV file (cust_address_cleansed.csv) into the designer (Source Analyzer) as a source.

1. Select the file type as delimited

2. Check import field names from first line

3. Start Import at Row field will be automatically updated to 2

4. Select delimiter as Comma (,)

5. Select Text Qualifier as Double Quotes

6. Set the data types as below:

Column	Data type	Length	Scale	Width
ADDR_ID	Numeric	38	0	10
CUST_ID	Numeric	10	0	10
ADDR_LINE_1	Text	255	-	-
ADDR_LINE_2	Text	255	-	-
CITY_ID	Numeric	10	0	10

c. In the target designer, go to Targets menu →Create

1. Select the database type as Flat File and provide a name as "addr_cleanse_upd_audit" and click Create and click Done

2. Double click the target to edit it

    a.   In the Flat file information, select `Fixed Width`

    b.   Then click `Advanced`...

    c.   Replace the `NULL` character from `*` to space ( )

    d.   Select `Repeat NULL character` and click OK

    e.   Add new ports as below

Column	Data type	Prec	Scale
ADDR_ID	int	8	0
CUST_ID	int	8	0
ADDR_LINE_1	string	128	-
ADDR_LINE_2	string	128	-
CITY_ID	int	8	0
ACTION	string	3	

    d.   Now, create a mapping `m_CustDB_Addr_Cleanse_Updates`

    e.   Drag the sources `CUST_ADDR` table and `cust_address_cleansed` flat file in to the mapping

    f.   Add two expressions. From each source qualifier drag all ports into each of the expression. Prefix all the flat file columns in the expression with `ff_` and prefix all the table columns in the corresponding expression with `tbl_`

    g.   Rename the expressions as `exp_File_Prefixer` and `exp_Table_Prefixer`

    h.   Drag the target `addr_cleanse_upd_audit` into the mapping

    i.   Create a joiner

        1.   Drag the columns from `exp_Table_Prefixer` (as detail) and then from the exp_File_Prefixer(as master) into the joiner

        2.   Edit the joiner

            a.   Rename it as `jnr_Addr_n_Cleansed`

            b.   Make it a detail outer join so that all records from the cleansing system (flat file) are retained

      c. Create a join condition to match it with `ADDR_ID`

 For the joiner to be successfully created, the data types for the columns participating in the joins must be identical.

  j. Create a new expression and drag all the ports from the joiner into it

      1. Edit the transformation and rename it as `exp_Derive_Action`

      2. Create a new output only port called `o_Action` as string(3) with the expression:

         a. `IIF(IsNull(tbl_ADDR_ID), 'INS',IIF('' ||`
              `ff_ADDR_LINE_1 || ff_ADDR_LINE_2 ||`
              `To_Char(ff_CITY_ID) = '',`
              `'DEL',IIF(tbl_ADDR_LINE_1 != ff_ADDR_LINE_1 OR`
              `tbl_ADDR_LINE_2 != ff_ADDR_LINE_2 OR`
              `tbl_CITY_ID != ff_CITY_ID,'UPD','REJ')))`

  k. Create a new router transformation

      1. Drag all the ports from expression into the Router

      2. Edit the router:

         a. Rename the router as `rtr_Audit_Deletes`

         b. Create a new group in the groups tab

         c. Rename the `NEWGROUP1` as `DELETES` and set its expression as `o_Action = 'DEL'`

  l. Drag the `add_cleanse_upd_audit` target into the mapping

  m. From the `DELETES` group, drag the `tbl_` ports (that originated from the `CUST_ADDR` table) to the target along with the `o_Action`

  n. Create a new update strategy transformation

  o. Drag all the ports in the `DEFAULT` group with prefix `ff_`(originated from the flat file) and drop them in the update strategy

p.   Link the o_Action from the DEFAULT group to update strategy

q.   Edit the update strategy

1.   Rename it as upd_Mark_Action

2.   Remove the number suffixes at the end. Address Line attributes have a number at the end. Be careful not to remove those. To avoid any accidental deletes, remove only the last digit from each port name

3.   In the properties tab, set the Update Strategy Expression as:

a.   Decode(o_Action, 'INS', DD_Insert, 'UPD', DD_Update, 'DEL', DD_Delete, DD_Reject)

4.   Uncheck the Forward Rejected rows

5.   Close the dialog, transformation

r.   Drag the CUST_ADDR target into the mapping. If not already imported, import it from the CustomerDB. Note that earlier we had imported this table as a source. Now we need to import it as a target

s.   Link all the ports between update strategy and the router except o_Action2 and ACTIVE

t.   Validate and save the mapping

u.   Go to workflow manager

v.   Create a new workflow called wf_CustDB_Address_Updates

w.   Create a new session linking to the mapping m_CustDB_Addr_Cleanse_Updates

x.   Edit the session

1.   Set the DI_Ora_CustomerDB connection to CUST_ADDR source and target connections

2.   For the customer address flat file source, set the following properties

a.   Source File Directory: $PMSourceFileDir\

b.   Source File name: cust_address_cleansed.csv

3.   Set the target addr_cleanse_upd_audit properties as following:

a.   Output Type: File

b.   Output file directory: $PMTargetFileDir\

      c.   Output file name: `addr_cleanse_upd_audit.log`

      d.   Reject file directory: `$PMBadFileDir\`

      e.   Reject file name: `addr_cleanse_upd_audit.bad`

    4.   Change the target load type as Normal for the `CUST_ADDR` target

    5.   In the properties tab, set the Treat Source rows as "`Data Driven`"

y. Now, upload the source file cust_address_cleansed.csv file onto your Informatica PowerCenter server to the location `$INFA_HOME/server/infa_shared/SrcFiles`, where `$INFA_HOME` is the location where PowerCenter server is installed

z. Run the workflow

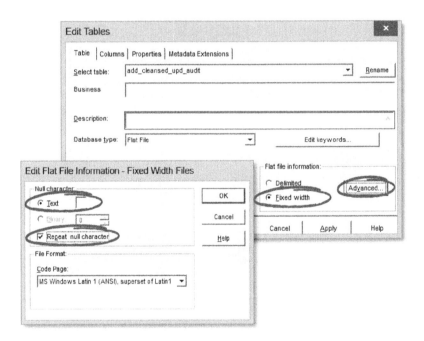

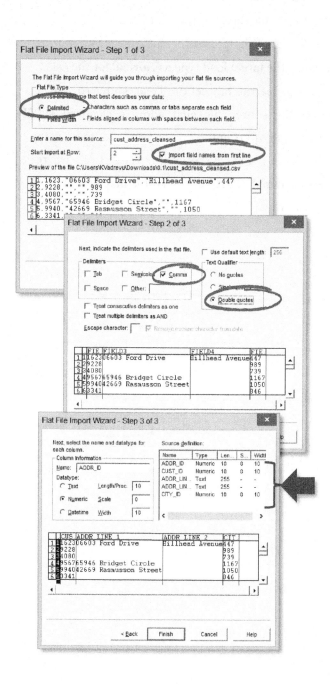

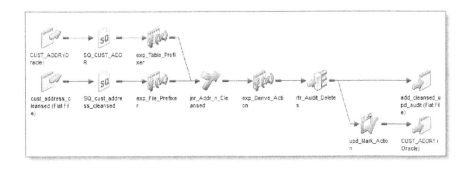

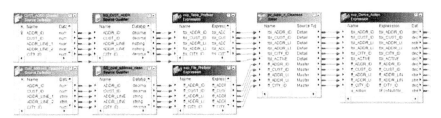

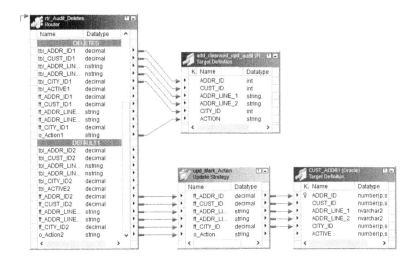

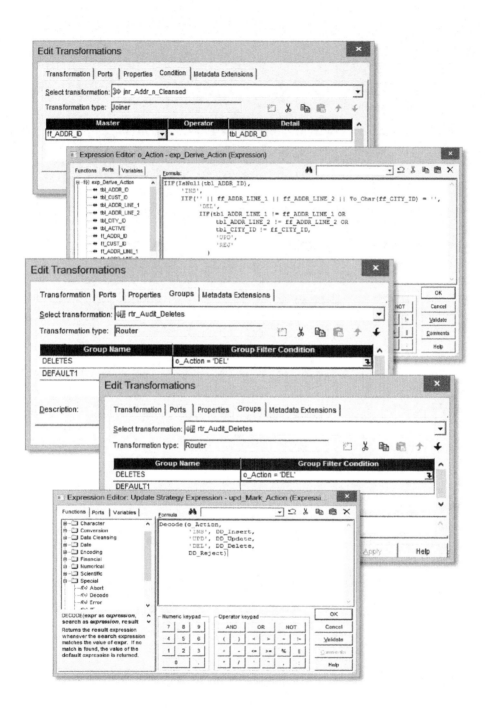

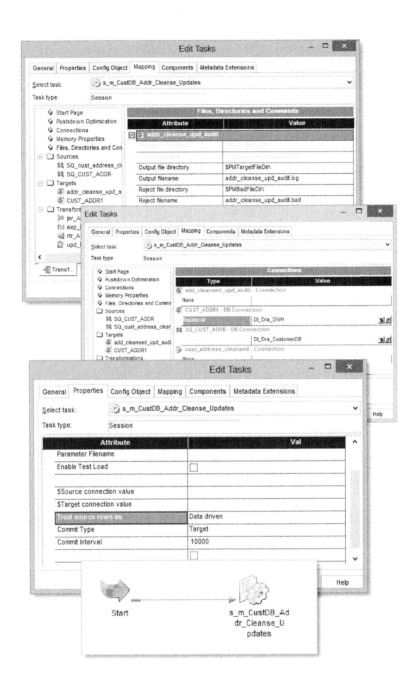

8.7 Advanced delimited file handling

The advanced properties can be accessed by opening the file definition in the Source Analyzer or Target Designer and clicking `Advanced...` in the `Table` tab.

8.7.1 Line sequential – Fixed width across files

By default, a fixed-width definition means that each column is made up of some bytes even if those bytes contain line termination characters such as carriage return and line feed. In such a case, Integration Service will continue to read the data from the next line until it reads specified number of bytes. This functionality is helpful when all columns in the file always have their defined width and some columns may have line termination characters as part of their data. Now, the line termination character is simply read like any other character and processed. Now consider a scenario where you expect all but the last column to have fixed width and the last column may have either the number of characters defined or less than that. In such case, you would like the line termination characters to be treated as true line termination characters. The line sequential file format option allows us to control this behavior. When checked, integration service will treat line termination characters as true line termination characters and not as part of data. If the line termination character appears before reading all the columns from the file, remaining columns are populated with NULL.

```
Input

1---|---10----|---20----|---30----|---40----|---50
900 Mickley Rd, Unit 203        NewCity    PA      08816
900 Mickley Rd,
Unit 204       NewCity      PA      08816
```

Output, when line sequential is off…

Row	Addr Line	City	State	Zip
1	900 Mickley Rd, Unit 203	NewCity	PA	08816
2	900 Mickley Rd, Unit 203	NewCity	PA	08816

Output, when line sequential is on…

Row	Addr Line	City	State	Zip
1	900 Mickley Rd, Unit 203	NewCity	PA	08816
2	900 Mickley Rd,	NULL	NULL	NULL
3	Unit 204	NewCity	PA	08816

8.7.2   Skip trailing blanks

In fixed-width files, since every column is expected to start and end at specific positions, if the column data falls short of the length, it is padded with spaces. When processing these in the PowerCenter, these spaces can cause unwanted results – especially when joining or comparing data. Hence, check this box to let Integration service automatically trim trailing spaces for you.

8.7.3   Repeat NULL character

While reading from or writing to fixed width files, absence of a column's data is usually represented by a NULL character (default is *). If you prefer to have the column filled with spaces instead, set the NULL character to space and check the Repeat NULL character.

8.8   Advanced fixed with file handling

8.8.1   Using special characters as delimiters

To use unprintable characters such as tab as a delimiter, go to table properties in Designer, click "Advanced...". In the Edit flat file information dialog, click "..." in the Column Delimiters section. Then choose a delimiter from the Insert delimiter drop down and click Add.

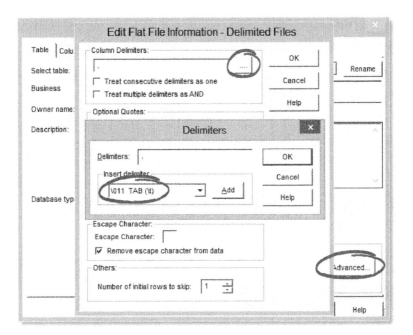

8.8.2   Multi-character delimiters

In general, delimited flat files have only one character as their delimiter. An example is a comma in a CSV file. Multiple characters can be provided in the delimiter field of table definition. Integration service then treats all of those characters as delimiters and treats the data as end of column as soon as it sees any one of these. To specify a group of characters as a delimiter, instead of single character, check the box `Treat multiple delimiters as AND`.

8.8.3   Delimiter as data

At times, delimiter itself is a part of the data and is required to be treated as data instead of delimiter. Look at the example mentioned. Here, `900 Mickley Rd, Unit 203` is all part of the `AddressLine` field. However, since the file is a comma delimited, `Unit 203` will now be treated as `City`, `NewCity` as `State` and `PA` as `zip` – causing data errors. So, to distinguish the delimiter within the data from a true delimiter, we can define an escape character in front of the delimiter where it appears as data. The character after the escape character is no longer treated as a delimiter, but simply as the data itself.

CSV file data

```
900 Mickley Rd, Unit 203,NewCity,PA,08816
```

CSV file data with escape character

```
900 Mickley Rd\, Unit 203,NewCity,PA,08816
```

Output data

Row	Addr Line	City	State	Zip
1	900 Mickley Rd	Unit 203	Ne	

* State data is truncated at 2 characters

Output data (when escape character is used)

Row	Addr Line	City	State	Zip
1	900 Mickley Rd, Unit 203	NewCity	PA	08816

9

XML file processing

9.1   Introduction to XML

XML stands for eXtended Markup Language. It is a markup language very similar to HTML. Unlike HTML, XML is designed to store the data and not to display it. Hence, XML tags are not predefined and are user defined. XML can be referred to as contemporary structured data format. XML is not a processing engine but just an advanced data format. In simple terms, it can be thought of as a natural evolution from the fixed-width and delimited file formats with a more structured format to hold relational information. Though most widely used in Web, it is also used in many other software architectures including SOA implementations due to its portability and interoperability. Let's take a look at this sample XML below

```
<BBank>
      <eaddr custId='39784120'>
            <emails>
                  <email type='Work'>johndoe@comp.com</email>
                  <email type='Home'>john@personal.com</email>
            </emails>
            <phones>
                  <Phone type='Work'>673 8270794</Phone>
                  <Phone type='Home'>946 2879376</Phone>
                  <Phone type='Mobile'>726-095-3856</Phone>
```

```
                </phones>
        </eaddr>
        <eaddr custId='39784120'>
                <emails>
                        <email type='Work'>janedoe@comp.com</email>
                        <email type='Home'>jane@personal.com</email>
                </emails>
                <phones>
                        <Phone type='Work'>673 8270794</Phone>
                        <Phone type='Home'>946 2879376</Phone>
                        <Phone>726-095-3856</Phone>
                </phones>
        </eaddr>
</BBank>
```

9.1.1   XML elements, attributes

XML consists of elements. Each element contains a start tag, end tag and data within it. An element can also optionally consist of attributes. Attributes are placed within the element's start tag to qualify or provide additional information about element data. Attributes are name value pairs separated by an 'equals to' sign (=). Look at this sample element from the XML above:

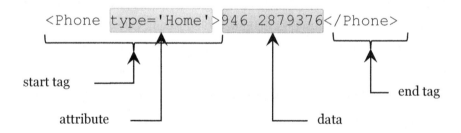

9.1.2   XML relationships

Elements can contain other elements forming parent-child relationships. Whether a parent can hold one occurrence of the child or more is defined in the XML Schema Definition. The top most element in an XML is called root element and the element that does not contain any children is called leaf element. Children of the root are generally known as global elements.

```
<BBank>
    <eaddr custId='39784120'>
            <emails>
        <email type='Work'>Shafira@netus.com</email>
        <email type='Home'>Shafira@netus.com</email>
            </emails>
            <phones>
                    <Phone type='Work'>673 8270794</Phone>
                    <Phone type='Home'>946 2879376</Phone>
                    <Phone type='Mobile'>726-095-3856</Phone>
            </phones>
        </eaddr>
</BBank>
```

root   global element – child to the root

9.1.3   DTDs and XSDs

Data Type Definitions (.dtd files) contain data type related metadata associated with an XML file. DTD provides basic grammar of the XML file. DTD's main focus is to define the data types of the elements and attributes in the XML document. XML Schema Definitions (.xsd files) contain schema definitions of an XML file. XSD is to XML what DDL is to a relational table – only difference being that DDL creates a physical object, whereas XSD is a separate living document that contains metadata to properly interpret and parse XML files. An XSD contains data types for each element, valid values, constraints on occurrences of children within a parent, relationship between elements and so forth. XSD is a more comprehensive document as it involves much more than data type information. But XSD can also become overhead at times due to the overwhelming details when something really simple needs to be implemented. An XML document can refer to either a DTD or a XSD as shown below

```
<?xml version="1.0"?>

<!DOCTYPE documentelement SYSTEM "cust_eaddress.dtd">


  <?xml version="1.0"?>

<BBank xmlns="http://pccr.edu"
xmlns:xsi="http://www.w3.org/2001/XMLSchema-instance"
xsi:schemaLocation="http://www.pctcr.edu
 cust_eaddress.xsd">
```

9.2   XML Sources and targets

PowerCenter can process XML documents using XML sources and XML targets. An XML definition can be imported into PowerCenter designer in more than one way. If the XML file or its XSD or DTD is available on your local machine, choose Local file option. If the XML file or its XSD or DTD is available on a remote location (such as a website), choose, URL option. If you do not have an XML definition ready, you can choose Non-XML Sources or Non-XML Targets and PowerCenter will create an XML definition based on the relational schema you selected.

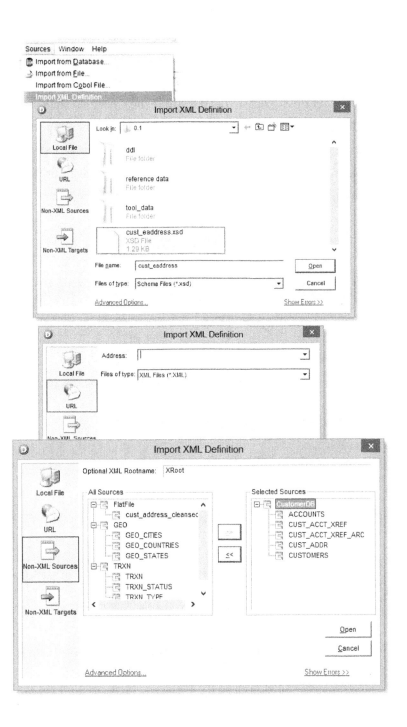

9.2.1   Before importing a XML definition...

Before importing an XML definition, click the advanced options. While importing, if the schema definition you are using does not contain lengths for any attributes or elements, PowerCenter requires that a default value be specified that can be assigned to them. To do so, click on the Advanced option in the Import XML definition dialog box. Then check the `Override all infinite lengths with value` and set it to a default value of your choice. If you have not done so, PowerCenter will prompt you to specify a default length.

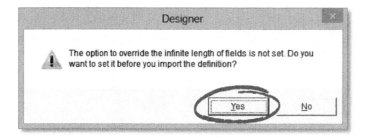

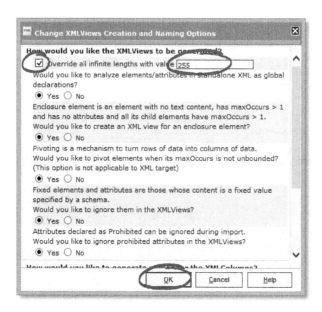

9.3   XML views

When a XSD/DTD/XML is imported, PowerCenter generates XML views. Each XML view is analogous to a relational table. Hence, the way the views are generated affects the way PowerCenter interprets an XML and hence the way it processes the XML at runtime. PowerCenter allows us to import the XML definitions in different ways. In this section, we will look at the same XSD imported with different options and examine the differences.

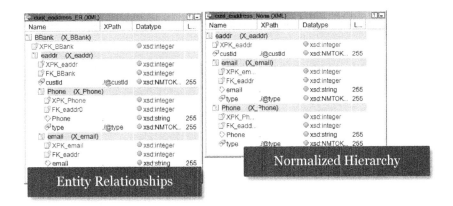

Entity Relationships

Normalized Hierarchy

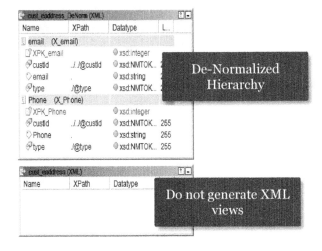

De-Normalized Hierarchy

Do not generate XML views

Note that each XML view is considered as a logical table in PowerCenter. Hence to join data from two XML views, a joiner transformation must be used

9.3.1 Entity relationships

In this model, PowerCenter will generate views for global elements and any multiple occurring elements. From the snapshot, we gather that in the ER model, each parent element is created as a view.

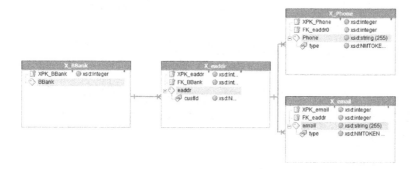

9.3.2 Normalized views

In this model, PowerCenter will try to create a relational set of views that resemble a relational representation of the schema.

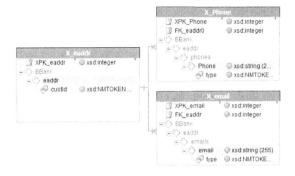

9.3.3 De-normalized views

In this model, PowerCenter will try to create a flat (de-normalized) view that resembles a flattened out representation of the schema.

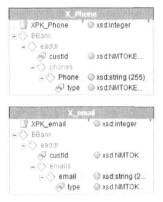

9.4 XML definition wizard

Import the XML definition into PowerCenter as source or target using an XML Schema definition. This is the recommended way of importing an offline XML document. However, the process remains the same, whether you use an XML

Schema or DTD or XML file itself. In the step 1 of the wizard, provide a name to the XML file. Step 2 provides options on different ways of creating XML views in PowerCenter including Entity Relationships, Normalized Hierarchical and De-Normalized Hierarchical methods. Once imported, the XML views generated can be viewed by clicking `Edit XML Definition` on the right click menu of the source or target.

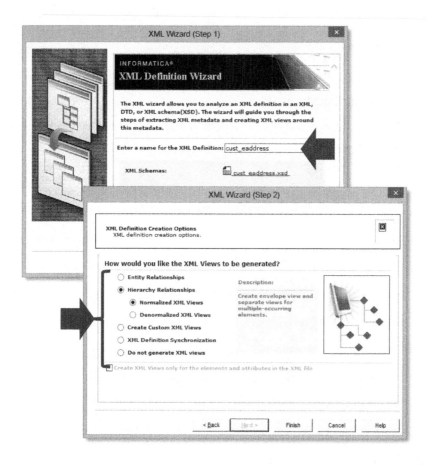

9.5   Lab 9 – XML files

Business requirement:

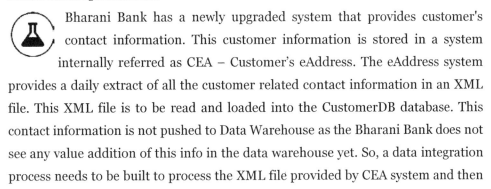 Bharani Bank has a newly upgraded system that provides customer's contact information. This customer information is stored in a system internally referred as CEA – Customer's eAddress. The eAddress system provides a daily extract of all the customer related contact information in an XML file. This XML file is to be read and loaded into the CustomerDB database. This contact information is not pushed to Data Warehouse as the Bharani Bank does not see any value addition of this info in the data warehouse yet. So, a data integration process needs to be built to process the XML file provided by CEA system and then load it into the Customer DB database.

Challenges:

a.   Read and consume XML file.

b.   Each XML file contains one or more phone numbers and email addresses belonging to each customer. These need to be flattened out and loaded to a relational table.

c.   The phone numbers and email addresses are present in different XML view in the XML file. These need to be transposed into columns so that they can be loaded to a relational table.

Technical solution:

XML files are read using XML source qualifier. Data that is read using an XML source qualifier is then transposed into columns using an expression and aggregator. Expression is used to populate the data from different rows into different columns. Aggregator is then used to collapse multiple contact records into a single record per customer. The aggregator will have group by ports but we will not have any aggregation functions because we do not need to aggregate, but just need to collapse the records into one.

Steps for solution:

    a.   Login to the designer and switch to Source Analyzer

    b.   Import the `cust_eaddress.xsd` as normalized hierarchical

    c.   Import the target table `CUST_EADDR` in the CustomerDB database

    d.   Create a new mapping called `m_CustDB_eAddress`

    e.   Drag the XML Source `cust_eaddress` into the mapping

    f.   Create a new expression

        1.   Drag `XPK_eaddr` and `custId` into it

        2.   Rename the expression as `exp_CustIDs`

    g.   Create a new expression

        1.   Drag the `XPK_email`, `FK_eaddr`, `email`, `type` into it

        2.   Rename the expression as `exp_Emails`

        3.   Create the following ports **in this order** at the end:

Port name	Data type	Type	Expression
v_FK	bigint	var	FK_eaddr
v_Email1	string(64)	var	IIF(type = 'HOME', email, IIF(v_FK != v_PrevFK, NULL,v_Email1))
v_Email2	string(64)	var	IIF(type = 'WORK', email, IIF(v_FK != v_PrevFK, NULL,v_Email2))
v_PrevFK	bigint	var	v_FK
o_Email1	string(64)	out	v_Email1
o_Email2	string(64)	out	v_Email2

    h.   Create a new expression

1. Drag the XPK_Phone, FK_eaddr0, phone, type into it

2. Rename the expression as exp_Phones

3. Create the following ports *in this order* at the end:

Port name	Data type	Type	Expression
v_FK	Bigint	var	FK_eaddr0
v_WorkPhone	string(64)	var	IIF(Upper(type0) = 'WORK', Phone, IIF(v_FK != v_PrevFK, NULL, v_WorkPhone))
v_HomePhone	string(64)	var	IIF(Upper(type0) = 'HOME', Phone, IIF(v_FK != v_PrevFK, NULL, v_HomePhone))
v_CellPhone	string(64)	var	IIF(Upper(type0) = 'CELL' OR Upper(type0) = 'MOBILE', Phone, IIF(v_FK != v_PrevFK, NULL, v_CellPhone))
v_PrevFK	Bigint	var	v_FK
o_WorkPhone	string(64)	out	v_WorkPhone
o_HomePhone	string(64)	out	v_HomePhone
o_CellPhone	string(64)	out	v_CellPhone

i. Create a new aggregator transformation

1. Drag FK_eaddr, o_Email1 and o_Email2 from exp_Emails into it

2. Rename it as aggr_Emails

3. Set FK_eaddr as group by port

j. Create a new sorter transformation

1. Drag all ports from aggr_Emails in to it

2. Rename it as srt_Emails

3. Set FK_eaddr as sort key

k. Create a new aggregator transformation

    1. Drag `FK_eaddr0`, `o_HomePhone`, `o_WorkPhone`, `o_CellPhone` from `exp_Phones` into it

    2. Rename it as `aggr_Phones`

    3. Set `FK_eaddr0` as group by port

l. Create a new sorter transformation

    1. Drag all ports from `aggr_Phones` into it

    2. Rename it as `srt_Phones`

    3. Set `FK_eaddr0` as sort key

m. Create a new joiner transformation

    1. Drag all ports from `srt_Emails` into it

    2. Check the `Sorted Input` property in the `Properties` tab

    3. When PowerCenter warns about the joiner condition, ignore it and click `yes`

    4. Drag all ports from `exp_CustIDs` into it

    5. Create a new join condition so that `XPK_eaddr = FK_eaddr`

    6. Ensure this is a normal join

    7. Rename the joiner as `jnr_Cust_n_Emails`

n. Create a new joiner transformation

    1. Drag all ports from `aggr_Phones` into it

    2. Edit the properties and set it as `Sorted Input`. Ignore the warning and click `yes`

    3. Rename it as `jnr_Cust_n_Phones`

    4. Drag all ports from `jnr_Cust_n_Emails` into it

    5. Create a new condition and set it as `FK_eaddr0 = XPK_eaddr`

o. Drag the `cust_eaddr` target table into the mapping

p. Connect the transformations as below:

Source object	Port	Target table	Column
jnr_Cust_n_Phones	XPK_eaddr	CUST_EADDR	EADDR_ID
	CUST_ID		CUST_ID
	o_Email1		EMAIL1
	o_Email2		EMAIL2
	o_HomePhone		HPHONE
	o_WorkPhone		WPHONE
	o_CellPhone		MPHONE

q. Validate and save the mapping

r. Go to the workflow manager and create a new workflow called `wf_CustDB_eAddrress`

s. Create a new session for this mapping

t. Link the start task to this session

u. Edit the session

    1. Go to mapping tab, select source `XMLDSQ_cust_eaddress`

    2. Set the source filename as `cust_eaddress.xml`

    3. Set the target connection to `DI_Ora_CustomerDB` and change its target load type to `Normal`

    4. Set the `Truncate Target Table` option if you have enough permissions. Otherwise, empty the table manually

v. Upload `cust_eaddress.xml` file to your server at `$INFA_HOME/server/infa_shared/SrcFiles` directory

w. Run the workflow and verify the results

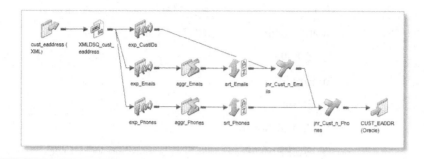

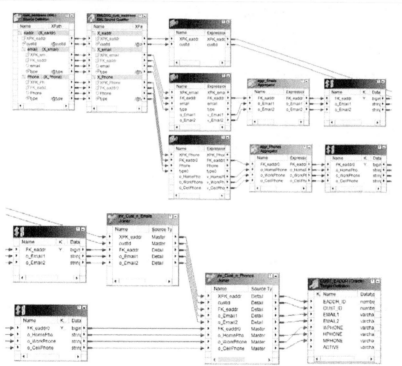

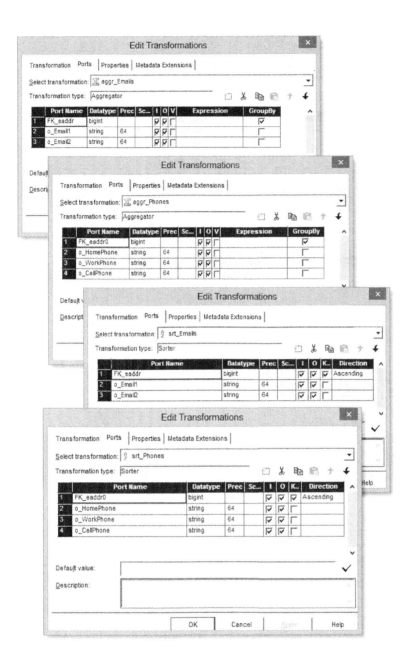

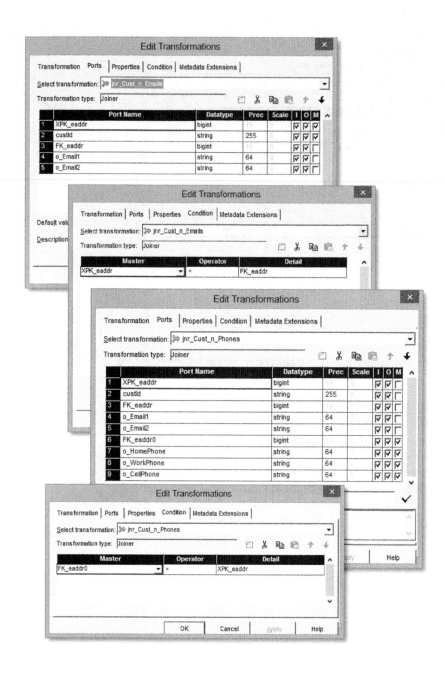

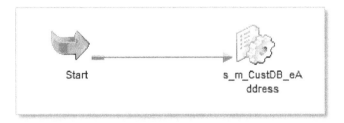

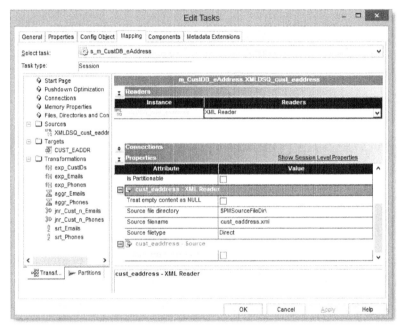

10

Change detection,
Slowly changing dimensions

10.1 Change detection

Change detection (also known as Delta Detection) is the process of identifying the changes happening in a source system (deltas) and applying only necessary changes to the target system. There are many ways of identifying the changes – some simple, some complex. All the approaches can be categorized into the following groups:

10.1.1 Notification based

In notification based change detection, source system already knows what has changed. Once it has processed the changes, it creates a file and pushes the changes to all the systems depending on it. No matter what the means of data exchange is, in this approach, the target systems rely on the source to let them know what changed. The target system simply needs to apply the changes as directed. This approach is very useful when there is more than one target system depending on the same source. A near real time consumption of these notifications can also be implemented by using Queues or other messaging framework for the notification exchange.

10.1.2   Identification based

In this approach, the source system's responsibility ends after identifying the changes and applying to itself. It is up to the target systems to intermittently check what changed and process the changes. The source system usually records the rows that changed in a flag or a date field or some sort of description so that it is easy for the target systems to identify these records. While this approach is not as close to real time as notification based changed detection, this is also a viable and often implemented approach because this approach does not require reading of all the source data. A set of predefined filters can be applied to identify the changed rows and hence limit the amount of data read from the source.

10.1.3   Comparison based

In this approach, the source system has usually no way of communicating the changes to the target system(s). Hence, the target systems read/receive a full extract of the source. They then compare every record and determine what has changed. This approach is typically applied when the source systems are legacy systems which are not easy to change and hence a notification or identification based change detections are not feasible.

10.1.4   Agent based

In this approach, a 3rd party software agent is usually installed in the source environment. This agent captures all the changes as and when they happen in the source and publish them in the target. The source and target in this approach are usually relational databases. Examples of such agents are Informatica PowerExchange CDC for Oracle. This is a real-time change detection that helps the source and target databases to be in sync with least impact on either. Since these agents operate at a much lower level, the administration of these agents is comparatively higher. But when speed and reliability are a matter of concern, agent based change detection is first in line.

 This book only discusses notification, identification and comparison based change detections.

10.2   Implementing change detection

Implementation of a change detection process involves two steps: identifying the differences and applying the updates. In this section, we learn how to implement different change detection techniques we discussed so far.

10.2.1   Notification based

In this approach, usually the source system marks those records with a change, which makes it relatively easy for the DI process to apply the changes. Snapshots below are examples of implementing such change detection.

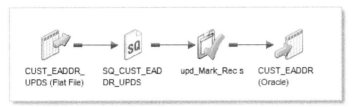

CUST_EADDR_   SQ_CUST_EAD   upd_Mark_Rec s   CUST_EADDR
UPDS (Flat File)   DR_UPDS   (Oracle)

10.2.2   Identification based

In this approach, source has marked the records that are changed. The DI process needs to select only those records and apply the changes to the target database. As seen in the example snapshot, filter condition is applied in the source qualifier to select only records that have changed (in this example either effective date or end date is within last 24 hours). Then we set the record status to Insert, Update or Delete accordingly.

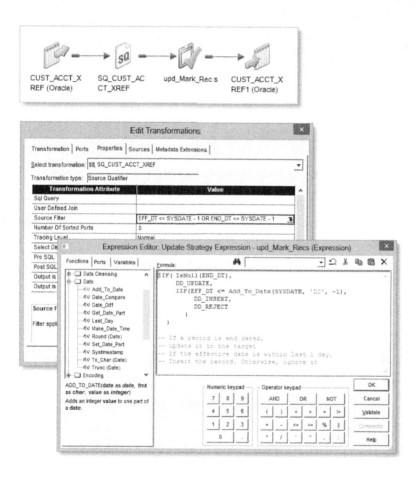

10.2.3   Comparison based

In this approach, we read the entire source data set and then compare record by record to the target. If there is any change in the information from source, we update the record in the target, otherwise we ignore it. We can use a lookup transformation to identify the record present in the target and then use an update strategy to change the row operation.

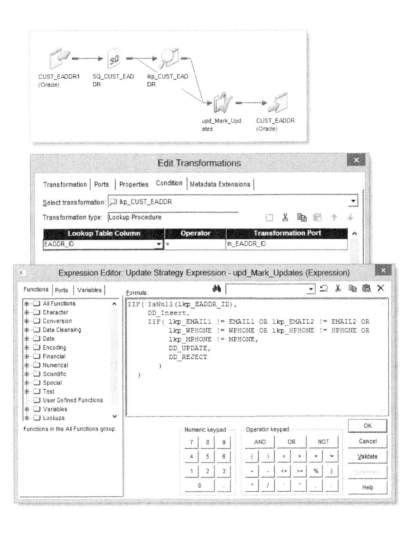

10.3   SCD - Slowly Changing Dimensions

A dimension is a logical group of similar data and a slowly changing dimension is a dimension where the data doesn't change often on a pre-defined schedule but changes slowly over time. Slowly changing dimensions are widely used in Data Warehousing. There are many types of slowly changing dimension implementations, out of which, Type 1, Type 2 and Type3 are most commonly used.

In the previous section of change detection, we focused on different approaches to identify changes in the sources. In this section, we discuss different approaches of applying the changes on to the target database.

10.3.1   Type 1 – Overwrite

In a type 1 dimension, existing data is overwritten. Therefore, no history is maintained. All new records are inserted and all changes are updated in place of existing records. Lab 8 on flat files and update strategy covers this type of dimension.

10.3.2   Type 2 – Complete history

In a type 2 dimension, every change is maintained. So, every change is inserted as a new record into the database. The old records are archived by flagging them or updating their timestamp. When using a flag, the flag is typically set to 0 (Zero) or N (No) or I (Inactive) to represent an inactive state and the new record is inserted typically with 1 or Y (Yes) or A (Active) to represent an active record. In a timestamp mode, the record having the latest timestamp is treated as active record and all other records are treated as inactive records.

10.3.3   Type 3 – 1 level of history

In a type 3 dimension, only one level of history is maintained, typically for high valued columns. Therefore a current value column and previous value columns are maintained. Every time a change is received, the previous value column is updated with current value column and current value column is updated with input data.

10.3.4   History tables

Another commonly used approach to track history is to use history tables. Typically, history tables have similar layout as their main tables with additional metadata to indicate when they are archived. Database triggers are used to automatically copy a record into the history table before the record in the main table is updated.

10.4   Implementing a Type 1 dimension

As part of type 1 dimension, we need to overwrite existing data. For smaller tables, a lookup can be used to identify whether the record exists in the target table. For larger tables, a database level or PowerCenter level join can be used. Lab 8 on update strategy has used level 1 type technique to apply changes to the target. Let's take a look at it again. The update strategy determines the actions (Insert or Update or Delete) and applies it to the rows.

10.5 Implementing a Type 2 dimension

In a type 2 dimension, a new record is created for each change. The latest records are identified using a flag or a timestamp. Let us take a look at the customer account cross reference table (CUST_ACCT_XREF – partial listing):

CUST_ID	ACCT_ID	EFF_DT	END_DT
1	1	23-SEP-2000	04-AUG-2011
1	2	04-AUG-2011	[null]

Above data represents the following business:

→ Customer with Customer ID 1 has opened an account on September 23, 2000

→ Customer with Customer ID 1 has closed his account on August 4, 2011 and opened a new account on the same day

Now, we can understand by looking at the data that on August 4, 2011, a new record is inserted into the cross reference table and an existing reference is end dated. This table is a true SCD Type 2 dimension that keeps continuous history. Note that there may be more than one ways to implement this.

10.6 Lab 10 – Implementing Type 2 SCD

Business requirement:

Bharani Bank has a cross reference table that maps customers and accounts and their active and inactive associations. We have already completed a one-time load of this table. We will now have to keep it live. In the source, if a customer closes an account and opens a different account, the current cross reference will be end-dated and a new entry will be created with the corresponding new account number. If a customer simply closes an account, existing record is updated to reflect this status. However, if the status of the customer-account relationship is changed, same record will be updated. When a customer-account status changes, the status is updated in the CustomerDB. This data then needs to be updated in the data warehouse. The corresponding record in the data warehouse must be end-dated and then a new record must be created with the updated status.

Challenges:

    a.   Identify if a record exists in the target

    b.   If a cross reference exists for the same customer-account combination, end-date it

   c. Create a new record for the same customer-account combination

Technical solution:

We will read the customer-account cross reference table where either the effective date or the end date is updated within last 1 day. This data will then be looked up on the target table. If this combination does not exist, we will treat this record as insert. If this combination exists and the status of the combination is different, we will then update the current record to end-date it and then insert a new record. To do so, we will use a router transformation and we will have two targets in the mapping, both pointing to the same physical target table.

Steps for solution:

   a. Create a new mapping called `m_DWH_CDC_Load_CustAcctXref`

   b. Drag the `CUST_ACCT_XREF` source into the mapping

   c. Change the source qualifier

      1. Rename the source qualifier as `__SQ_CUST_ACCT_XREF`

      2. Set the Source Filter as `EFF_DT >= (SYSDATE - 1) OR END_DT >= (SYSDATE - 1)`

 `SYSDATE` is an oracle keyword representing today (current date). If you are using a different database, use the appropriate keyword. Note that source filter in source qualifier is passed on to database as-it-is. PowerCenter transformation language cannot be used here.

   d. Create a lookup transformation

      1. Select `Target➔Customers`

      2. Drag `CUST_ID` from source qualifier into it

      3. Rename the lookup as `lkp_DWH_Customers`

4. Change the input `CUST_ID(CUST_ID1)` from source qualifier as `in_CUST_ID` and make it an input only port

5. Set the condition as `CUST_ID = in_CUST_ID`

6. Delete all ports except `in_CUST_ID`, `CUST_ID`, `CUST_KEY`

e. Create a lookup transformation

1. Select `Target→Accounts`

2. Drag `ACCT_NR` from source qualifier into it

3. Rename the lookup as `lkp_DWH_Accounts`

4. Change the input `ACCT_NR (ACCT_NR1)` from source qualifier as `in_ACCT_NR` and make it an input only port

5. Set the condition as `ACCT_NR = in_ACCT_NR`

6. Delete all ports except `in_ACCT_NR`, `ACCT_NR`, `ACCT_KEY`

f. Create a lookup transformation

1. Select `Target→CUST_ACCT_XREF` table

2. Drag `CUST_KEY`and `ACCT_KEY` from `lkp_DWH_Customers` and `lkp_DWH_Accounts` into this lookup

3. Rename the lookup as `lkp_DWH_CA_XREF`

4. Rename the ports from `lkp_DWH_Lookups` as `in_CUST_KEY` and `in_ACCT_KEY` and convert them as input only ports

5. Create a lookup condition as:

    a. `CUST_KEY = in_CUST_KEY`

    b. `ACCT_KEY = in_ACCT_KEY`

6. Setup the Lookup Source Filter as `END_DT IS NULL`

7. Delete all ports except `CUST_KEY`, `ACCT_KEY`, `CA_KEY`, `in_CUST_KEY`, `in_ACCT_KEY` and `STATUS`

g. Create a new expression called `exp_Actions`

1. Drag the `CA_KEY`, `CUST_KEY`, `ACCT_KEY`, `STATUS` from `lkp_DWH_CA_XREF`

2. Rename the `STATUS` from `lkp_DWH_CA_XREF` as `lkp_STATUS`

3. Drag all ports from source qualifier into the expression

4. Create a new output only port called `o_Action` **String(3)** and set its expression as `IIF(IsNull(CA_KEY), 'INS', IIF('' || STATUS != '' || lkp_STATUS, 'UPD', 'IGN'))`

h. Create a new router transformation called `rtr_Inserts_n_Updates`

   1. Drag all ports from `exp_Actions`

   2. Create 2 groups:

      a. `INSERTS` with condition `o_Action = 'INS'` or `o_Action = 'UPD'`

      b. `UPDATES` with condition `o_Action = 'UPD'`

i. Create a new update strategy called `upd_Inserts`

   1. Drag all ports from `INSERTS` group of the router into it

   2. Set the update strategy expression as `DD_INSERT`

j. Create a new update strategy called `upd_Updates`

   1. Drag all ports from `UPDATES` group of the router into it

   2. Set the update strategy expression as `DD_UPDATE`

k. Create a new sequence generator called `seq_CUST_KEY`

   1. Set its start value and current value as `20000`

l. Create a new expression called `exp_InsertDate`

   1. Drag the `nextval` from sequence generator into the expression

   2. Drag the `CUST_KEY, ACCT_KEY, STATUS1` (not the lkp_Status) into it from upd_Inserts

   3. Create a new output port called `o_Today` (date) and set its expression as `SYSDATE`

m. Create a new expression called `exp_UpdateDate`

   1. Drag the `CA_KEY3, STATUS3` from the `upd_Updates` into it

   2. Create a new output port called `o_Today` (date) and set its expression as `SYSDATE`

n. Drag the `CUST_ACCT_XREF` target into the mapping

1. Rename it as ins_CUST_ACCT_XREF

2. Match the columns as follows:

exp_InsertDate	Target
NEXTVAL	CA_KEY
CUST_KEY1	CUST_KEY
ACCT_KEY1	ACCT_KEY
STATUS1	STATUS
o_Today	EFF_DT
o_Today	LAST_UPD_DT

o. Drag the CUST_ACCT_XREF target into the mapping

    1. Rename it as upd_CUST_ACCT_XREF

    2. Drag matching columns from exp_Updates into it and connect CA_KEY, o_Today to END_DT and also to LAST_UPD_DT in the target. Do NOT connect the status field.

p. Validate the mapping and save it

q. Go to workflow manager

r. Create a new workflow called wf_DWH_CDC_Loads

    1. Create a new session called for this mapping

    2. Go to mapping tab and setup the connections

        a. Point the sources to DI_Ora_CustomerDB

        b. Point the targets and lookups to DI_Ora_DWH

s. Save the workflow

t. Update a couple of rows in the customer account cross reference to set the date as sysdate (today's date)

u. Run the workflow and validate the results

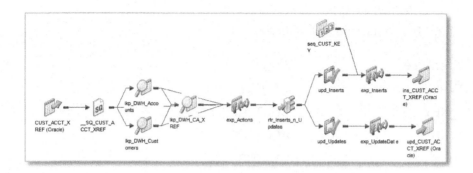

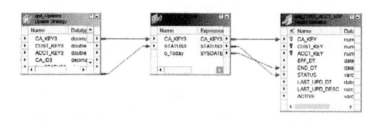

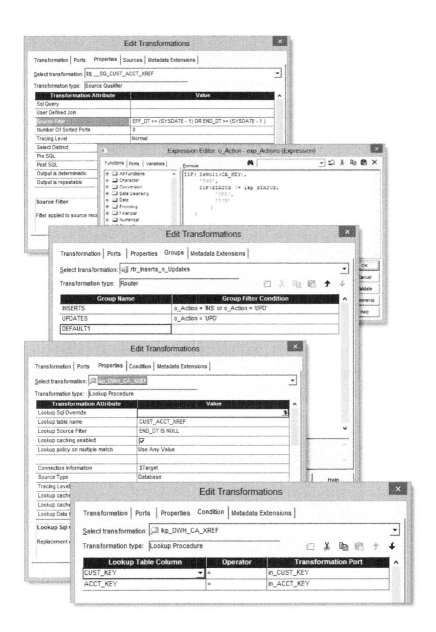

10.7   Lab 11 – Implementing Type 3 SCD

Business requirement:

Customers, at times, may change their names. Changing last name after marriage is the most common scenario. But there are also other scenarios when customers change their names and wish to update their names in the Bank database. Bharani Bank allows its customers to change their names online after accepting a name change agreement. These changes are reflected regularly in the CustomerDB. As part of the Data Warehouse that is being built, Bharani Bank would like to store the original name with which a customer registered himself/herself, their current name and the most recent name they used before their current name, where applicable. The customer dimension in the Data Warehouse contains 3 sets of attributes to store these names. When a customer changes his/her name, the original name in the Data Warehouse needs to be retained. The current name in the Data Warehouse is to be copied into the previous name columns. If the previous name columns already contain a value, they can be overwritten. Then the incoming update must be updated in the current name columns.

Challenges:

    a.   Maintain 3 levels of history: original, current and previous
    b.   Document that a name change occurred for the customer

Technical solution:

CustomerDB Customers table is read and data from this table is looked upon the customers dimension. When a matching Customer ID is found, the names are compared in a lookup transformation to see if there has been an update. All records that do not have a name change are then filtered out using a filter transformation. An expression transformation is used where with appropriate links of the data ports, current name and previous name are assigned appropriately. Only the names' columns and metadata fields such as last update date and last update description are updated in the target table. Since in this mapping we only process updates, we set the Treat Input rows as session property to updates. Then by default, PowerCenter will consider all incoming rows as updates. This will eliminate the need to use Update Strategy transformation.

Steps for solution:

a. Create a new mapping called m_DWH_CDC_Load_Customers
b. Drag the source CustomerDB→CUSTOMERS in to the mapping
c. Create a new expression called exp_Placeholder
d. Drag all columns from source qualifier into it
e. Create a new lookup transformation
   1. Rename it as lkp_DWH_Customers
   2. Drag CUST_ID from exp_Placeholder into the lookup
   3. Rename CUST_ID1 (CUST_ID from exp_Placeholder) as in_CUST_ID
   4. Create condition CUST_ID = in_CUST_ID
f. Create a new expression transformation
   1. Rename it as exp_Type3_SCD
   2. Drag CUST_KEY, FIRST_NAME, LAST_NAME from lookup and prefix them with lkp_
   3. Drag all ports form exp_Placeholder into the exp_Type3_SCD
   4. Rename the CUST_TYPE as in_CUST_TYPE
   5. Rename the GENDER as in_GENDER
   6. Create the following ports:

Port name	Data type	Type	Expression
o_Action	String(5)	O	IIF(IsNull(lkp_CUST_KEY), 'INS', IIF(lkp_FIRST_NAME = FIRST_NAME AND lkp_LAST_NAME = LAST_NAME, 'REJ', 'UPD'))
o_Cust_Type	String(1)	O	IIF(in_CUST_TYPE = 1, 'P', 'B')
o_GENDER	String(1)	O	Decode(in_GENDER, 1, 'M', 2, 'F', 'U')
o_Last_Update _Date	Date/time	O	SYSDATE
o_Last_Update _Desc	String(255)	O	'Name change'

g. Create a router called `rtr_Insert_Update`

   1. Drag all columns from the `exp_Type3_SCD` into it

   2. Create a group called `INSERTS` with expression as `o_Action = 'INS'`

   3. Create a group called `UPDATES` with expression as `o_Action = 'UPD'`

h. Create a new update strategy transformation

   1. Drag all ports from Router (`INSERT` group) into the update strategy

   2. Rename it as `upd_Mark_Inserts`

   3. Set the update strategy expression as `DD_INSERT`

i. Create a new update strategy transformation

   1. Drag the ports from router (`UPDATES` group) into the update strategy transformation

   2. Rename it as `upd_Mark_Update`

   3. Set the update strategy expression as `DD_UPDATE`

j. Create a new sequence generator transformation

1. Rename it as seq_CUST_KEY
2. Set the start value and current value as 30000

k. Drag the (DWH) CUSTOMERS target into the mapping

1. Rename it as ins_CUSTOMERS
2. Connect the sequence generator next value to CUST_KEY
3. Connect the FIRST_NAME and LAST_NAME to both the name fields and the original name fields
4. Connect other columns as below:

upd_Mark_Inserts	Ins_CUSTOMERS
o_GENDER1	GENDER
o_Last_Update_Date	CREATE_DT
in_CUST_TYPE1	CUST_TYPE

l. Drag the (DWH) CUSTOMERS target again into the mapping

1. Rename it as upd_CUSTOMERS
2. Connect the following ports from upd_Mark_Updates to the target:
   a. Lkp_CUST_KEY3to CUST_KEY
   b. lkp_FIRST_NAME3to FIRST_NAME_PREV
   c. lkp_LAST_NAME3 to LAST_NAME_PREV
   d. FIRST_NAME to FIRST_NAME
   e. LAST_NAME to LAST_NAME
   f. LAST_UPDATE_DATE to LAST_UPDATE_DATE
   g. LAST_UPDATE_DESC to LAST_UPDATE_DESC

m. Validate the mapping, save it

n. Open the workflow manager and open the workflow wf_DWH_CDC_Loads

1. Create a session in the workflow

o. Run the session and validate the results

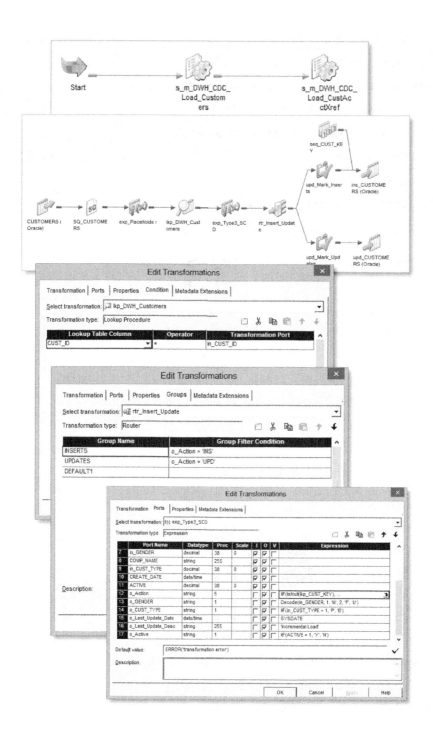

11

Parameter files

11.1   Mapping parameters

Mappings often read data from one or more sources and write to one or more targets. In real life, more often than not, it is important for these mappings to be dynamic. We can configure mappings to have parameters. These parameters can receive values from parameter files. Contents of parameter files are read during the session initialization and the values are assigned to the mapping parameters. These parameters are then consumed within the mapping. There are many use-cases for mapping parameters. Some examples are: dynamic - where clause for source qualifiers compare some computed values in expressions with a parameter, etc... Mapping parameters are used in the context of a mapping – meaning that a mapping parameter defined is only available within that mapping. Mapping Parameters are read only attributes that can only receive values into the mapping from the parameter files. Mapping Variables are read-write parameters – meaning that mapping variables values can be updated by transformations within the mapping.

11.2   Defining mapping parameters

Mapping parameters can be defined using the `Mappings` menu →`Parameters and Variables` (🔣). This will open the Declare Parameters and Variables dialog box. Click the new parameter icon (🔲). This will add a new row. Mapping parameter names must begin with a `$$`. Name the parameter as something meaningful. It can be of type Parameter or Variable. Native PowerCenter data types are supported. For string types, precision must be provided. If the `IsExprValue` is set to `TRUE`, the mapping parameter/variable will be evaluated as PowerCenter transformation expression before the value is used within the mapping. An initial value can be provided to a mapping parameter when it is defined. If the mapping parameter value is not defined in the parameter file, the initial value will be used.

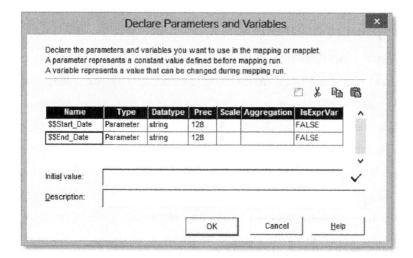

11.3   Parameter files: definition and format

To be able to completely understand the mapping parameters, it is also important to understand how they are passed into the mapping. In this section, let us look at the structure of a sample mapping parameter file. A parameter file contains sections of information. A parameter file can contain any number of sections. Each section has a header followed by name value pairs of the mapping parameters. A header consists of the following elements: Repository folder name, workflow name and session name. Header is enclosed within square brackets []. All parameters listed below a header are applicable to the workflow/session listed in the header. Workflow name is prefixed with the keyword WF: and session task name is prefixed with ST:. Parameter file does not differentiate between a mapping parameter and a mapping variable. Same guidelines apply to both. Parameters start with a $$ symbol. Parameters and their values are separated by equals sign (=). Any spaces after the equals to sign are considered part of the value. Any line starting with a hash sign (#) is considered as a comment.

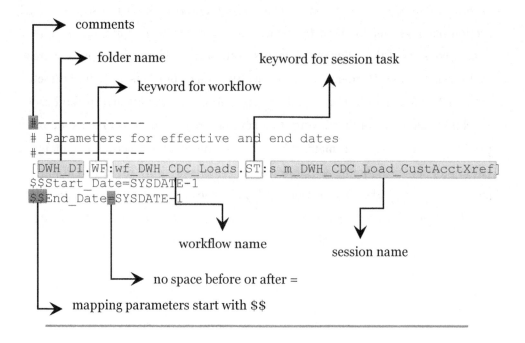

```
#--------------
# Parameters for effective and end dates
#--------------
[DWH_DI.WF:wf_DWH_CDC_Load.ST:s_m_DWH_CDC_Load_CustAcctXref]
$$Start_Date=SYSDATE-1
$$End_Date=SYSDATE-1
```

→ section header

→ section content

```
#--------------
# Parameters for Customers
#--------------
[DWH_DI.WF:wf_DWH_CDC_Loads.ST:s_m_DWH_CDC_Load_Customers]
$$Run_Date=SYSDATE-30
```

11.4   Configuring parameter files

Parameter files can be configured at both workflow level and at a session level. Parameter file configured at a workflow level is by default used for all the sessions in the workflow. To configure a parameter file for a session, go to session properties, properties tab and provide a mapping parameter file name with the path. Integration Service variables such as $PMSourceFileDir can be used to specify a relative path.

11.5   Mapping parameters at runtime

So, how do we know if a mapping parameter is resolved properly at run time? May be there is a typo, maybe we defined it as a number and passed a string value. Simple, you can look in the session log. Session log is almost always the starting point to look for run-time information. Let us take a look at what kind of information about parameters is available in the session log. If a parameter file is not properly configured, the session will throw a PETL_2409 error indicating it is unable to read the parameter file. When the parameter file is opened, Integration Service logs it in the workflow log as

VAR_27085 - Parameter file [*filename*] is opened for [session[*workflow.session*]]. This is followed by

LM_36488 - Session task instance [*session*] : [VAR_27028 Use override value [*param value*] for mapping parameter:[*param name*].]

We can see in the session log the following:

VAR_27028 - Use override value [*param value*] for mapping parameter : [*param name*].

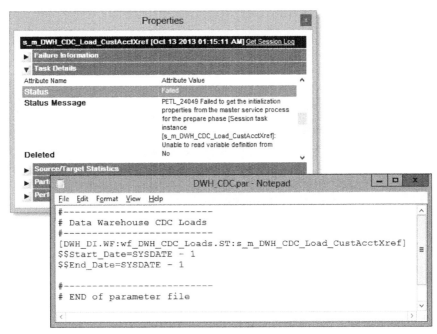

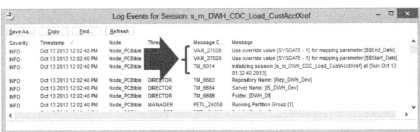

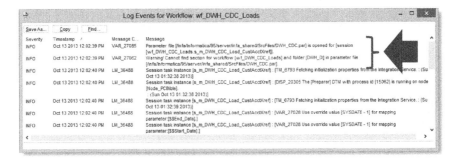

11.6   Expressions as mapping parameters

PowerCenter expressions can be passed as mapping parameters. To distinguish between expression parameters and simple string parameters, we need to set the `IsExprValue` property to `TRUE`. When this property is set to `TRUE`, PowerCenter will evaluate the parameter value as expression before passing the value to the appropriate transformation.

11.7   Mapping variables

Mapping variables are very similar to mapping parameters. Mapping parameters are used to provide dynamic values into the mapping. However, mapping parameters are read-only and hence cannot be changed during the mapping execution. But sometimes, it is required to update the mapping parameters so that an updated value can be used later on. For example, when executing incremental loads that are run at regular intervals, it is important to track when the mapping last ran, so that we can pull all the delta records from the last point of execution. This is precisely where mapping variables come into play. Mapping variables are simply writeable mapping parameters. A mapping variable can be updated *once* in the course of mapping execution. To update the mapping variable's value, we use the transformation functions `SetVariable`, `SetMaxVariable`, `SetCountVariable`. `SetVariable` takes a mapping variable and a value as input and sets the variable to that value.

11.8   Workflow/worklet variables

Workflow/worklet variables are quite similar to mapping variables and they only vary in their scope. Workflow/Worklet variables can be only used in workflows/worklets respectively. They are not visible at the mapping level. They can be used at the workflow level to control the execution of the tasks. They can be used to temporarily store values such as session task's status and then use it later to decide whether not to execute other tasks. We will discuss the further use of these workflow variables when we discuss assignment tasks later in this book.

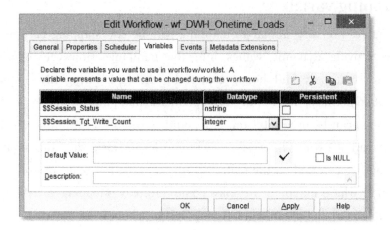

11.9   Lab 12 – Using mapping variables

<u>Business requirement</u>:

Bharani Bank's Data Warehouse receives updates for its customers' accounts cross references regularly. The schedule is not defined yet. They would like the CDC mapping to run at these regular intervals. However, to eliminate manual execution, they would like to build the CDC process such that every time it runs, it automatically picks up the data that has been changed from the last time. The current CDC logic is also not finalized. Hence Bharani Bank wants the logic to be flexible and to be updateable without a code change.

<u>Challenges</u>:

→ The mapping should be able to automatically keep track of its last execution date.

<u>Technical solution</u>:

We use mapping variables to keep track of the execution date. We use a mapping parameter to perform the insert/update logic calculation. This mapping parameter will be provided a value from the parameter file.

<u>Steps for solution</u>:

    a. Open the mapping `m_DWH_CDC_Load_CustAcctXref`

    b. Go to `Mappings` → Parameters and Variables menu item

    c. Click the new icon (⬚)

    d. Create the following mapping parameters/variables:

Name	Type	Datatype	IsExpValue
$$Run_Date	Variable	String(32)	False
$$CDC_Logic	Parameter	String(4096)	True

    e. Set the default value for `$$Run_Date` as `'01-01-05'`

    f. Click `OK` to close the dialog

    g. Edit the source qualifier:

        1. Set the source filter to `EFF_DT >= $$Run_Date OR END_DT >= $$Run_Date`

    h. Edit the expression `exp_Actions`

        1. Change the output port o_Action and set its expression as `$$CDC_Logic`

    i. Edit the expression `exp_UpdateDate`

        1. Create a new variable port of `string(128)` and set its expression as `SetVariable($$Run_Date, To_Char(SYSDATE, 'DD-MM-YY'))`

2. The above example uses ORACLE syntax as we are using it in the source qualifier. If you are using a different database, please change the format accordingly

j. Save the mapping

k. Edit the session in the workflow (wf_DWH_CDC_Loads)

1. Set the parameter file name in the properties tab as $PMSourceFileDir/DWH_CDC.par

l. Save the session and the workflow

m. Create a new parameter file at the $PMSourceFileDir location

1. Name it as DWH_CDC.par

2. Set its content as shown below (↵ symbol is used to represent newline character.):

```
#---------------------------↵
# Data Warehouse CDC Loads↵
#---------------------------↵
[DWH_DI.WF:wf_DWH_CDC_Loads.ST:s_m_DWH_CDC_Load_C
ustAcctXref] ↵
$$Run_Date='01-01-05'↵
$$CDC_Logic=IIF(IsNull(CA_KEY), 'INS', IIF(STATUS
!= lkp_STATUS, 'UPD', 'IGN')) ↵
#---------------------------↵
#END of parameter file↵
#---------------------------↵
```

3. Change the $$Run_Date value to current date on your system

4. The above example uses ORACLE syntax as we are using it in the source qualifier. If you are using a different database, please change the format accordingly

n. Save the file

o. Run the session/workflow

p. Right click on the session and click on View Persistent Values. Today's date will appear next to the mapping variable

q. If you run the session again immediately, it will read zero records as there is no data on today's date

12

Logging, Debugging & Exception handling

12.1 Row Indicators

PowerCenter maintains a row-level flag called Row Indicator. Row Indicator is used to represent the operation that the Integration Service will perform for this row in the target table viz. Insert, Update, Delete or Reject (log and skip). By default, when PowerCenter reads rows, it treats them all as inserts. This can be changed in the session properties or in the mapping (by defining an update strategy transformation). By defining in the session, we change the row indicator for all records processed by the session. To change the row indicator based on a condition or data values, we set it in the mapping using an update strategy transformation. When we use Update Strategy transformation, we must set the session property `Treat sources rows` as `Data Driven`. Update strategy gives great flexibility to mark a row to be insert, update or delete at run time based on data conditions. More than one update strategy can be used in a mapping. However, if more than one update strategy is used in the same pipeline, only the last one takes effect. More than one update strategy can be used in different pipelines to perform different operations on their corresponding targets.

 Row Indicator is visible when using Debugger in the PowerCenter Designer tool. We will discuss Debugger later in the book.

In session properties, we can configure to read all the records as inserts (default), updates or delete. If we have a mapping that only performs updates to the existing data, instead of defining an update strategy transformation, we can use the session properties to treat the records as updates. In this case, PowerCenter integration service will issue an `UPDATE` statements instead of `INSERT` statements for every row flowing to that target.

12.2   Bad files/reject files

When PowerCenter performs an action on a target database such as Insert, it is possible that the target database may reject this operation. This can happen due to several reasons. One of the most common being NULL passed to NOT NULL columns. For example, we are reading from a flat file and loading the data to a relational database. Since files have no relational integrity or data integrity checks, there may a record with NULL as value for a specific column. The mapping will not reject this record and will process it just like any other record. But when this row reaches the target database, it may be rejected due to a NOT NULL constraint on the column. More often than not, rejections happen at the target database level, but they can also occur anywhere in the mapping pipeline. For example, imagine a business requirement that specifies the developer to not load a row if it does not have an account number. So, the developer can implement an update strategy transformation where each record is verified to see if the account number has a value. If no value is present in the account number field, the update strategy will set its row indicator to DD_REJECT causing the record to be rejected. In both the scenarios above, PowerCenter has already processed (or at least partially processed) the record, it will log into what is known as a Bad File. Bad Files contain records rejected by the mapping, sources or targets. A Bad File contains all the rejected data with metadata, indicating the cause of the rejection.

12.2.1   DONTs

There are four common scenarios when a rejection happens and they are collectively known as DONTs.

Data Driven:

A data driven reject is when the row meets a certain condition and the update strategy sets its row indicator to DD_REJECT thus requesting the PowerCenter Integration Service to reject the record and write it into a Bad File.

Overflow:

An overflow occurs when the data is larger than the column it is being loaded to. For example, a numeric overflow occurs when a big integer data is loaded into a small integer. Similarly, an overflow might also occur when decimal data such as (12.38) is attempted to be loaded to an integer value.

NULL:

A NULL value is attempted to be loaded into a NOT NULL column and the database engine and hence the writer thread rejected the record.

Truncate:

Very similar to overflows, but occurs with the strings. When a string value with less precision is loaded to a column/port , truncation occurs.

12.2.2   Configuring bad files

Bad files are automatically configured in session properties for every target. When a session is created or a target is added to a mapping and the session is refreshed, PowerCenter Workflow Manager automatically adds a default Bad File name. The default Bad File name is same as the target name in the mapping with a .bad extension. Every target will have a corresponding Bad File and hence the number of Bad Files a session has equals the number of targets. If no rejections happened in a session run, a zero byte file is created with no data in it. In scenarios where rows need to be rejected but do not have to be logged, Developers can configure the session property `Reject overflow or truncated data`. For data driven rejections, the `Forward rejected records` property in update strategy can be used to configure whether or not a reject is written to the Bad File.

12.2.3   Location and format

By default, Bad Files are located in `$PMBadFileDir`. `$PMBadFileDir` is an Integration Service level variable that defines the path where Bad Files will be created. The default value for this variable is `%INFA_HOME%\server\infa_shared\BadFiles` in Windows environments and `$INFA_HOME/server/infa_shared/BadFiles` in non-Windows environments, where `INFA_HOME` represents the directory where Informatica services are installed. This can be customized in sessions and a different path can be provided to each target in the session properties. Bad Files are in text format and are human readable. In this section, let us look at the format of the Bad File. As an example, imagine we are processing a dataset containing Customer ID, First

Name, Last Name and Gender – all columns are of NOT NULL nature. Now, if a row arrives with NULL last name, the record gets rejected. Let us examine a line in the reject file:

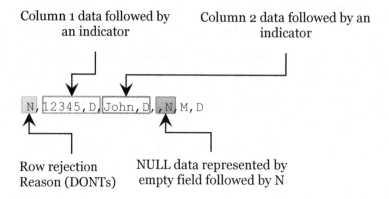

Contents of this file are in this order: Row Rejection Reason (N for NULL), Customer ID, column indicator (D for Data) First name (John), column indicator (D), last name (NULL / empty), column indicator (N for NULL), gender (M), column indicator (D)

 A reject file is created for each target in the mapping. If there are no rejections, they will be zero byte files.

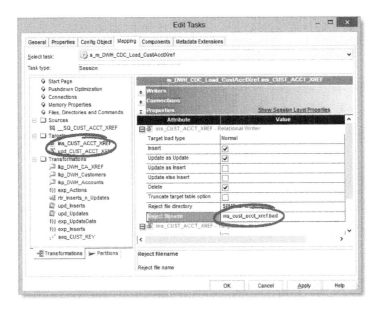

12.3   Logging levels in PowerCenter

From a programmer's perspective, Data Integration jobs are probably not as easy to debug as jobs developed in programming languages. In programming languages such as Java, one can simply write an echo statement and printout necessary information. When the program runs, developer can look at the console to understand the values of variables and the current state of the program. With DI jobs, it is much more complex than that. DI jobs typically process millions of records in production. Understanding what is happening inside a DI job at a certain state of its execution may appear to be quite complex. If you are under similar impression, this section of the chapter will prove you wrong and you'll be happy about it.

12.3.1   Understanding workflow logs

Workflow logs contain information on how the tasks have been executed within a given workflow. Workflow logs primarily focus on whether particular tasks have been executed and their end status. The detailed logs for session tasks can be found in the session logs. Workflow logs are of the same format as session logs.

12.3.2   Understanding session logs

Luckily, PowerCenter provides various levels of insight into a session's execution. A session log consists of various details of every step the session goes through along its execution. To understand this better, let us first look at the contents of session log. Each line in the session log contains primarily four elements: Severity, timestamp, message code and the message. Severity specifies the importance of the information. `INFO` severity for example, refers to general information that is written in the log file just for your reference. `WARN` refers to Warnings generated either by PowerCenter or the source/target databases when processing this data. `ERROR` refers to any errors occurred during the processing. Timestamp refers to the timestamp when an event is logged. The event can be an information or a warning or an error. But this is the time when it occurred.

Severity: Debug/Info/Warning/Error

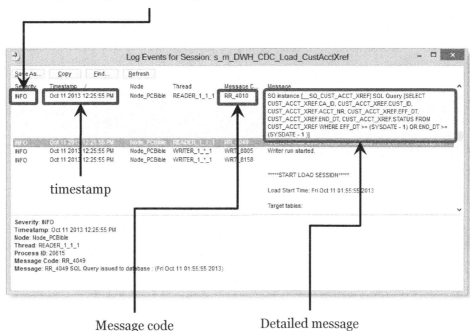

timestamp

Message code   Detailed message

Message code is a unique reference to each type of message and the message description is the detailed message. Based on the severity, message could vary drastically. In the example snapshot shown, the message description consists of SQL query PowerCenter issued to the source database. In case of ERROR severity, description usually consists of error caused by PowerCenter or the source/target database such as Primary Constraint violation.

12.3.3 Trace levels

PowerCenter allows us to change the severity level at which Integration Service logs messages in session logs. This setting is known as trace level. This property can be changed at session level and transformation level. Following are the different trace levels available:

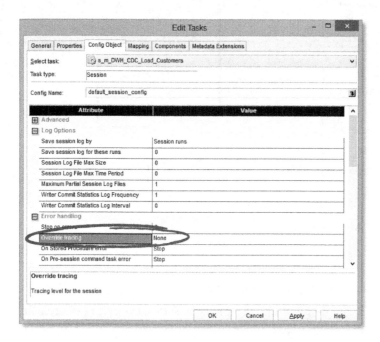

Terse:

This is the highest level of tracing where minimal information is recorded into the session log viz., only initialization messages and error messages. Notifications about events such as rejections are recorded without any data.

`Normal:`

This is the default level of tracing, logging where along with errors and initialization messages, useful information such as `SELECT` queries issued to source database, syntax of `INSERT` / `UPDATE` queries fired on the target database etc., are recorded in the session log.

`Verbose Initialization:`

In addition to normal information, detailed information during session initialization is recorded. This level is very helpful while establishing connectivity to new sources or targets.

`Verbose Data:`

This is the most granular level of information that the Integration Service can record. In this mode, Integration Service logs every row in and out of every transformation.

 Setting the trace level to `Verbose Data` writes huge amount of information into the session log and at the same time causes the session to slow down due to the extra logging.

12.4 Debugger

PowerCenter Debugger allows developers go through a step-by-step execution of their mapping to examine all transformations, their evaluation of various expressions as at run time. Debugger helps identify, troubleshoot various conditions – both data and code related. Debugger relies on Integration service to run the sessions and developers can choose to discard the target data. Developers can choose an existing session to use with a debugger or create a new session for the debugger run.

12.4.1 Debugger wizard

Debugger wizard starts with a summary of debugger activity. In step 2, we are prompted to choose an integration service and option to whether or not to use an existing session or create a new one for the debugging purpose. If we chose to reuse an existing session, Debugger Wizard will display all sessions that are linked to the current mapping. Developer can also choose to create a new temporary session with default configuration for debugging. The last step is to specify whether or not we want to save the data that is processed as part of the debugging. Choose discard target data to ignore all data loaded by the debugging run. In the last step, we can also choose the targets that we want to monitor in real time. Debugger, once started, will show the data that is being sent to these selected targets in real time. When you click Finish, debugger initiates itself. You can see the initialization messages in the output window debugger tab.

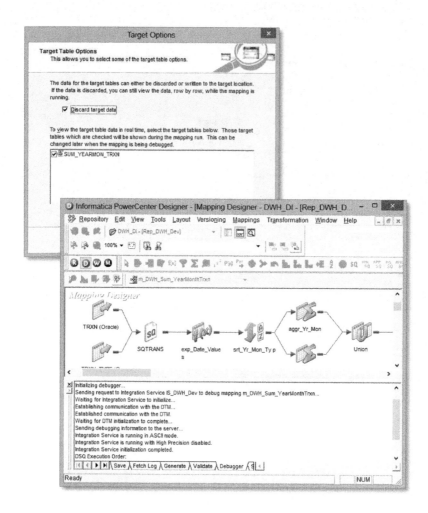

12.4.2   Debugger workspace

As soon as you start the debugger, you will notice that the workspace adjusts itself for the debugger. Before we begin working with debugger, let us understand the User Interface. Debugger will automatically display the Target Data window (a) and Instance Data Windows (b). If they are not displayed, you can turn them on from View menu →Debugger sub menu. Mapping Designer still remains in the workspace (c). To start the debugger click `Next Instance` (⌗). Next Instance command is used initially to start the debugger and also to ask Integration Service to move on to the next step in the execution. Now, you will notice that a green and yellow arrow with animation appears on source qualifier (d). This represents the active transformation where debugger paused.

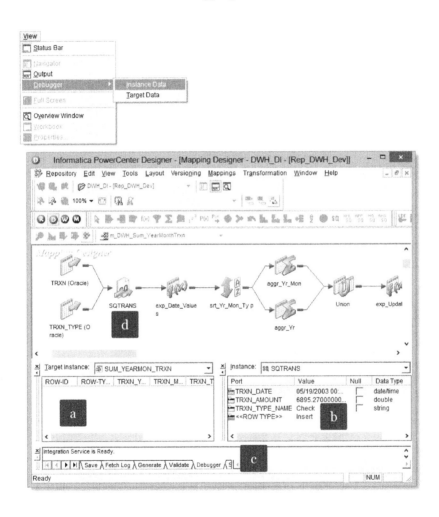

12.4.3 Debugger commands

The following debugger commands are available in `Mappings` → `Debugger` menu:

	Menu item	Description
	Next Instance	Continue debugger to next transformation or until a breakpoint is hit
	Step to Instance	Continue till data reaches selected transformation
	Show current instance	Highlight the current transformation in the mapping designer
	Continue	Run until a breakpoint is hit or all data reaches targets
	Stop debugger	Shutdown debugger

12.4.4 Breakpoints

You can add breakpoints to debugger. A breakpoint can be either simple or based on a condition. For example, if you are interested in only one transformation during the debugging, add a breakpoint to that transformation by right clicking on it and clicking `Edit Breakpoints` (   ).

With a simple breakpoint, debugger will pause as soon as the data reaches the specified transformation. With a conditional break point, debugger will pause only when one or more rows match the condition specified in the breakpoint. Use the `Remove All` to remove all breakpoints in a mapping with a single click. In the Edit Breakpoints dialog, click Add / Remove (a) to add a breakpoint or remove it. Click the port icons to add new conditions (b). When breakpoints are added, the transformation will show a STOP icon (   ).

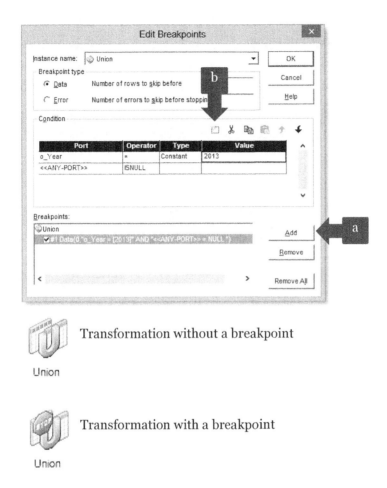

Transformation without a breakpoint

Union

Transformation with a breakpoint

Union

12.4.5   Evaluating expressions

When debugger is paused, you can evaluate different expressions to see their run time status. These do not have to be variable defined in a transformation. These just have to be valid expressions as per transformation language. Select any transformation that supports expressions such as expression and aggregator. Right click and click the menu item Evaluate Expression. This will open an expression dialog editor. Provide a valid expression and click Validate. This will validate the expression at the current runtime context.

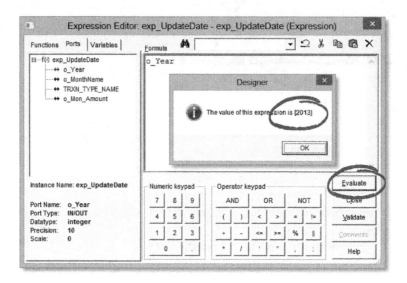

12.5   Row level errors

Row level errors that occur in a session are by default logged in the session log. While a session log is very easy to read and understand, it cannot be easily used to automate any error recovery scenarios. PowerCenter provides an ability to redirect all row level errors into a set of tables or files for automation and better reporting. But before we get in to the details, we must first understand what PowerCenter write when an error occurs. Let us look at a sample mapping:

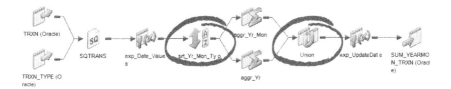

In the above picture, (a – sorter) and (b – union) are two possible points of failures. While a row can have an error virtually at any transformation in a mapping, we are currently focusing on two points for keeping the concept simple. Now, if a row has an error and is rejected at (a), the information written to the log file will be different than when a row is rejected at point (b). Why? The answer is quite simple. The transformations at point (a) and point (b) do not have the same structure. In fact even the data flowing through these transformations is not the same.

When a row level error happens, the data typically has not reached its target yet and may have already been transformed from its source. Hence, PowerCenter cannot write row level error data either as it is read from the source or as it will be written to target. Hence, it has to write the data as-it-is at the intermittent level. As shown in the pictures above, the data structure(ports) at point (a) and point (b) is not the same. Two aggregators in between summarize the data and hence, point (b) receives lesser data than point (a). Now, based on the complexity of the mapping, there may be many more significant differences between any point (a) and point (b). Hence it is practically impossible for PowerCenter to write any row level data at these two points into a common structure. So, what does PowerCenter do? It simply writes the data at any rejection point in a delimited format. While this makes it a little hard to read manually, it makes it easy to automate reporting and recovery operations. The actual data resembles to that in the bad file or reject file.

Each line consists of row indicator (DONTs) followed by each column's data and a column indicator (DONTs).

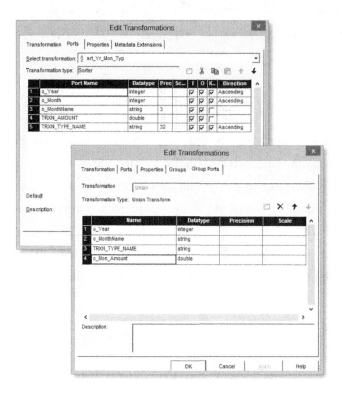

 When a row level error occurs, PowerCenter writes the data as of the most recent active transformation towards the originating source.

The error logging properties can be setup in each session in the session properties (config object tab). To change the default logging for all sessions, edit the default session configurations.

The overhead of the row level error logging may impact session performance due to the additional overhead.

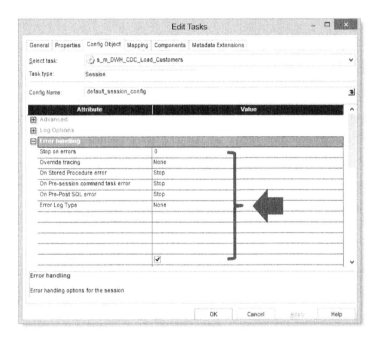

12.6   Error logging tables

PowerCenter provides 4 relational tables that can be optionally created and configured to contain all row level error information. Once row level logs are maintained in a table or file, PowerCenter Integration Service will no longer write them to a session log. These 4 tables can be created in any database and need not necessarily remain the session's source or target. Row level errors for more than one session can be populated and stored in the same set of tables.

12.6.1 PMERR_SESS

This is the master table that contains session related information including repository, folder, workflow, (optionally) worklet and session name and mapping name.

12.6.2 PMERR_TRANS

This table contains transformation level information such as transformation name where the error occurred, group name (for example, in a router did the error happen in an INPUT group or OUTPUT group?), port names (and data types, separated by a :). If there are no active transformations between the transformation where an error occurred and its source qualifier, the source qualifier name is also listed here.

12.6.3 PMERR_MSG

This Table contains the true error messages that occurred during session runs. Each row level error that occurred is logged into this table along with references to the session, mapping and transformation that caused it. The error timestamp (when the error occurred) is logged in both local to the Integration Service node and the Universal time (GMT). The error type field contains the following values:

Error type	Description
1	Reader error
2	Writer error
3	Transformation error

12.6.4   PMERR_DATA

This table contains detailed data for the errors that are logged in the PMERR_MSG table. Some of the important fields in this table are:

TRANS_ROW_DATA:

This contains the row data in a delimited fashion. Each column is followed by a column indicator that represents the type of data. Each column is separated by a pipe (|). Within each column, data and the indicator is separated by a colon (:)

SOURCE_ROW_TYPE:

Row type	Description
0	Insert
1	Update
2	Delete
3	Reject

SOURCE ROW DATA:

This contains the data that is being sent into the transformation where the error occurred. The data format is similar to TRANS_ROW_DATA.

A table name prefix can be specified (up to 11 chars) for the error log tables. This provides the ability to have more than one set of tables in the same schema.

If any error data is more than 2000 characters, PowerCenter logs them as different rows. These can be collected together using the LINE_NO column.

12.7 Error logging file

Instead of logging to relational tables, you can also choose to let PowerCenter log row level errors into a flat file. The file contains similar data as the relational structure with a double pipe as delimiter (||). Row data is delimited by a single pipe (|).

If your DI processes are processing sensitive data that you do not wish to be logged into the error logging tables or files, but you still want to enable the logging of error messages, you can do so by unchecking the Log Row Data and Log Source Row Data in session properties → Config Object tab.

12.8 Debug ready mappings

PowerCenter provides detailed logs and additional error logging capabilities. Data Integration jobs process millions of records every day. Typically when a DI solution is developed and deployed in production, during its stabilization phase, several data issues are found. These are fixed and the DI solution eventually becomes error-free. During the stabilization phase, most of the time is usually spent in analyzing the data differences and attempting to reproduce the issues in test environments. Typically, these issues are hard to reproduce in test environment due to lack of real-life data. Hence, it is important to build debug-ready techniques into the mappings so that when a data issue occurs, the necessary data sample can be taken from production. This data represents the state of the code when the data is being processed and hence helps analyze the situation and reproduce the issue in test environment with similar data.

In this technique, we write certain important variables to an output file for a post-session analysis. Important ports from different transformations are thus collected and written to a log file along with primary keys. When a data issue happens, this log file can be consulted for understand how different variables were evaluated when the row was processed. We can use mapping parameters to turn this log file on or off. When turned on, this additional information is written to the file. When turned off, a zero byte file is created with no log contents.

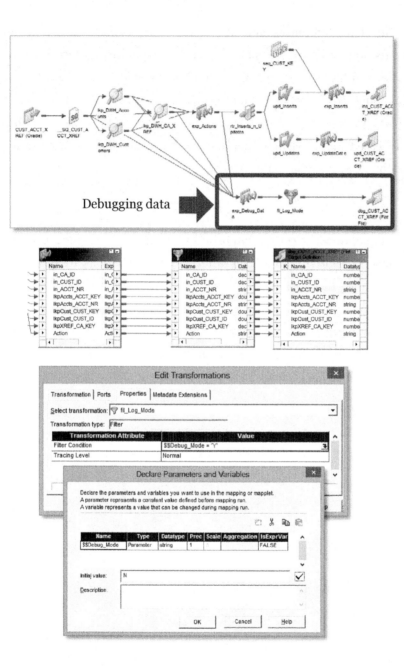

In the example shown (Customer Account Cross Reference table load), a new expression called `exp_Debug_Data` is created. This expression contains data from the input source qualifier (`in_` ports), DWH Customers lookup (`lkpCust_` ports), DWH Accounts (`lkpAccts_` ports) and DWH Customer Account Cross Reference lookup ports (`lkpXREF_` ports) and the action code (`Action`). This data is then passed on to a filter transformation. This filter has an expression depending on the mapping parameter. If mapping parameter `$$Debug_Mode` is set to `Y`, then filter will allow this debug information to be written to a flat file. If this mapping parameter is set to any other value(for example, `N`), filter will ignore all the records in this pipeline. In either case, the main target is not impacted. If there is ever a data issue, the `$$Debug_Mode` can be set to `Y` in the parameter file so that the production mapping captures this debug data. This data is then analyzed to understand how the data has flown through the mapping and can be arrived at a conclusion. If there are many ports, an expression can be built to capture this data as name value pairs and then can be written to a generalized target.

13

Workflow Tasks

Workflow is a logical order of tasks execution. So far, we have focused entirely on sessions. Sessions are one type of tasks, but a workflow is capable of executing many other type of tasks. These tasks can be executed along with sessions. A session is runtime configuration of a mapping. However, we seldom need to execute mappings alone. In a data integration project, the data integration processes such as mappings, run hand in hand with many external components. For example, a data integration mapping may need to look at the list of files in a directory and then process them in the order they were created. To do so, mappings need to interact with operating system shell and execute some operating system commands. We can do so by executing a command task from a workflow. Similarly, we often need to invoke a data integration mapping as soon as a file arrives in a directory. We can use event wait task in a workflow to wait for the file and then immediately run a mapping as soon as the file arrives.

13.1   Command tasks

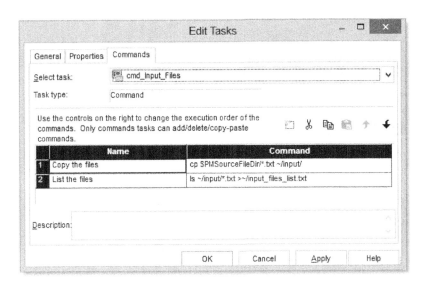

Command tasks are used to execute valid operating system commands and shell (or DOS) scripts. More than one operating system command/script can be executed in a command task in an order. Output of these commands/scripts can be redirected to files and/or pipes as long as they follow a valid syntax. By default, workflow will continue even if one or more commands have failed. `Fail task if any command fails` checkbox needs to be checked to change behavior.

13.2   Pre-session and Post-session tasks

Command tasks can also be executed as pre or post session execution. These are known as pre-session command task and post-session command task respectively. Different command tasks can be executed upon session success and session failure. These can be configured in session properties → `Components` tab. Both reusable and non-reusable command tasks can be created as part of pre-session and post-session tasks.

13.3 Email tasks

 An email task can be used to send emails from within workflows. To be able to use the email tasks, email must have already been configured in the Integration Service. As part of the email task, email username (email address), subject and text (body) can be configured.

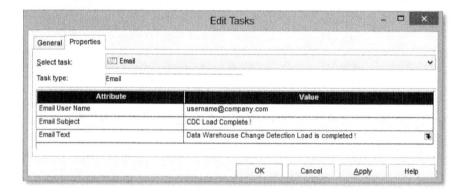

To be able to use email task, your administrator should have already configured the Integration Service to be able to send mail.

13.4   Decision tasks

A decision task is used to evaluate a condition in the workflow and then define conditional flows based on its result. A condition written in a decision task evaluates to TRUE or FALSE. A simple use-case is to determine whether or not to execute a transaction load based on the success criteria of other sessions that load the dimension. Typically, decision task has two outgoing links – one for TRUE path and one for FALSE path, based on the condition evaluation.

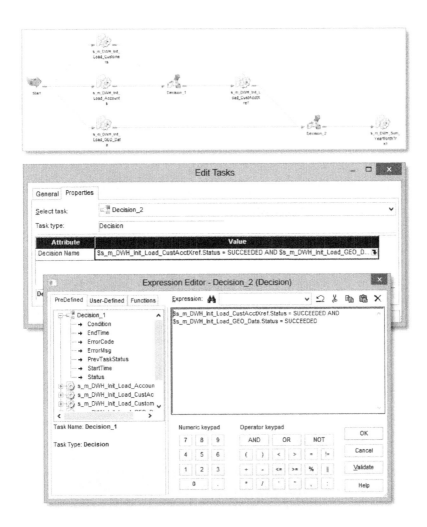

13.5 Timer tasks

A timer task is used in a workflow to introduce time delays / schedules in the workflow. For example, say we have two sources providing data at 4 AM. The third source data load should begin at 6 AM irrespective of the first two. Now, we can introduce a timer task and set its time to absolute time. We can also use a workflow variable to calculate the wait. Similarly, if we have database such as re-indexing operations happening in between data integration tasks, we can use a timer task to let the workflow "sleep" for sometime and then resume its activities later. The relative time can be relative to start of the workflow or worklet or the task itself.

13.6 Control tasks

A control task is used to dynamically set the status of the workflow. For example, when one or more sessions in a workflow fail, we might want to set the workflow status as FAILED. But when some sessions fail, we may simply want to log the error and continue. To change the status of the workflow, we can use a control task. A control task can be used to set the following statuses:

Status	Meaning
Fail me	Status of the current object is set to failed
Fail parent	Status of the parent object is set to failed. If the control task is in a workflow, workflow is set to failed. If it is in a worklet, worklet status is set to failed
Stop parent	Parent object is stopped – all currently running children are given 60 seconds to close their source/target connections
Abort parent	Parent object is immediately terminated
Fail top-level workflow	If the control is in a worklet, changes the top most workflow status as failed
Stop top-level workflow	If the control is in a worklet, changes the top most workflow as stopped
Abort top-level workflow	If the control is in a worklet, changes the top most workflow as aborted immediately

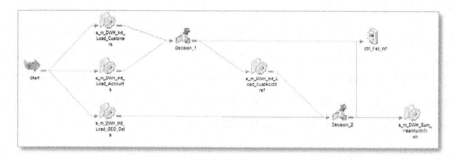

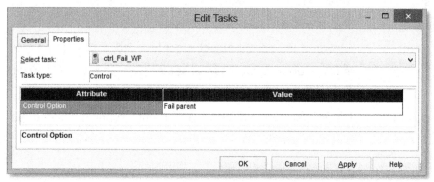

13.7 Assignment tasks

An assignment task is used to assign values to workflow/worklet variables. These assignments can be made after evaluating valid PowerCenter expressions. To be able to use assignment task, it is mandatory to define workflow/worklet variables.

13.8   Event raise and event wait tasks

Events represent incidents. In data integration processes, events play a vital role. Sometimes, we need to execute steps asynchronously. During asynchronous execution, the workflow does not wait for a step to complete before moving on to another. This also happens when we execute several steps in parallel. These asynchronous steps can communicate with each other using events. Let's look at an example to understand it better.

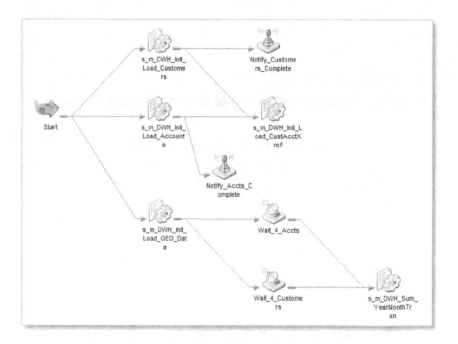

In the above example, we can notice that we execute the customers and accounts in parallel to geography dimension. However, the transactions need to wait until both customers and accounts are completed. This can be achieved by raising events when customers and accounts are completed. Transactions flow finishes the geographies dimension and then waits for the customers and accounts to complete. If customers and accounts are already completed by then, it will simply move on. To build this kind of logic, we first have to create unique events – each event representing the completion of customers and accounts. We do so by creating events in the workflow properties → Events tab. Then we create event 'raise tasks' in workflow after customer and accounts sessions. In each of these, we select appropriate events to be raised. We then create a two event wait task just before the transactions session. Each of these tasks waits for one event. In the events tab of the event wait task, we select the event we want the task to wait for. We select user defined events and choose an event from the list. Now, if the GEO dimensions complete before the customers and accounts, the event waits will be in a running state until they receive their corresponding events from the event raise tasks.

14

Caches

PowerCenter transformations such as Lookup and aggregator cache the data for better performance and extended functionality. Cached data is stored in a proprietary memory structure. An index is also built to speed up access to this data structure. Caches can be categorized in different ways.

14.1   Non Persistent cache

By default, all caches are non-persistent i.e. the data that is cached at the beginning of the session (as part of session initialization) and is disregarded at the end of the session. Though caching the data takes some time at the beginning of the session, the performance gain usually outweighs the initial cache time. A non-persistent cache is used when the lookup data changes often and between mapping runs. For example, if a mapping uses a lookup to cache, the geography data that is updated by other processes, then every time the mapping runs, it has to re-cache the data.

14.2   Persistent Cache

Persistent caches are used when the data that is being cached is large in volume. When using a persistent cache, PowerCenter Integration Service saves the cache file at the end of the session run. The cache file is then loaded at the beginning of the session into the memory. By loading the cache file at the beginning session, we avoid reading the whole data from the source all over again. Since the cache and its index are already prebuilt, the time to reload the cache file(s) into memory again will be minimal. Persistent caches are most commonly used in two scenarios: lookup with large volumes of data that cannot be re-cached and incremental aggregation.

14.3   Named cache

Persistent caches are by default named after their transformation IDs. However, this makes it very difficult to manage the lookup files on the disk. Hence, a prefix can be added to the cache file names, for example, lookups used by a data warehouse application.

14.4   Lookup caches

By default, lookup transformation caches the data it reads from its source. If the lookup is based on a relational table, developers can choose whether or not to cache the lookup data. When a cached lookup transformation is used, PowerCenter Integration service caches the lookup data.

The cached data and the index are written into files in the $PMLookupFileDir\directory. All the cached data is written to .dat files and the index files are written to .idx files.

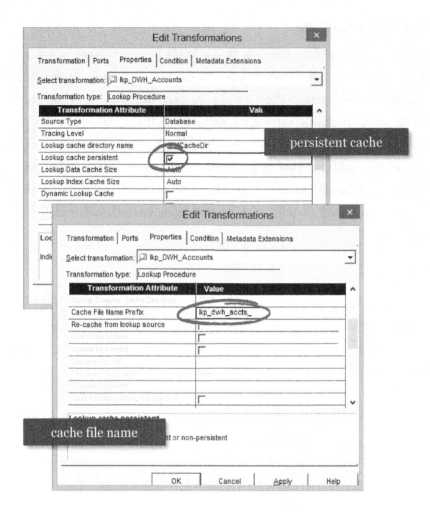

14.5 Static lookup cache

By default, all lookup caches are static. A static lookup cache is one that does not change during a session run. Depending on whether the lookup cache is persistent or non-persistent, the lookup cache is built or loaded at the session initialization. The cache will stay the same throughout the session run.

14.6   Dynamic lookup cache

A dynamic lookup cache can be updated during a session run. Initially, during the session initialization, the lookup cache is created and during the session run, every incoming record is looked up and if it does not already exist in the cache, it is added to the cache. Such records are marked so that the same action can also be performed in the corresponding targets. When a lookup is marked as dynamic, a new port called `NewLookupRow` is created. This new `NewLookupRow` port contains the value 0 when the integration service did not change the cache. The `NewLookupRow` port contains 1 and 2 when the integration service inserts the record into the cache and updates the cache respectively.

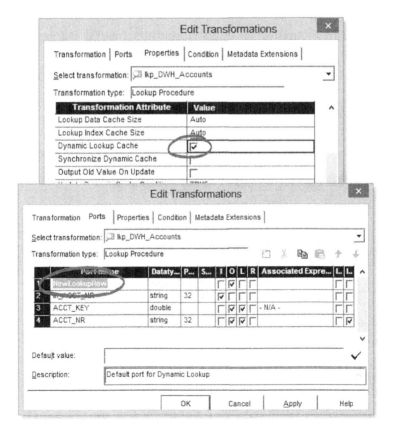

14.7   Incremental aggregation

Aggregation is one of the active transformations that cache the input data. By default, the aggregation caches are non-persistent. So, they are built during the session run and are deleted at the end of successful execution of the session. An aggregator cache can be configured to be incremental. When an incremental cache is configured, Integration Service retains the cache files on disk and reloads the cache files for subsequent runs. In the subsequent runs, aggregations computed in the current run are incrementally added to the historically computed values that are stored in the cache. At the end of the run, the cache is updated with the updated values. Incremental aggregation can be configured in session properties → `Properties` tab. To reinitialize an already built incremental aggregation, select the `Reinitialize aggregate cache` property.

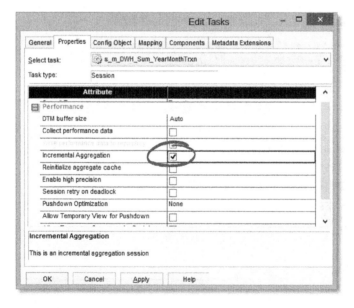

15

Deployment

PowerCenter has more than one way to deploy objects between environments. Many levels of objects can be deployed from one PowerCenter environment to another. Individual objects such as sources, targets, mappings and workflows can be exported as XML and imported into other repositories either within the same domain or a different one.

15.1 Drag and drop

Objects can be dragged from the source repository (using repository navigator) source folder and dropped into a different folder in the same/different repository. This is the simplest way of deploying objects from one repository/folder to another.

 When using drag-n-drop, press SHIFT to move the objects instead of copying.

15.2   Export objects as XML

Sources and targets can be exported from the Designer into XML files. Expand the sources in the repository navigator. Select the sources you would like to export and select export objects menu item. Use advanced options to determine whether or not to export primary/foreign keys. Mappings can also be exported as XML files just like any other objects. Go to `Repository` Menu →`Export Objects` to export the mappings as XML. Workflows can be exported to XML files from workflow manager.

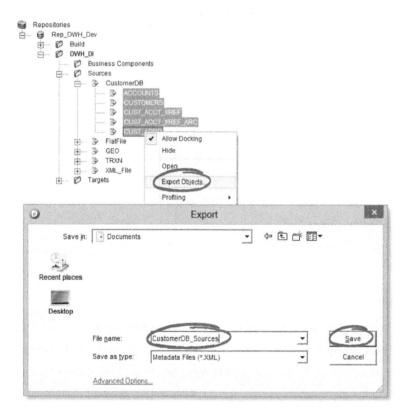

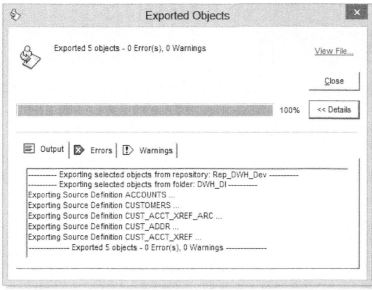

15.3   Exporting multiple objects

Repository manager, as the name suggests, is used to manage the repository. Deploying objects is one of the most common activities performed using repository manager. When we export objects from Designer or workflow manager, we can choose only one object at a time. More than one object can be exported at the same time from the Repository Manager. Use SHIFT key to make continuous selection and CTRL key to make individual selections.

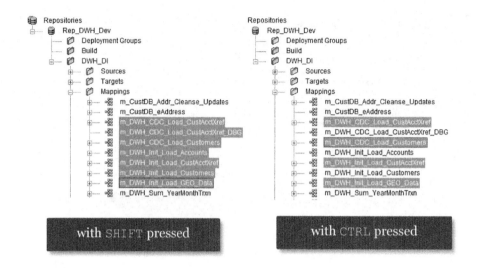

15.4 Exporting all dependencies

When objects are exported from repository manager, by default, all dependent objects are also exported. For example, when a workflow is exported from repository manager, all the sessions, mappings, sources, targets and other dependent objects are also exported along with the workflow.

15.5 Importing exported objects

When objects are exported, an XML file is created. This XML file contains definitions of the objects exported. This XML file can be imported in another repository (in same or another domain) or even in the same repository in a different folder. To do so, go to Repository Manager, connect to the repository where you would like to import the objects, select the destination folder. Then go to Repository Menu →Import Objects… Import Wizard appears. Browse and select the XML file you would like to import. To perform selective import, select the specific objects on the left hand side and click Add>>. To import all objects, click

Add All>>. In the Match Folders screen, choose the destination repository/folder, where you would like these objects to be imported. You can then define rules on how to handle conflicts. A conflict occurs when one or more objects you are trying to import already exist in the destination repository. If you do not want to define any rules, simply, click on Next. If the import wizard finds any conflicts it will automatically load the Conflict Resolution Wizard. In this wizard, you can select the objects that have conflicts and define to perform any of the following actions:

Action	Meaning
Rename	The conflicted object already exists in the destination repository/folder. You can rename the new object and import it with a different name. When you check the Rename checkbox, PowerCenter will automatically generate a name for you. To change it, click Edit.
Replace	The conflicted object already exists in the destination. The existing object will be overwritten with the new object definition from the XML. By default, This action cannot be undone after the deployment.
Reuse	The object definition in your XML will be ignored and the object already in the destination repository/folder will be reused. For example, if you are trying to import a mapping and a source definition has a conflict, by clicking reuse, you are asking PowerCenter to import the mapping but use the existing source definition in the destination repository. So, the source definition in the XML file is discarded.
Skip	The conflicted object is not imported. If the object you are trying to import depends on this conflicted object, it will be invalidated.

Once all the conflicts are resolved, Conflict Resolution Summary will be displayed. After closing the window, the import will start. The import log is displayed on the screen along with the status of the imports. Once the import is complete, click Done to close the import wizard.

 To be able to import objects into a repository/folder, you need write access to it. Contact your PowerCenter administrator if you do not have write access on the destination repository/folder

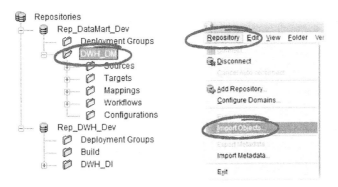

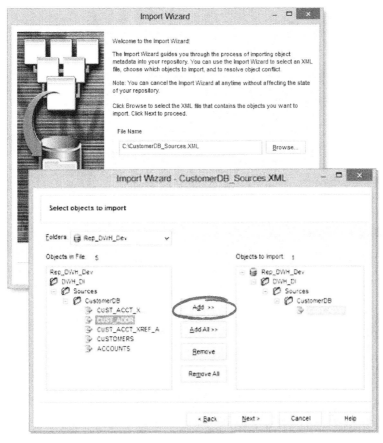

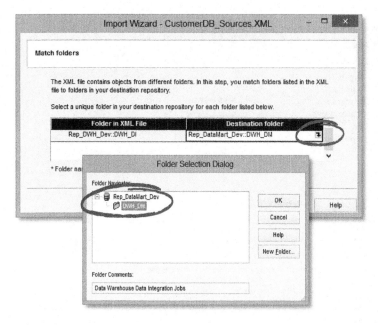

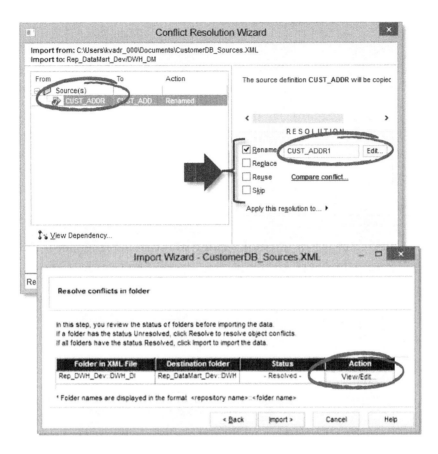

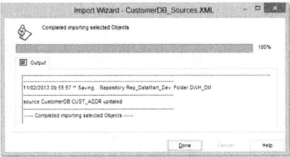

15.6   Starting folder copy wizard

Folder copy wizard is used when you want to copy the entire contents of a repository folder instead of selected objects. When performing a folder copy, all the objects within the folder are copied to the destination repository/folder. A conflict resolution wizard (similar to the one that appears in the import object wizard) is used to resolve any conflicts while performing the folder copy.

There is more than one-way to initiate the folder copy wizard:

15.6.1   Drag and drop

Connect to the repository from where the folder is to be copied. Connect to the repository where the folder is to be copied. Now, drag the folder you would like to copy and drop it in the repository where you would like it to be copied.

While dropping the folder, drop it on the destination repository – not on a folder within the repository.

15.6.2   Copy and paste

Connect to the repository from where you want the folder to be copied. Select the source folder and select the menu `Edit` → `Copy`. Now, select your destination *repository*, which can be the same as source. Now select the menu `Edit` → `Paste`. Folder copy Wizard will initiate

You can also use the windows shortcut `CTRL+C` to copy and `CTRL+V` to paste.

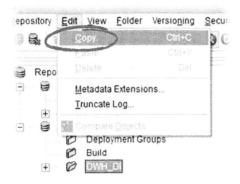

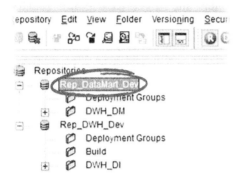

15.7 Folder copy wizard

Folder copy wizard is used to copy a folder from a source repository to destination repository. The destination can be same as the source repository. The following list contains different steps in the wizard. Please note that depending on the folder(s) you are trying to copy and its contents, some of these steps may be optional.

a. The folder copy wizard starts by prompting whether or not to use typical options.

b. We are then prompted with any related folders and an option to replace an existing folder.

c. If you choose a folder in the list and don't choose the replace option, PowerCenter will confirm if you want to replace the folder.

d. If you choose to replace, PowerCenter will prompt to analyze the source and destination folders.

e. If they are related, it will prompt whether or not the destination folder has been changed since its previous deployments.

f. It will then compare the folders and present you with a summary of the changes, if any.

g. Choose the owner of the folder in the destination repository. By default, owner of the destination folder will be the user with which we logged in at the time of folder copy.

h. We are prompted to copy the persistent values for all mapping variables. If the checkbox is ticked, persistent values of mapping variables are copied from the source repository to the destination repository.

i. PowerCenter will then prompt you whether you want to retain persistent values of existing mappings. By checking this box, you let PowerCenter know that while copying the persistent values to destination repository, if the objects in the destination already have a persistent value, it should retain the value. If not, it must copy from the source folder. Typically, while copying a folder to production, you check "Retain persisted values for all mapping variables".

j. In production, usually jobs run at regular intervals and hence mappings execute more frequently than in other environments. So, the values of sequence generators, normalizers and XML transformations are different from those in other environments. We choose to "Retain Sequence Generator, Normalizer or XML key current values". If this box is checked, PowerCenter will keep the existing values for these transformations in the destination repository as it is.

k. A list of connections used by the objects within this folder is then displayed. Each connection is suffixed either with 'Match found' or 'No match found' indicating whether or not a connection with the same name already exists in the destination repository. If the connection does not exist in the destination, it is copied over.

l. If the mappings contain dependency information, you are prompted to copy over the dependencies.

m. By default, workflow run history is not copied over. To copy this information, check the box "Copy session or workflow run history". Typically, when copying a folder to production, this checkbox is left *unchecked*.

n. In the last screen before deployment, we are presented with the option to save the deployment options we selected into an XML file. It is defaulted to `deployOptions.xml`. We can also choose to start the deployment immediately (default). If you wish to use the `deployOptions.xml` to deploy a folder from command line at a later time, uncheck Ready to start deployment. The `deployOptions.xml` file is by default saved at `clients\PowerCenterClient\client\bin` sub directory in the PowerCenter Client Installation location.

o. If you choose to deploy immediately, the deployment status is displayed on the screen.

p. It is then followed by the deployment result in the message window at the bottom of the screen.

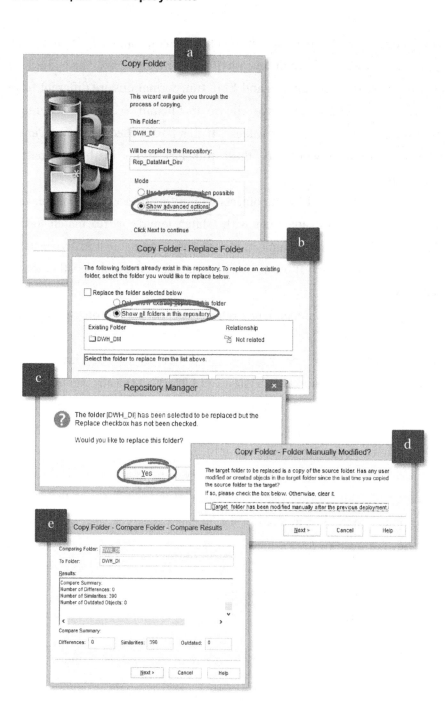

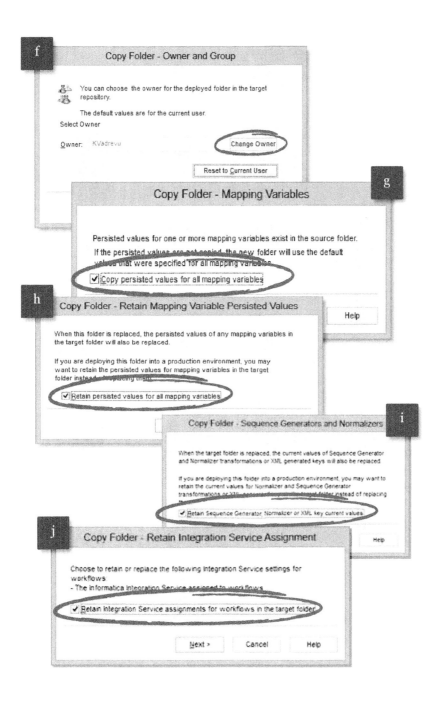

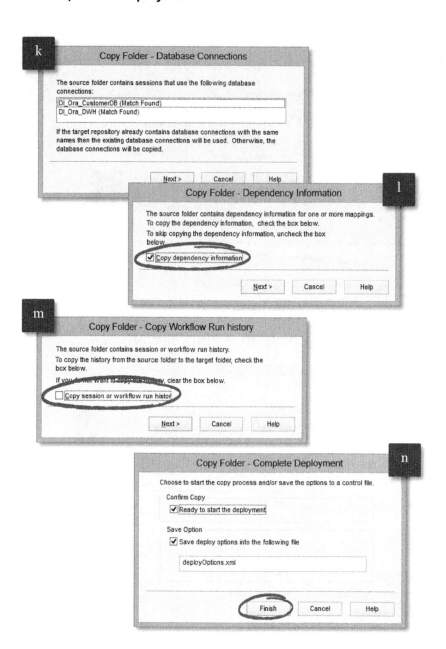

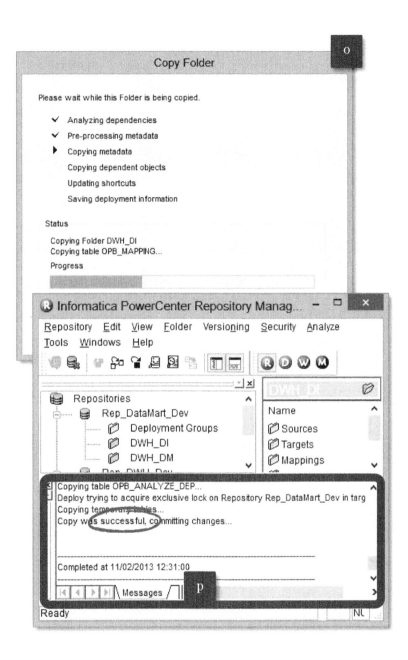

15.8 Deployment groups

A deployment group represents a set of objects from one or more folders that need to be deployed as a unit. Deployment groups (DGs) are of two types: static and dynamic. In a static deployment group, the developer adds the objects manually. In a dynamic deployment group, an object query is built and all objects that are returned as a result are considered to be part of the deployment group. Deployment groups can be accessed in Repository Manager `Tools` menu → `Deployment` menu → `Groups`. Once a static deployment group is created, developers can drag and drop the objects that they want to add to the deployment group. Each time an object is added to the deployment group, a dependency dialog box appears. Developers can choose to add all dependencies/reusable dependencies along with the object. To copy a DG from a repository, simply drag it and drop on a destination repository. Copy Deployment Group wizard will appear. This wizard is very similar to Folder Copy Wizard with the following additional options:

Option	Meaning
Deployment folders	As part of copying a DG, the wizard will require you to provide a matching folder in the destination repository for every folder the deployment group contains.
Clear contents of the source deployment group	If this option is checked, at the end of the successful deployment, the original DG is emptied out.
Copy deployment group definition	Check this box, if the destination repository is not your final repository. For example, when copying from Development to test repository, you may want to copy the DG definition so that it can eventually be copied over from test to production.

Option	Meaning
Validate objects in the target repository	If checked, at the end of successful deployment, all objects deployed as part of the DG will be validated in the target repository.

Dynamic deployment groups are created when there are numerous objects that need to be added to the DG and manually adding them could lead to human errors. To create a dynamic deployment group, you must first create an object query. Object queries can be created in `Repository Manager` → `Tools` → `Object queries` → `New`. In the query editor, select the appropriate options from the drop down and save the query.

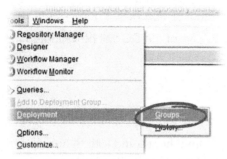

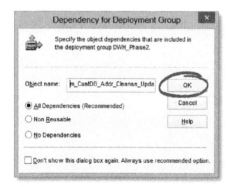

PART 4

ENTERPRISE

DATA INTEGRATION

16

Team based development, Versioning

Team based development enables versioning in PowerCenter repository. With versioning enabled, developers can check-in and check-out objects directly in the PowerCenter IDE. PowerCenter keeps track of all the versions and developers can revoke back to the earlier versions as needed.

16.1   Versioned or not...?

Before we start, it is important to understand that the team based development/versioning is a one-way street. It is either enabled for a repository or it is not. Once enabled, a versioned repository cannot be un-versioned, at least not simply. To know whether a repository is versioned or not is easy. If you are in repository manager, right click on the repository, if you see versioning related menu items enabled, your repository is versioned. In Designer and Workflow

Manager, open the `Versioning` menu. If `Find Checkouts` menu item is enabled, your repository is versioning enabled.

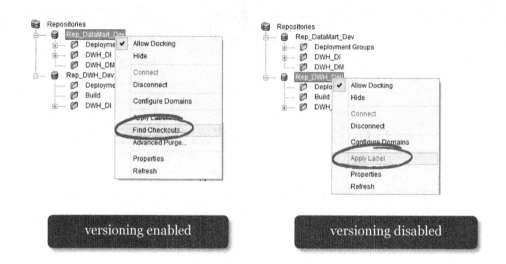

16.2 Check in and check out

By default when an object is created in a versioned repository, its status is checked out. Developer can save the object without having to check it in. However, other users cannot see the object until it is checked in. A checked out object has a green checkmark next to it in the repository navigator. For example, a checked out mapping will have the icon ( ) where as a checked in mapping will have the icon ( ). To check out an object that is already checked in, right click on the object in the repository navigator and go to the `Versioning` menu →`Check out`. A Check out dialog box appears. Type a comment to represent why the object is being checked out. Once the changes are complete, check in the object by right clicking on it in the repository navigator and going to `Versioning` menu →`Check` `in`. A check in dialog box will then appear. Type in a comment to note the changes made. Objects can be checked out or checked in using the `Versioning` menu as well.

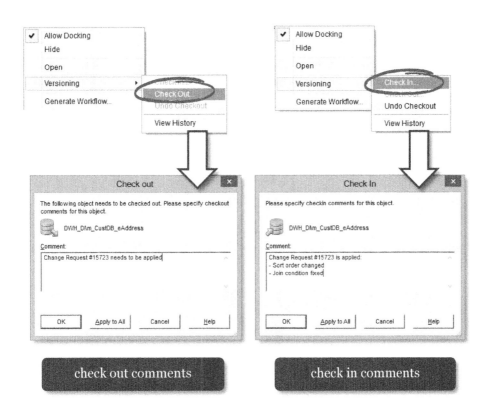

16.3 Working with history

The beauty of the versioning is realized when we need to go back and take a look at a previous version of the same object. In a non-versioned repository, this is hard to do so and is maintained manually, if at all. To view an object's history, right click on the object in the repository navigator and go to `Versioning` menu →`View history`. View History window opens up. The History window shows all the versions of the object available in the repository along with comments (at the bottom). Right click on any version of the object and click `Open in workspace` to view the object in the workspace. You can also compare it with the previous version using the `Compare` menu →`Previous version`. You can also, alternatively, select more than one versions (use `CTRL` key to make multiple selection) and then choose the `Compare` menu →`Selected versions`.

16.4   Labels

Labels are used to logically group versioned objects. Labels are user friendly names attached to versioned objects. Some examples of labels are: "CR 15723", "DWH Phase 2". So, in these examples, the objects that are to be deployed as part of Data

Warehouse Phase 2 implementation can be attached to that label irrespective of their individual version numbers. In this case, a mapping may be of version 20, while its source definition is still version 15. Labels can be created in Repository Manager, Versioning menu. To apply a label to an object, it must be viewed in the version history window. To view the history of an object, right click on it in the repository navigator, go to `Versioning` menu and then select `View History`. Right click on the version to which you want to apply label. Click `Labels`→`Apply Label` and select a label.

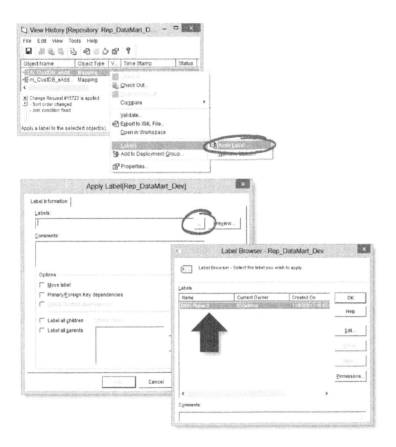

17

ODBC

ODBC stands for Open DataBase Connectivity. ODBC is an API, originally developed by Microsoft to provide applications to write database independent programs. PowerCenter ships with DataDirect ODBC drivers for most of the common databases. In a way, we have already used ODBC connections to import our source, target definitions into the repository. In this chapter, we will look at ways to process data using ODBC sources/targets.

17.1   ODBC on client vs. ODBC on server

When we imported sources and targets into the Designer, we already used ODBC connections. However, these connections are only used to import the table definitions and are not retained in the PowerCenter repository. To be able to process ODBC data, ODBC connections must be first configured on the host PowerCenter Integration Service is residing on. These connection details are then configured within the Workflow Manager to be used in the sessions. At runtime, the PowerCenter Integration Service will look for this ODBC connection details and establish a connection to its underlying database. These connection details or the

ODBC name need not match the connection/name used to import the table definitions in the designer. PowerCenter ships with the DataDirect ODBC drivers for most of the databases. You can also use the ODBC drivers provided by the corresponding database vendors such as Oracle and Microsoft.

17.2   Configuring ODBC on windows

ODBC can be configured in Windows using the Windows Control Panel → Administrative Tools. If you are running 32-bit windows, you will only see one ODBC Data Source. If you are on a 64-bit platform, you will notice ODBC Data Sources (32-bit) and ODBC Data Sources (64-bit). You must choose the appropriate platform on which your Informatica PowerCenter is running.

 If you have 32-bit PowerCenter and you configure a 64-bit ODBC Data Source or vice-versa, your session will fail. Contact your Informatica Administrator to find out the right platform on which your PowerCenter is hosted.

Follow these steps to create an ODBC connection in Windows:

a.   Go to Control Panel → Administrative Tools

b.   Open the ODBC Data Sources (32-bit) or ODBC Data Sources (64-bit) depending on the platform hosting your PowerCenter

c.   Go to the System DSN tab

d.   Click Add

e.   Fill in the details provided to you by your DBA

f.   Test the connection and save it

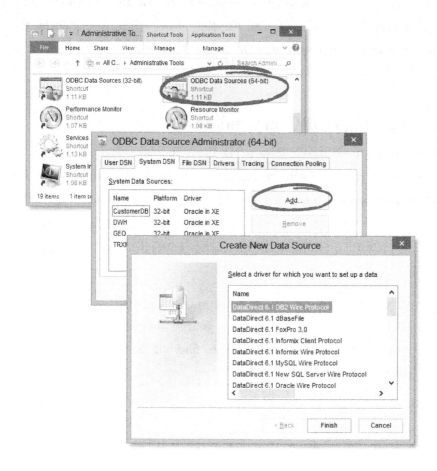

17.3 Configuring ODBC on UNIX/Linux platforms

PowerCenter ships with DataDirect ODBC drivers. These can be found in the PowerCenter server installation directory ($INFA_HOME). ODBC 6.1 (or ODBC7 based on the PowerCenter version you have) directory is present within the $INFA_HOME. This ODBC directory is referred as $ODBCHOME. The odbc.ini file within the `$ODBCHOME` should be updated to contain ODBC entries that correspond to ODBC connections. A sample odbc.ini file is as shown below. A template for each database supported is present in the file. Copy the template of the database for which you want to create a connection. Update it with the database values provided to you by your DBA. Restart the Integration Service for the changes to take effect.

17.4   Configuring ODBC connections in PowerCenter

Once the ODBC connections are configured on the PowerCenter Server (Windows/UNIX platforms), a connection must be created in the Workflow Manager pointing to the ODBC connectivity. The connectivity defined at the server level is used by PowerCenter Integration Service at runtime to read/write data. There can be more than one ODBC connection configured at the server level. To specify a specific connection to be used in a session, we will still have to create a connection in the Workflow manager and point it to the configuration defined at the server level. This connection will be used in the sessions that will connect through the ODBC drivers to the database.

Follow these steps to create an ODBC connection in PowerCenter Workflow Manager:

a.   Go to Workflow Manager

b.   Connect to the repository

c.   Go to the `Connections` menu →`Relational`

d.   `Relational Connection Browser` appears. Click `New`

e.   Select `ODBC` and click `OK`

f.   `Connection Object Definition` dialog box appears

g.   Fill the details as follows:

Property	Value
Name	Provide a unique name representing the source to which you are connecting. You will use this name in your sessions
Username	Username to connect to the database
Password	Corresponding password
Connect string	On Windows: This should be the name you provided for your ODBC connection you created in Control Panel On UNIX: This will be the exact name you provided to your ODBC connection in odbc.ini
Code page	Code page under which your database is running. Contact your DBA for details

h.   Click OK and then click close to close the dialog boxes

17.5   Using ODBC connections in sessions

You can use ODBC connections just like any other relational connection. Open the session properties, go to `Mapping` tab. Select the source/target. On the right hand side, within `Connections` horizontal bar, click on the selection icon (⬇) and select the ODBC connection you want to use. Save the session and run the workflow.

18

FTP / Secure FTP

(S)FTP is a (Secure) File Transfer Protocol. (S)FTP is used to exchange files between nodes, usually within the firewall. Typically (S)FTP requires a username and password to connect to the destination server. (S)FTP protocol transfers files directly between the servers without landing. FTP uses a default port number 21 and SFTP uses a default port number 22. If you have different port configuration, you can provide the same in the workflow manager connection.

18.1   Integration service and the (S) FTP

When (S)FTP connections are used, Integration Service will attempt to perform a (S)FTP from the server hosting PowerCenter Integration Service. Hence, the ports of communication must be opened between these servers. If you intend to FTP a source file from a server, process it and then FTP the output file to another server, the ports of FTP communication must be open between the Integration service and source server and the Integration Service server and the destination server.

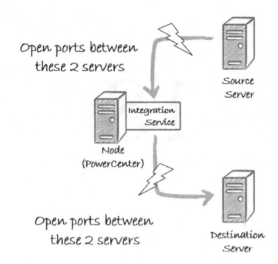

18.2 Creating (S)FTP connections

(S)FTP connections can be created in the Workflow manager client by following these steps:

    a.   Go to the `Connections` menu → `FTP`

    b.   This opens the `FTP Connection Browser`. Click `New`

    c.   Fill in the details for the connection

Property	Value
Name	Provide a unique name to the connection. This name will be used in the sessions to represent this connection.
Username	Username to connect to the remote host. This is typically the OS user (sometimes a service account) with (S)FTP privileges.
Password	Corresponding password
Hostname	Hostname of the server that integration service will FTP from (if used in source) or will FTP to (if used in target).

	This server MUST be accessible from the server hosting integration service. Optionally, a port number can also be specified. If port number is specified, use a semi colon (:) as a separator between hostname and port number.
Default remote directory	The default directory where files will be FTP'ed from/to.
Use SFTP	If checked, PowerCenter Integration Service will use Secure FTP instead of FTP. If your server uses private/public key authentication, provide the key file name and password.

d. Click OK and Close to close the dialog boxes

e. Open the session properties, where you would like to use the (S)FTP connection

f. Go to Mapping tab and select the *Flat File* source/target

g. On the right hand side, in the Connections horizontal section, change the connection from None to FTP. Click the selection icon (⬛) and select the FTP connection

h. Save the workflow and run

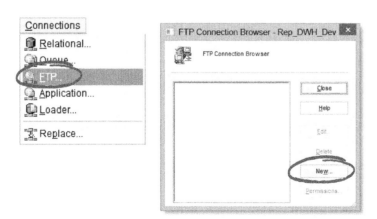

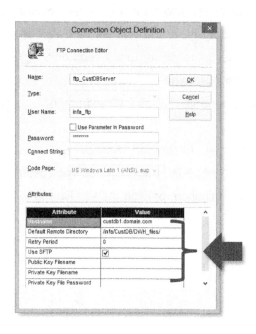

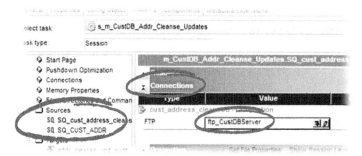

19

High Availability

PowerCenter High Availability framework consists of Resilience, Grid Computing and Load Balancing features. High availability refers to the ability to maintain uninterrupted availability of the environment. While High Availability involves all components internal and external to Informatica environment, this book focuses only on the Informatica PowerCenter aspects of it. High Availability concepts and concerns regarding external components such as Operating System, File System etc are out of scope.

19.1   Resilience

Resilience is the system's ability to tolerate temporary failures. These temporary failures may have happened for a number of reasons. Resilience is primarily of two types: Design-time Resilience and Run-time Resilience.

19.1.1   Design time resilience

Design-time resilience refers to the ability of the domain and the PowerCenter clients to handle temporary interruption of the services. For example, when a developer is working on a mapping and has lost the connectivity to the repository service, design-time resilience refers to the Designer's ability to connect to the repository service once it is back up and save the changes as if the interruption / failure never happened.

19.1.2   Run-time resilience

Run-time resilience refers to the ability of the domain and its services to handle temporary interruption of the services they depend on while executing workflows. Runtime resilience is typically configured in the database/(S)FTP connections used by the sessions. This includes retry count and the time out periods.

19.2 Load Balancing

Load balancing is the ability to balance the workflows execution such that system resources across all nodes are optimally utilized. In a multi-node domain, if too many workflows are executed on the same node, the system resources on that node max out impacting the workflow performance even though there are ample resources on the other nodes within the domain. When an Integration Service is configured to execute on a Grid, PowerCenter intelligently allocates the workflows to different nodes such that the resources on the systems and the workflows' demand for resources are optimally addressed. To make a workflow grid-aware, it must be executed on an Integration Service running on the Grid. No other design time configuration is necessary from the developer's point of view to enable load balancing.

19.3   Fail-over

When the services on a node fail / are interrupted, the workflows running on the node can be failed over to another backup node or can be restarted on the same node, once it's services are back up and running. The workflows can resume their state of operation upon recovery.

19.4   Workflows – HA recovery

HA Recovery can be enabled for workflows in Workflow properties. To do so, open the workflow for which you want to enable HA Recovery. Go to `Workflows` menu →`Edit` Workflow properties are displayed. Go to Properties tab and check the `Enable HA Recovery` checkbox. The following properties are then enabled:

Property	Meaning
Automatically recover terminated tasks	When checked, if a task terminates, Integration Service will automatically attempt to recover it. Recovery strategy for the tasks can be set at task level.
Maximum automatic recovery attempts	Defaulted to 5, this indicates the number of times the Integration Service will try to recover the terminated tasks before giving up.

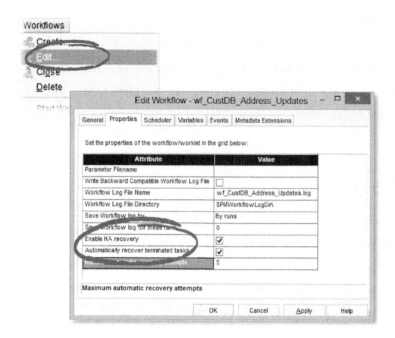

19.5   Session recovery strategy

When HA Recovery is enabled for workflows, session tasks can be configured of recovery strategy. The following options are available for a task recovery strategy.

Strategy	Meaning
Fail task and continue workflow	Default. Integration Service will log the failure and move on to the next task in the workflow. It will not attempt to recover the task.
Resume task from last checkpoint	Once the services are up and running (on same node or on backup node), integration service will resume the task from the last commit point
Restart task	Integration service will restart the task once the services are available

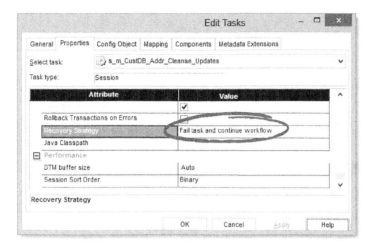

19.6   Session on GRID

By default, when a workflow is assigned to an integration service running on Grid, PowerCenter dynamically decides on which node each subsequent task will run. But at any given time, each session task will be executed only on one node. But when there is a complex processing within the session that can be distributed across multiple nodes, you can turn on the SONG – Session OnGrid. When Session On Grid is enabled, PowerCenter Integration Service will distribute the threads within the task to multiple nodes. If not used with caution, for session that requires less computing power, the overhead to distribute the session across multiple nodes may be more than the gain in performance. Hence, session on grid must be used after thorough analysis.

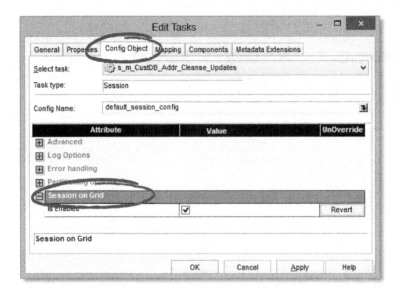

20

Command line utilities

PowerCenter comes with several command line utilities to perform tasks that are typically performed through GUI. Command line utilities provide a way to automate tasks without manual intervention. While there are several administration related utilities available, in this chapter, we only discuss the command line utilities that are focused on developer. Most of these commands rely on the domain connectivity information. When we configure the PowerCenter clients, the domain connectivity information provided to them is stored in a file called domains.infa. The location of this file is set in an environment variable so that the command line interface can read domain information (such as gateways, ports, ...) without having to be specified in each command.

20.1 Location

The command line utilities are available on PowerCenter server. They are also installed along with PowerCenter client at the location.

```
<PowerCenter Client Installation directory>\clients\
PowerCenterClient\CommandLineUtilities\PC\
server\bin
```

20.2 pmpasswd

pmpasswd utility generates encrypted strings for the given input. When passwords are to be provided from a command line or from parameter files, it is always recommended to provide encrypted passwords.

<u>Syntax:</u>

```
pmpasswd<password>
```

<u>Example:</u>

```
pmpasswd MyPassword
```

20.3 pmcmd

pmcmd is one of the most widely used PowerCenter commands. pmcmd has the ability to perform several runtime operations including start workflows, stop workflows, etc. pmcmd can be executed in two ways: console mode and command mode.

20.3.1   Console mode

In console mode, the developer first executes pmcmd to enter into the pmcmd console. A pmcmd prompt appears. Developer will then execute all the subsequent commands and finally exit using the exit command. This will take him/her back to the operating system shell.

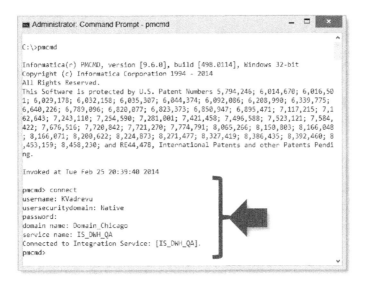

20.3.2   Command mode

In command mode, pmcmd returns back to operating shell after execution of every command. This is very helpful to script programs around the pmcmd commands and their outputs. In this method, all commands are executed asynchronously and hence the connectivity details and the login credentials must be passed to each command separately.

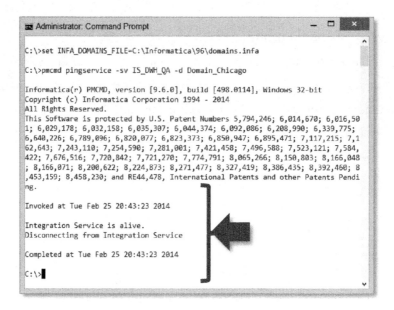

20.3.3   Integration service status

Description: This command verifies if the integration service is up and running.

Command	Pingservice
Syntax	pmcmd pingservice -sv <serviceName> -d

	<domainName>
Examples	→ pmcmd pingservice -sv IS_DWH_DEV -d
	Domain_DWH_Dev

20.3.4   Help, list of all commands

Description: This command lists all the valid pmcmd commands or show help for the command specified.

Command	Help
Syntax	pmcmd help [command]
Examples	→ pmcmd help
	→ pmcmd help pingservice

20.3.5   Version

Description: Shows the version of PowerCenter. PowerCenter version is by default displayed with any pmcmd command.

Command	Version
Syntax	pmcmd version
Examples	→ pmcmd version

20.3.6   Integration service properties

<u>Description</u>: Displays the integration service properties.

Command	`getserviceproperties`
Syntax	`pmcmd getserviceproperties -sv <serviceName>` `-d <domain>`
Examples	→ `pmcmd getserviceproperties -sv IS_DWH_DEV` `-d Domain_DWH_Dev`

20.3.7   Runtime statistics

<u>Description</u>: Displays statistics of what is running and what is not in Integration Service.

Command	`getservicedetails`

Syntax	`pmcmd getservicedetails -sv <serviceName>`
	 `-d <domain> -u <username> -p <password>`
	 `-usd<securityDomain>        [-all|-running|`
	 `-scheduled]`

Examples	→ `pmcmd getservicedetails -sv IS_DWH_DEV`
	     `-d Domain_DWH_Dev -u KVadrevu`
	     `-pv MyPassword -usd Native -all`

In this example, we have set the environment variable `MyPassword` to the encrypted password and passed the environment variable name as input to the `pmcmd` command. `-running` can be used instead of `-all` to fetch statistics of the sessions/workflows that are currently in running state. Similarly `-scheduled` will provide list of workflows that are scheduled to run.

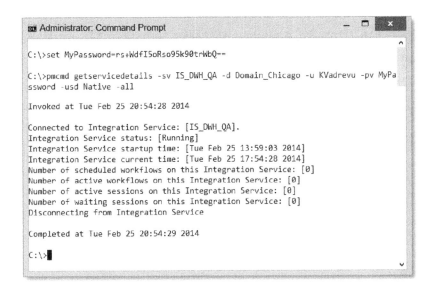

```
Administrator: Command Prompt                                    _  □  x

C:\>set MyPassword=rs+WdfI5oRso95k90trWbQ==

C:\>pmcmd getservicedetails -sv IS_DWH_QA -d Domain_Chicago -u KVadrevu -pv MyPa
ssword -usd Native -all

Invoked at Tue Feb 25 20:54:28 2014

Connected to Integration Service: [IS_DWH_QA].
Integration Service status: [Running]
Integration Service startup time: [Tue Feb 25 13:59:03 2014]
Integration Service current time: [Tue Feb 25 17:54:28 2014]
Number of scheduled workflows on this Integration Service: [0]
Number of active workflows on this Integration Service: [0]
Number of active sessions on this Integration Service: [0]
Number of waiting sessions on this Integration Service: [0]
Disconnecting from Integration Service

Completed at Tue Feb 25 20:54:29 2014

C:\>
```

20.3.8   Start a workflow

<u>Description</u>: This command can start a workflow from the beginning or from a specific task.

Command	`startworkflow`

Syntax	`pmcmd startworkflow -sv <serviceName>`
	 `-d <domain> -u <username> -p <password>`
	 `-usd<securityDomain> -folder`
	 `<folderName><workflowName>`

Examples	→ `pmcmd startworkflow -sv IS_DWH_DEV`
	   `-d Domain_DWH_Dev -u KVadrevu -pv`
	   `MyPassword -usd Native -folder DWH_DI`
	   `wf_DWH_Initial_Loads`

This command will start the workflow and immediately return to the operating system shell. If you want the command to rather wait until the workflow is complete, add -wait before the workflow name.

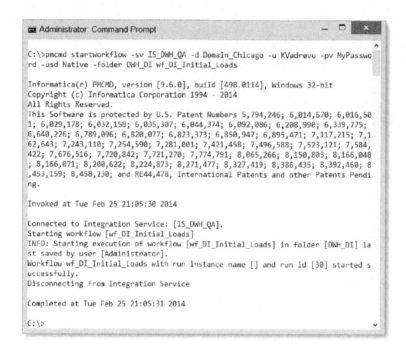

20.3.9   Start a workflow and wait

<u>Description</u>: This command can start a workflow from the beginning or from a specific task.

Command	startworkflow
Syntax	pmcmd startworkflow -sv <serviceName>
	-d <domain> -u <username> -p <password>
	-usd<securityDomain> -folder <folderName>

```
-wait<workflowName>
```

Examples → pmcmd startworkflow -sv IS_DWH_DEV

-d Domain_DWH_Dev -u KVadrevu

-pv MyPassword -usd Native -folder DWH_DI

-waitwf_DWH_Initial_Loads

This command will start the workflow and immediately return to the operating system shell. If you want the command to rather wait until the workflow is complete, add -wait before the workflow name.

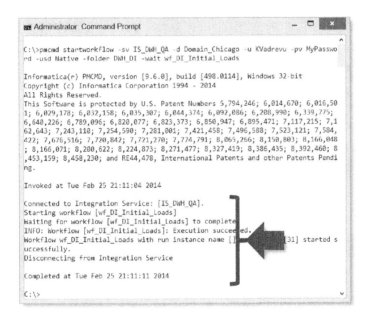

20.3.10 Start a workflow from a session

<u>Description</u>: This command can start a workflow from a specific task.

Command	`startworkflow`
Syntax	`pmcmd startworkflow -sv <serviceName> -d <domain> -u <username> -p <password> -usd<securityDomain> -folder <folderName>-wait-startfrom <taskPath><workflowName>`
Examples	→ `pmcmd startworkflow -sv IS_DWH_DEV` `-d Domain_DWH_Dev -u KVadrevu` `-pv MyPassword -usd Native -folder DWH_DI` **`-startfrom`** **`s_m_DWH_Init_Load_Accountswf_DWH_Initial_`** `Loads`

This command can be used to start a workflow from somewhere in between. In the `taskPath`, provide the name of the session to start workflow from task.

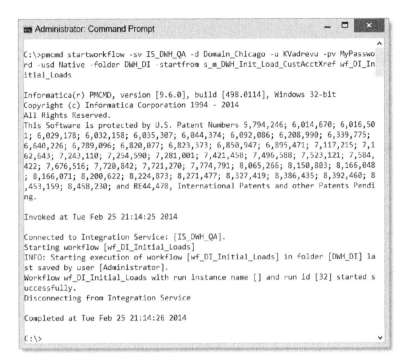

```
C:\>pmcmd startworkflow -sv IS_DWH_QA -d Domain_Chicago -u KVadrevu -pv MyPasswo
rd -usd Native -folder DWH_DI -startfrom s_m_DWH_Init_Load_CustAcctXref wf_DI_In
itial_Loads

Informatica(r) PMCMD, version [9.6.0], build [498.0114], Windows 32-bit
Copyright (c) Informatica Corporation 1994 - 2014
All Rights Reserved.
This Software is protected by U.S. Patent Numbers 5,794,246; 6,014,670; 6,016,50
1; 6,029,178; 6,032,158; 6,035,307; 6,044,374; 6,092,086; 6,208,990; 6,339,775;
6,640,226; 6,789,096; 6,820,077; 6,823,373; 6,850,947; 6,895,471; 7,117,215; 7,1
62,643; 7,243,110; 7,254,590; 7,281,001; 7,421,458; 7,496,588; 7,523,121; 7,584,
422; 7,676,516; 7,720,842; 7,721,270; 7,774,791; 8,065,266; 8,150,803; 8,166,048
; 8,166,071; 8,200,622; 8,224,873; 8,271,477; 8,327,419; 8,386,435; 8,392,460; 8
,453,159; 8,458,230; and RE44,478, International Patents and other Patents Pendi
ng.

Invoked at Tue Feb 25 21:14:25 2014

Connected to Integration Service: [IS_DWH_QA].
Starting workflow [wf_DI_Initial_Loads]
INFO: Starting execution of workflow [wf_DI_Initial_Loads] in folder [DWH_DI] la
st saved by user [Administrator].
Workflow wf_DI_Initial_Loads with run instance name [] and run id [32] started s
uccessfully.
Disconnecting from Integration Service

Completed at Tue Feb 25 21:14:26 2014

C:\>
```

20.3.11   Start workflow with parameter file

Command	`startworkflow`
Syntax	`pmcmd startworkflow -sv <serviceName>` `-d <domain> -u <username> -p <password>` `-usd<securityDomain> -folder <folderName>` `[-wait	-nowait] -startfrom <taskPath>` **`-paramfile <parameterFileName>`**`<workflowName>`

Examples	→ `pmcmd startworkflow -sv IS_DWH_DEV`
	    `-d Domain_DWH_Dev -u KVadrevu`
	    `-pv MyPassword -usd Native -folder DWH_DI`
	    `-paramfile`
	    `/infa/95/wf_DWH_Init_Loads.parwf_DWH_Initial_Lo`
	    `ads`

This command can be used to start a workflow with a parameter file. Parameter file must be valid, accessible from the Integration Service server and in a valid format.

20.3.12   Stop workflow

<u>Description</u>: This command stops a running workflow.

Command	`stopworkflow`

Syntax	`pmcmd stopworkflow -sv <serviceName>`
	`-d <domain> -u <username> -p <password>`
	`-usd<securityDomain> -folder <folderName>`
	`[-wait
		-nowait] <workflowName>`

Examples	→ `pmcmd stopworkflow -sv IS_DWH_DEV` `-d Domain_DWH_Dev -u KVadrevu -pv`

```
MyPassword
-usd Native -folder DWH_DI
-waitwf_DWH_Initial_Loads
```

This command will attempt to stop the workflow. If the workflow does not stop within 60 seconds, it will be aborted.

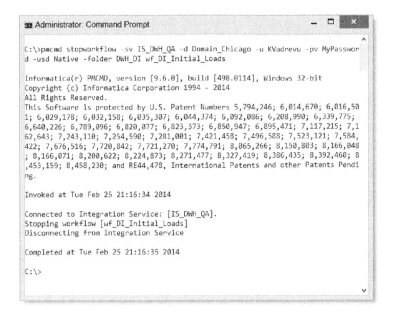

20.3.13 Abort workflow

Description: This command aborts a running workflow.

Command	`abortworkflow`
Syntax	`pmcmd abortworkflow -sv <serviceName>` `-d <domain> -u <username> -p <password>` `-usd<securityDomain> -folder <folderName>` `[-wait	-nowait] <workflowName>`
Examples	→ `pmcmd abortworkflow -sv IS_DWH_DEV -d` `Domain_DWH_Dev -u KVadrevu -pv MyPassword -` `usd Native -folder DWH_DI -` `wait``wf_DWH_Initial_Loads`

This command will abort the workflow immediately. Any data currently in the memory is discarded.

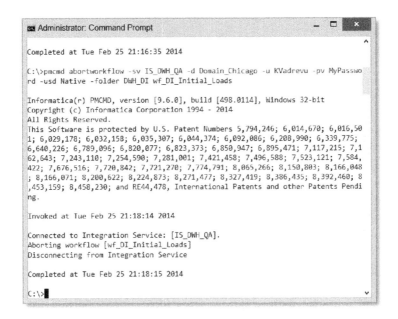

 List commands provided here is only for an overview. Please consult product manual for complete details

21

Scheduling

PowerCenter is equipped with a built-in scheduler. It is important to note that PowerCenter is not intended to be an enterprise scheduler; it serves the needs of scheduling for Data Integration environments within an enterprise. This includes the ability to schedule workflows to run on a specific day/time or at regular intervals or when specific events occur such as when PowerCenter Integration starts up.

21.1   Reusable and non-reusable

PowerCenter allows you to create both reusable and non-reusable schedules. Non-reusable schedules are created within a workflow, whereas reusable schedules are created outside the workflows. To create a reusable schedule, go to `Workflows` menu → `Schedulers...` `Scheduler Browser` dialog box opens up. Click `New...` to create a new schedule and `Edit...` to edit an existing schedule. To create a non-reusable schedule, open the workflow you want to schedule. Go to `Workflows` menu → `Edit....` Then go to the `Scheduler` tab. Click on the `Non Reusable`.

Then click the schedule button () to configure the schedule.

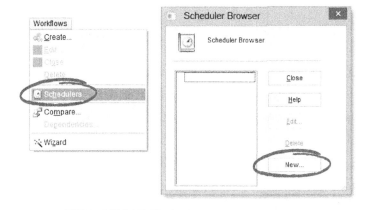

Creating reusable schedules

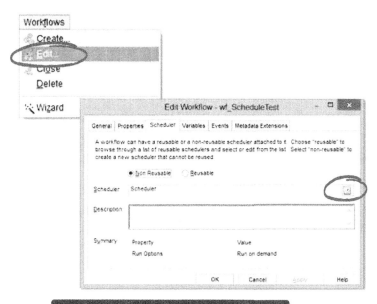

Creating non-reusable schedules

21.2 Run options

21.2.1 Run on IS Initialization

When this option is checked, the workflow is executed whenever Integration Service is (re)started. When an Integration service is (re)started, it looks for all the workflows that have schedules defined and schedules them accordingly. This run option is typically used to execute maintenance workflows to perform certain administrative activities at the beginning of the service and to execute event notification workflows to notify a group of members about the integration service startup.

 When an Integration Service is (re)started, it does not start any workflows whose schedules have already passed during the down time.

21.2.2 Run on demand

This is the default run mode for all workflow. Run on demand indicates that the workflow is not scheduled to run automatically and the developer(s) choose when to run the workflow either from the workflow manager or by using pmcmd command line interface.

21.2.3 Run on continously

With this option is checked, integration service will automatically restart the workflow as soon as the current run is complete. There are typically two use cases that can benefit from this option:

→ The incoming file's schedule is unexpected. So a polling workflow is needed. This polling workflow will continuously monitor the file system for the presence of a file. If the file is present it will invoke a subsequent workflow that will consume the file

→ A source system feeds 'n' number of files, where 'n' is a variable that changes every day and is typically a large number. However, to keep the system resource continuously engaged instead of peaking out during specific time windows, Administrator has constrained the system to run no more than a 'x' number of processes at any given time. In this case, a continuously running workflow is created to consume 'x' amount of files at any given time. This workflow is executed continuously until there are no more files to be consumed. It will then be unscheduled until next day's batch window opens up. When an integration service is (re)started, it will execute all workflows marked as 'Run continuously'.

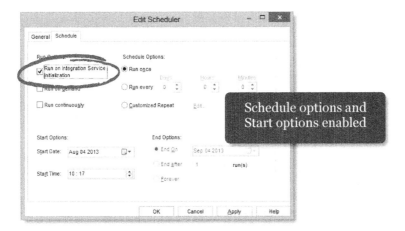

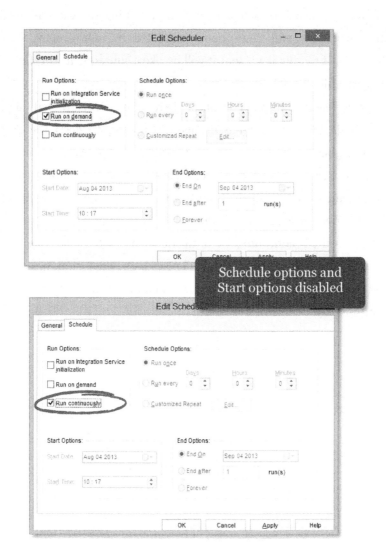

21.3   Schedule options

 Schedule options are not available when Run on demand or Run continuously options are selected. The schedule options can be used along with (though not mandatory) Run on Integration Service Initialization option.

21.3.1   Run once

You can schedule a workflow to run once at a specific day/time. When you select the Run once option, Start Options are enabled. Run once option is available when the workflow is not configured to be run on demand, and rather, run continuously. Integration service will run such a workflow only once at a specific date/time. If the integration service was not running at the scheduled time, it will not start the workflow when it comes up unless the Run on Integration Service Initialization option is checked.

21.3.2   Run at intervals (Run every...)

You can schedule a workflow to run at regular intervals. The intervals can be defined in any combination of Days, Hours and Minutes. When 'Run' every option is selected, the Start options and End options are enabled. While specifying the intervals, you can specify the start date from which the intervals would be in effect and the end date when the schedule should stop. An example would be to run a workflow every 1 hour starting from August 4 to September 4. You can specify the workflow to complete after specific number of runs by configuring the `End after… runs`.

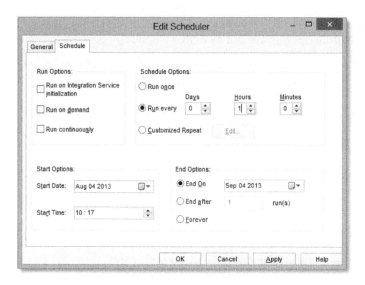

21.3.3   Customized repeat

Customized repeat option provides great flexibility in terms of when to schedule a workflow. In the customized repeat dialog box, we can schedule a workflow to run at intervals of days/weeks/months. Based on the selection, either Daily frequency / weekly / monthly options are enabled. When the Daily option is selected, developers can choose to run it once a day or specify intervals in hours/minutes. When the weekly option is selected, developers can choose the days of the week when the workflow can be executed. An example use-case of such an option is to run a workflow every Tuesday and Thursdays. When the monthly option is selected, developers can choose to run the job on a given day of the month (such as 1st, 2nd, 3rd, ..) or can also choose a specific day in each month. For example, run every Monday of the month or every second Tuesday, etc.

In customized repeat, daily options are available for daily, weekly and monthly schedules.

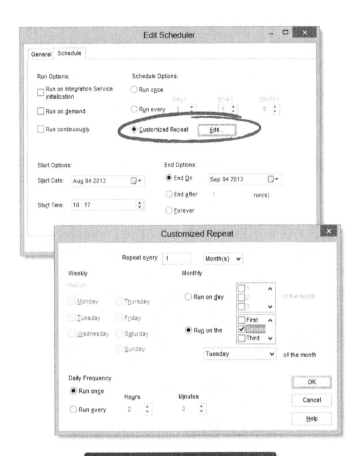

Customized Repeat

21.4 Advanced scheduling

21.4.1 Schedules and failures

When a workflow fails or aborts or terminates, it is automatically un-scheduled. When an integration service restarts or fails over, and if the workflow is not configured to be recovered, it is automatically un-scheduled by the integration service.

 When an Integration Service is running in safe mode, it does not execute any scheduled workflows.

21.4.2 Un-scheduling

You can unschedule a workflow manually without editing or deleting its schedule. Right click on the workflow in the repository navigator or open the workflow in the workspace and right click on the workspace (without selecting a session). Then select Unschedule workflow menu item.

21.4.3 Rescheduling

If you have un-scheduled a workflow, you must manually schedule it again before integration services continue normally with its schedule for that workflow. To do so, right click on the workflow in the repository navigator or open the workflow in the workspace and right click on the workspace (without selecting a session). Then select Schedule workflow menu item.

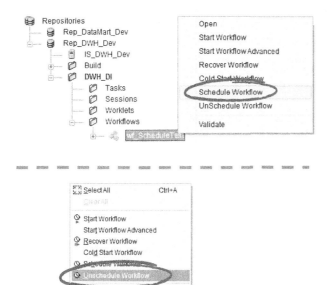

21.4.4   External schedulers

Workflows can be executed using external schedulers. To use external schedulers, developers typically rely on the `pmcmd` command line interface. The `pmcmd` `startworkflow` command is usually wrapped up in a wrapper shell/batch script. It is then invoked by the external scheduler to run the PowerCenter workflows. Such batch/shell scripts usually invoke an environment script (such as setenv.bat or setenv.sh) to load all the necessary environment variables. Look at sample workflow execution script below (Linux platform):

Wrapper script

```
$INFA_HOME/setenv.sh

pmcmd startworkflow

    -sv $DWH_PCIS -d $INFA_DOMAIN

    -u $DWH_USR -pv $DWH_PASS -usd $DWH_USRDOM

    -folder $DWH_FLDR

    -paramfile $INFA_HOME/wf_DWH_Initial.par

    -wait wf_DWH_Initial_Loads
```

setenv.sh

```
# ------------------------------
# Global PowerCenter variables
# ------------------------------
export INFA_DOMAIN=Domain_DWH_Dev



# ------------------------------
# Data Warehouse Project related
# ------------------------------
export DWH_PCIS=IS_DWH_DEV

export DWH_FLDR=DWH_DI

export DWH_USR=infauser

export DWH_PASS=*****

export DWH_USRDOM=Native
```

22

Web Services

Web Services are applications that interact via open protocols such as HTTP and XML and are interoperable with other services in the enterprise. Web Services use SOAP and XML as their basis of communication and information exchange. Due to their interoperability, they can be built in any technology that supports web services and can be consumed using any technology that supports web services. For example, a web service built using .net technology can be used by a java program with no changes to the service itself. This is possible due to the open technologies such as XML that form the foundation of web services.

22.1 SOAP

SOAP is an XML based protocol in which the web services communicate. A SOAP message consists of an envelope, header, body and optionally fault elements. Every SOAP message must have an envelope. Envelope contains information such as HTTP binding, location of the service, etc. Header contains information like authentication details, etc.

22.2 WSDL

WSDL describes the web services. Simply put, it is to web services what DDL is to relational tables. Major elements in WSDL are:

→ Types: defines data types definitions

→ Message: defines the data that is being communicated

→ PortType: contains set of operations. Each operation can be compared to function calls. Each function has one or more input/output messages.

→ Binding: protocol and data format specification

22.3 Web Service Provider & Consumer

Web services typically operate in a request-response mode. The program acting as a web service and serving the requests is called Web Service Provider. The program invoking the web service and consuming its responses is called the Web Service consumer. The web service provider and consumer need not be built on the same technologies. They just need to be SOAP and XML enabled.

22.4 Web Services Hub

Web Services Hub is the PowerCenter's gateway in the domain that handles all web service requests and responses. Web Services Hub hosts the web service providers built in PowerCenter and also acts as gateway for any requests made from PowerCenter mappings to external web services. When an external web service client invokes a PowerCenter web service, the request comes through the web services hub. WSH then communicates with the PowerCenter Integration Service to exchange information with the underlying DI workflow. The responses are then communicated from the PowerCenter Integration Service to the WSH which then passes on to the external client. This architecture allows the PowerCenter workflows to remain in the PowerCenter framework and operate as web services to serve external clients.

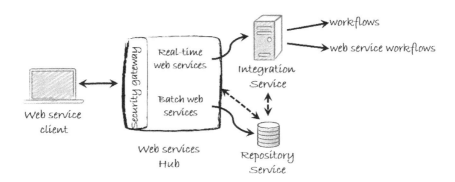

22.5 Web Services Hub console

The web services hub console is a web-based user interface for the WSH. This where the developers can view and test the published web service workflows. WSH Console hosts both Batch Web Services and Real-time Web Services. Batch Web Services are comprised of Metadata web services and Integration web services. Metadata web services consist of operations related to PowerCenter repository. Examples of such operations are `getAllFolders` (fetches a list of all PowerCenter repository folders), `getAllWorkflows` (fetches a list of PowerCenter workflows), etc. Integration web service consists of operations related to PowerCenter Integration Services. The operations within this web service include fetching session logs, starting workflows, etc. Real-time web services are created by Developers and published into the WSH.

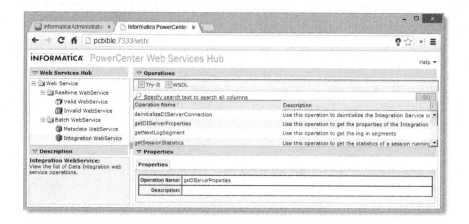

22.6 Developing web services

PowerCenter encapsulates most of the complexities involved in creating the web services – making it a simple and straight forward process. The steps associated with creating a web service are almost same as creating any DI workflow with few exceptions. Let us take a look at different steps involved in this process and understand each of them in detail:

a. The first and foremost step is to create a WSDL. If you already have a WSDL, you can import the same. If you don't, you can create a web service provider source and target using the designer's Create Web Service Definition wizard. In this wizard, you must specify what will be the input and output of your web service.

b. We then create a mapping that uses this input, performs processing logic and then writes to this output you created. You can use most of the transformations such as lookup to retrieve data from additional data sources.

c. We then create a workflow/session. In the workflow, we configure the workflow to be as a web service. When we do so, we provide a name to this web service. This name will appear in the Web Services Hub Console and will be the name that web service clients use to invoke this service.

22.7 Lab 23a – Web service provider

Business requirement:

Bharani bank would like to make their Data Warehouse a primary source of information for certain master data elements. They would like to begin this by making the customer information in the Data Warehouse as the primary customer master data across the enterprise. Bharani bank is planning to expose this customer information from the Data Warehouse as a Web Service so that other departments within the enterprise have access to it and still remain independent of the technologies used within the Warehouse.

Challenges:

a. A PowerCenter mapping must be built and published as a web service.
b. Other departments within the enterprise should be able to access the web service without any additional technical implementation complexities.
c. Applications that want to access this web service should have access to its WSDL easily.
d. The service must be visible in the PowerCenter Web Services Hub Console.
e. If the service is not running when a client invokes it, it must automatically be triggered and should process the request.

Technical solution:

We will develop a WSDL definition based on the Customer information within the Data Warehouse. We will then build a web service that complies to this WSDL.

Following which, we will develop a workflow/session associated with the mapping. We will configure the workflow to be a web service and mark it as visible (so that it is visible in the PowerCenter Web Services Hub console) and as run able (so that Integration Service can automatically start it, if it is not running already) when a request comes in.

Steps for solution:

    a.   Open the Designer

    b.   Connect to the repository

    c.   Open the `DWH_DI` folder

    d.   Go to Source Analyzer

    e.   Create WSDL

        1.   Go to the menu `Sources`→`Web Service Provider`→`Create Web Service Definition`

        2.   Provide the web service name as `ws_DWH_Customer_Info`

        3.   Create a new source port of name `Cust_ID` as `double(15)`

        4.   Ensure `Create Target` checkbox is checked

        5.   Click the Import from Source/Target icon (⬇)

        6.   Select `CUSTOMERS` table in the Targets and click OK

        7.   Click OK to create the WSDL

    f.   Source and Target definition can now be seen in the repository navigator

    g.   Create a new mapping

        1.   Name the mapping as `m_ws_DWH_Customer_Info`

        2.   Drag the source `ws_DWH_Customer_Info_input` into the mapping

        3.   Create a new expression as `exp_Source_Safe` and drag all the input ports from source qualifier into the expression

        4.   Create a new lookup transformation

            a.   Select `Targets`→`Customers`

            b.   Name the lookup as `lkp_DWH_Customers`

c. Drag the n_Cust_ID from exp_Source_Safe into the lookup

d. Go to the Condition tab

e. Create a condition such that CUST_ID = n_Cust_ID

5. Create a new expression transformation

a. Name it as exp_Process

b. Drag all the ports from exp_Source_Safe into exp_Process

c. Drag all the ports from lkp_DWH_Customers into exp_Process

d. Delete the n_Cust_ID1 port from the expression

6. Drag the target ws_DWH_Customer_Info_Output into the mapping

7. Connect all ports from the exp_Process into target except the n_CUST_ID in the expression exp_Process

h. Save the mapping

i. Go to workflow manager

1. Create a new workflow and name it as ws_DWH_Customer_Info

j. Create a new session

1. Select the mapping as m_ws_DWH_Customer_Info

2. Link the session from the start task

3. Edit the session: go to the mapping tab → select the lookup lkp_DWH_Customers→ click on the connection selection button (⬇) and choose the connection as DI_Ora_DWH

k. Edit the workflow properties and save the workflow

1. Go to the workflow → Edit to open the workflow properties

2. Check the Enabled checkbox in Web Services section

3. Config Service button will be enabled. Click on it

4. Set the service name as ws_DWH_Customer_Info

5. Check the `Visible` and `Runnable` checkboxes and click OK

6. Click OK to close the dialog box. You will notice that the `Configure Concurrent execution` button will also be enabled

7. Once you save the workflow you will notice that the workflow icon (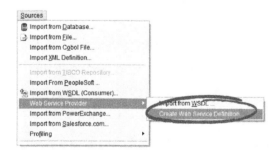) changes to a web service icon ()

l. Open an internet browser window and go the Web Services Hub Console URL. Typically this URL is http://<hostName>:7333/wsh where hostName is the name of the host where your web services hub is running. If you do not have this information, contact your Informatica Administrator

m. PowerCenter Web Services Hub console will open

n. Select your web service:

1. On the left, Select Web Service → Realtime Web Service → Valid Web Service

2. On the right hand side, you will notice the web service ws_DWH_Customer_Info will appear.

3. Click on the web service. Properties will be displayed below it

4. Click on the WSDL button (WSDL) to view the WSDL used by this Web Service

o. Go to workflow manager and run the workflow. It will run continuously

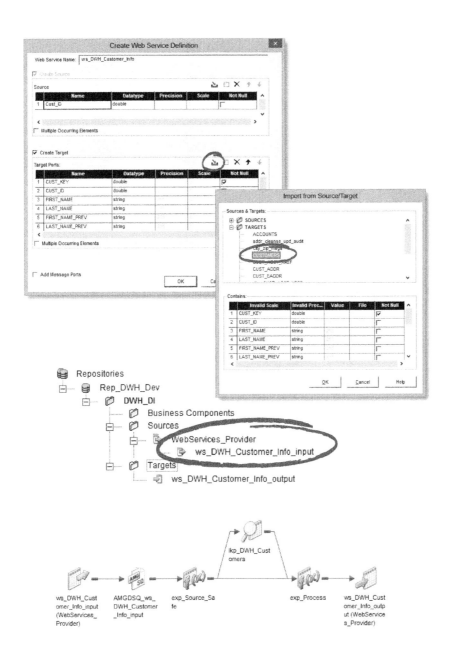

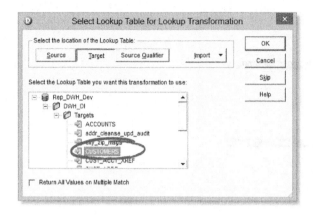

Start   s_m_ws_DWH_Customer_Inf o

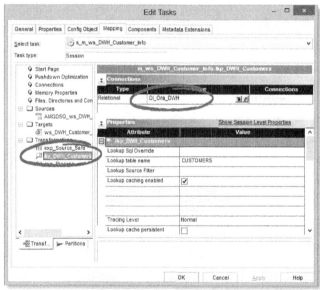

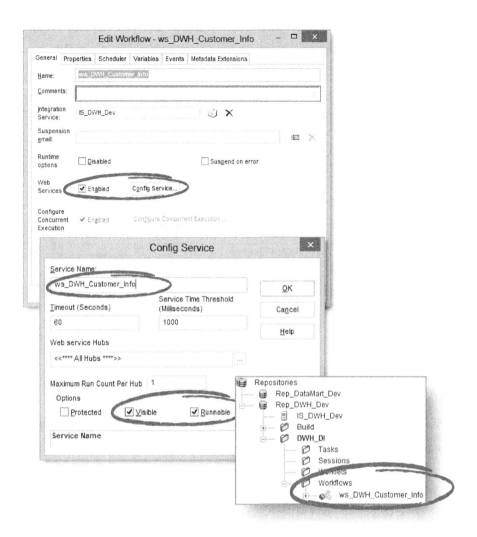

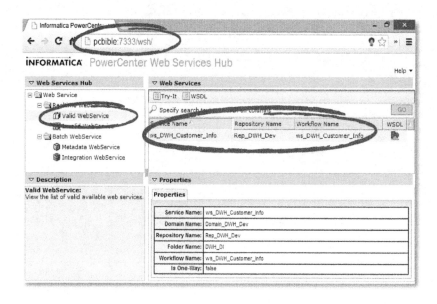

22.8 Developing web service consumer

A web service consumer is a program that executes a web service call and processes its response. Not all web services provide a response. Some web services are one-way. One-way web services receive a request and process them but do not send any acknowledgement back to the client/consumer. A web service consumer can be built in any technology, regardless of the technology in which the web service (provider) is built. To develop a web service consumer, we need the WSDL of the web service. WSDL contains definitions with which the web service communicates with its consumers.

22.9 Lab 23b – Web service consumer

Business requirement:

 Bharani bank would like to build a web service consumer to test the customer information web service built in the Data Warehouse project. This web service consumer will serve as a baseline for testing all the subsequent consumers that will be developed. This testing job will read all Customer IDs from CustomerDB and invoke the DWH Customer Info web service. The output from the web service is then written to a file.

Challenges:

   a.   Use the WSDL of the Web Service Provider previously developed
   b.   Write the output to a file

Technical solution:

We will develop a mapping with a web service consumer that uses the WSDL of the web service previously developed.

Steps for solution:

   a.   Go to Web Services Hub Console. WSH Console is typically located at `http://<hostName>:7333/wsh`
   b.   On the left hand side, click `Web Service`→`Realtime Web Service`→`Valid Web Service`
   c.   Select the web service `ws_DWH_Customer_Info` and click `WSDL` button
   d.   WSDL will open in a new browser window
   e.   Copy the URL of the WSDL. Example URL will be: `http://<hostName>:7333/wsh/services/RealTime/ws_DWH_Customer_Info?WSDL` to the clipboard.
   f.   Open the Designer
   g.   Login to the `Rep_DWH_Dev`

h. Open the folder DWH_DI

i. Create a mapping

1. Name the mapping as m_ws_Test_DWH_Customer_Info

2. Drag the source CUSTOMERS from Sources→CustomerDB into the mapping

3. Create an expression called exp_SrcSafe and drag CUST_ID from source qualifier into the expression

4. Create a new web services consumer transformation by clicking on the icon (🌐) in the transformation toolbar. You can also create this transformation by clicking the Transformation menu →Create menu item and choose web services consumer transformation

   a. Import from WSDL wizard appears

   b. Select URL button (🌐) on the left if it is not already selected

   c. In the address section, paste the WSDL URL we copied earlier. This URL will be in the format http://<hostName>:7333/wsh/services/RealTime/ws_D WH_Customer_Info?WSDL

   d. Click the Open button

   e. If you are prompted to override the infinite lengths, click Yes

   f. Check the box named Override all infinite lengths with value and specify 255 in the textbox next to it. Then click OK to close the dialog

   g. Web Services Wizard will appear:

5. Click on the operation ws_DWH_Customer_Info Operation (🔗) and click Next

6. Choose hierarchy relationships→Normalized views and click Finish

7. Web service consumer transformation is created in the mapping

8. Create a new sequence generator transformation

      a.   Name it as `seq_WS_Key`

      b.   Connect the `NEXTVAL` in the sequence generator to the `XPK_key` in the web services consumer transformation

      c.   Connect the `CUST_ID` from the expression `exp_SrcSafe` to the web services consumer transformation `n_CUST_ID` port

9.   Create a new expression transformation:

      a.   Name it as `ws_Output`

      b.   Drag all output ports from the web services consumer transformation to the expression transformation

      c.   Right click on the expression and click the menu `Create and Add Target`

      d.   A new target called `ws_Output1` is added to the mapping

      e.   Connect all ports from the expression to the target

10. Go to `Target Designer`

11. Drag the `ws_Output` into the workspace and edit it

      a.   Change the database type as `Flat File`

      b.   Click `Advanced...` to view advanced properties

      c.   Change the delimiter as pipe (|)

      d.   Click `OK` twice to close the dialog boxes

j.   Save the mapping

k.   Go to workflow manager

l.   Create a new workflow by the name `wf_Test_ws_DWH_Customer_Info` with a session pointing to this mapping

m. Create a new Application connection:

     1.   Go to `Connections` menu →`Application`

     2.   `Application Connection Browser` dialog box will appear

     3.   Click `New`→`Web Services Consumer`→`OK`

     4.   Provide the name as `ws_DWH_Customer_Info`

     5.   Set the end point URL. End point URL is typically the same as your WSDL URL, without the reference to the WSDL. For example,

`http://<hostName>:7333/wsh/services/RealTime/ws_DWH_Customer_Info`. Notice that there is no `?WSDL` at the end.

6. Provide username as `PMNullUsername` and password as `PMNullPassword`

7. Click `OK` and `Close` to close the dialog boxes

n. Edit the session properties:

1. Go to `Mapping` tab

2. Select the source and change connection to `DI_Ora_CustomerDB`

3. Select the target and set its file properties as:

   a. Output file directory is `$PMTargetFileDir\`

   b. Output file name is `ws_DWH_Customer_Info.out`

4. Select the web service consumer transformation

5. Change the `Connection Type` as `Application` and select (⏬) the `ws_DWH_Customer_Info` as connection

o. Save the workflow and run it

p. If your web service provider is not running at the time you run the consumer, you will notice that the provider workflow automatically gets triggered as we checked the `Runnable` property in the web service configuration

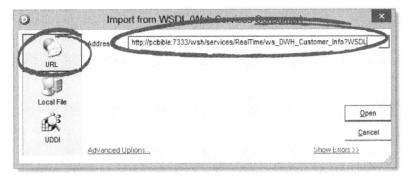

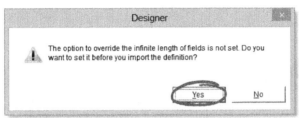

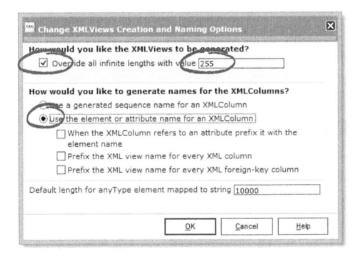

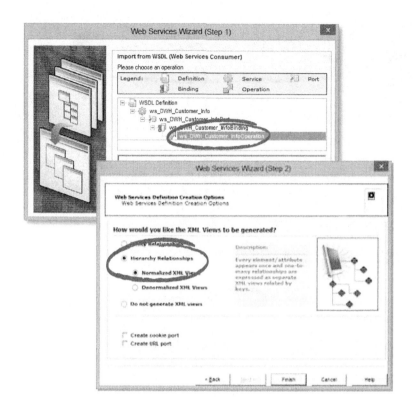

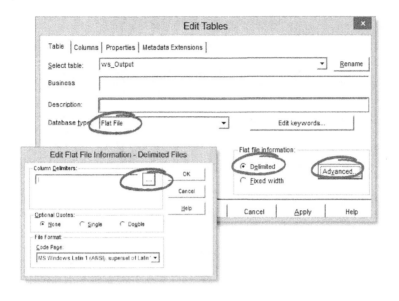

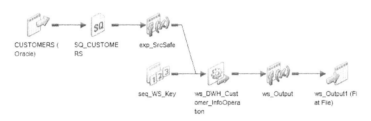

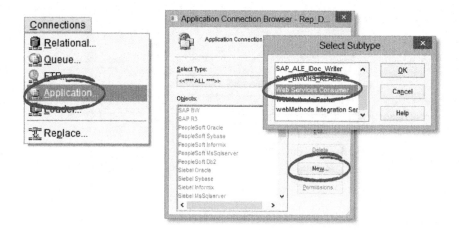

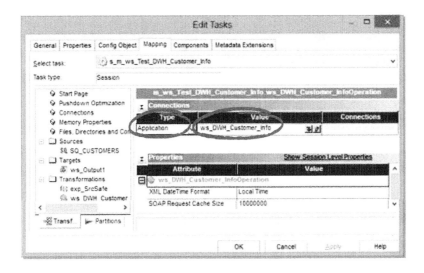

Snapshot showing Web Service Provider getting triggered when Web Service Consumer invokes it

22.10 Secure/Protected web services

Web services can be protected for secure access by authorized users. To develop secure web service providers, we configure the web service workflow as protected. Web service providers developed in Informatica PowerCenter use PowerCenter domain security aspects to authorize users. If a protected web service is developed in PowerCenter, any consumer accessing it must be authenticated with Informatica domain. To configure a protected web service, open the workflow in the workflow manager's workspace. Then go to Workflows menu →Edit. In the workflow properties, click Config Service in the Web Services section. Config Service dialog box appears. In the Options section, check the Protected checkbox.

To configure a secure web service in the web service consumer transformation, open the transformation Properties → web services consumer transformation properties → change WS Security Type as Password Text or Password Digest. When Password Text is used, password is sent as plain text or base 64 encoded password in the SOAP request.

23

External (bulk) loaders

"External loaders" is the term used by Informatica PowerCenter to represent corresponding database bulk loaders. A bulk loader is a database tool provided by the database vendor to load huge volumes of data at high speeds. Bulk loaders usually take a data file and a control file. Data file contains data in a specific format as required by the loader. Control file contains various options on how the data is to be loaded. In this chapter, we will look at a bulk loader example.

 This book uses Oracle bulk loader as an example. However, conceptually most of the major databases are configured similarly in PowerCenter.

23.1 Oracle SQL* Loader

SQL *Loader reads a delimited file with each record separated by line separator and loads them mto Oracle database. Control file contains instructions on the load.

SQL *Loader program is available in bin directory of oracle home as `sqlldr.exe` or `sqlldr` on windows and UNIX platforms. A sample control file's content is as shown below. For this example, data file is a comma delimited file with optional quotes around string values. The data file is placed at /home and is named as data.txt. This data is requested to be loaded into customers table.

```
Control file

load data

        infile '/home/data.txt'
into table customers

        fields terminated by ","

        optionally enclosed by '"'
( id, firstname, lastname )
```

SQL Loader can be executed as

```
sqlldr user/pass control=/home/control_file.ctl
```

SQL Loader by default requires the table to be empty. To append new records to a table already containing data, use the keyword `append` after the `infile` clause.

23.2 How to: configure SQL* Loader in session

To perform bulk loads using PowerCenter, developers can choose to leverage the Oracle SQL *Loader. This gives the flexibility of using PowerCenter to perform DI operations and to use SQL *Loader to perform a bulk load, thus achieving the best of both worlds. Bulk loaders such as Oracle SQL *Loader are typically used for Initial loads/seed loads. To use SQL *Loader, perform the following steps:

a. Go to Workflow Manager

b. Open the folder/workflow you want to edit

c. Create a new external connection

    1. Go to `Connections` menu →`Loader`

    2. `Loader connection browser` will appear

    3. Click `New`

    4. Select `subtype` as `Oracle External Loader` and click `OK`

    5. Provide a user name, password and connection string

    6. Change the `Load Mode` to `Truncate` to empty the table and load. Other options available are `Append, Insert` and `Replace`

    7. Click `OK` to close the connection and click `Close` to close the Loader Connection Browser

d. Change the session to point to the external loader connection

    1. Open the session properties

    2. Go to `Mapping` tab

    3. Select the target

    4. On the right hand side, `Writers` section → change the writer from `Relational Writer` to `File Writer`

    5. In the `Connections` section, change the `Type` from `None` to `Loader`

    6. In the `connections` section, change the value by clicking on the selection button () and choose a loader connection

    7. Click `OK` to close the session properties

e. Save the session and run the workflow

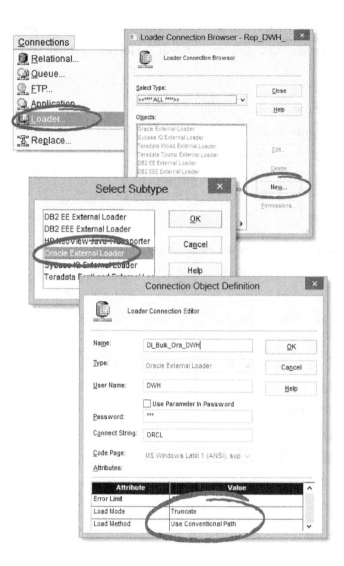

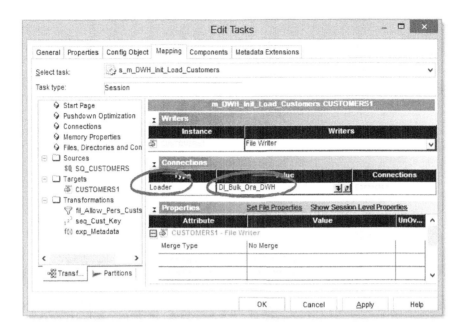

24

Pipeline Partitioning

A pipeline is a source/qualifier with all the downstream transformations that receive its data. By default, each pipeline has a single partition – meaning that each pipeline has a single reader thread, writer thread and a single DTM (Data Transformation Manager) thread. Pipeline can be partitioned to execute more than one thread to process data in parallel and hence achieve high performance. Let us try to understand the concept of partitioning in detail. Imagine a source table called Transactions containing Transaction ID, Date, Transaction type, description and amount. Now, imagine a summary target table called Transactions Summary with Transaction ID, Transaction Year, Transaction Month, Transaction type and amount. In this scenario, we are grouping the transactions by year, month and type and loading them to the target table. If the source table has a billion records, reading all of them and grouping them by year, month and type could take a long time. Let's say this session takes about an hour to complete. Now imagine that this session is split up in to 10 sessions – one for each transaction type (such as Debit card transaction, credit card transaction, bill pay, etc...). Each session is built with a source qualifier condition such that it reads one and only one transaction type from the source. If each session is processing one transaction type and transactions are evenly distributed, the entire billion transactions can be processed in 1/10th of the original load time – which is 6 minutes in this case. In essence, instead of one session processing a billion records, we now have 10 sessions each processing 100 million records and all of them are executed in parallel. Executing multiple threads in parallel to process heavy volumes of data – without impacting functional results is the core principle behind pipeline partitioning.

In pipeline partitioning, instead of physically creating multiple sessions, we specify the number of partitions we would like. At run time when the session initializes, PowerCenter Integration Service will initialize as many reader, transform, writer threads. In the previous example, we would have created 10 reader, transform, writer thread sets. Each reader, transform, writer set is processing data belonging to one transaction type.

24.1   Partitioning key

To be able to use pipeline partitioning effectively, it is very important to use the right partition key. A partition key is a set of one or more columns that form the basis of separating data into partitions. In the previous example, Transaction type is the partition key. By choosing partition key appropriately, we separate the data and eliminate any dependencies between the data across different partitions. Most optimal partition key distributes the data as close to equal as possible among all the partitions. The more the partitions are evenly distributed, the better the performance gain will be. Imagine distributing transactions by Transaction ID. In such a case, no two transactions will be in the same partition. Hence, to process a billion transactions, we will need a billion partitions. Same is the case if you choose account number as partition key. On the other hand, if you choose an attribute like transaction status (Pending, Hold, Cleared, …), you will have about 5 – 10partitions of data. In simple terms, a partition key should be a static column with limited value range. Attributes like transaction status, transaction type some good partition keys. Other examples for partition keys can be: customer state (address attribute), account type, etc.

24.2   Partitioning tables

The concept of partitions has been in databases for a long time now. Though conceptually similar, database partitions have different considerations than the DI tools using them. While storage is the primary consideration for database partitioning, performance and distribution are taken into consideration for partitioning DI jobs. Typically when data is partitioned in databases, it is done so for two primary reasons: to separate old/ready-to-archive data from new and to distribute data equally in partitions to improve read/write performance. Archival type partitioning is used when there is continuous stream of data and the data ages out with time. Examples are transactions. Transactions that occurred recently have higher demand for read/write operations than transactions that occurred a year ago. In such cases, data is partitioned by time. For example, a transaction table may have 8 partitions – one for each quarter of current and previous years. Every quarter, the oldest partition is moved for archiving and a new partition is created for the upcoming quarter. This way it is easy to archive data without affecting current data. In such case, DI jobs run faster at the beginning of the quarter (as the partition is empty) and become slower as we progress in the quarter. This is commonly used where write performance is more important than read performance and ability to archive seamlessly is very important. The second most common use case for database partitioning is performance. In this case, the transactions may be grouped by, for example, transaction type. This is usually used to evenly distribute the data. Hence, the reads and writes of transactional data for any transaction type are more or less same. But since the data is divided by transaction type, the read/write speed is 10 times faster (assuming there are 10 transaction types/partitions) than a non-partitioned table.

Whichever the case may be, it is useful enough to align the DI partitioning with the database partitioning for optimal performance. When the database and DI jobs are partitioned based on same approach, time taken to process the data and the time taken to write it to a relational table is improved linearly. Unless otherwise stated, this book discusses only pipeline partitioning in PowerCenter. For detailed information on the database level partitioning, please refer to corresponding database vendor manuals.

24.3 Partition points

A partition point is where PowerCenter Integration Service redistributes data. You can modify the number of partition points at allowed transformations. When you have active transformations, you can increase the partition points to improve their performance. Look at the snapshot below. It shows different transformations with the partition points. In this example, the mapping has two sources – each with different number of partition points. Router transformation has 4 partition points configured.

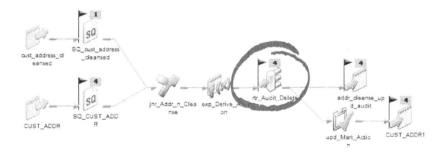

It is important to understand why we need to add partition points or change partition types at specific partition points. Consider a session reading from a transactions table that is partitioned at the database level on transaction date.

24.4 Partition stages

A partition stage can be defined as the processing between two partition points. In a simple mapping, there are only two partition points: one at source qualifier and one at target. In this case, we have 3 partition stages: Reader thread, the transformation thread and the writer thread.

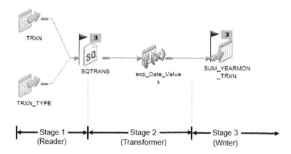

Now, consider another example: a mapping with 3 partition points as shown below. Now, we have 4 stages: a Reader thread, 2 transformer stages – one till the aggregator and another from aggregator to target and finally the writer thread.

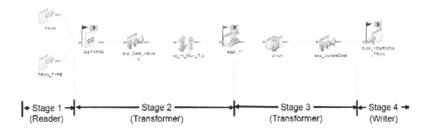

24.5   Partition types

A partition point can be partitioned in many ways depending on where it is being created. For example, certain relational sources and targets support database partitioning, pass through and round robin partitions are supported by most transformations. We will learn more about each of these in detail in the subsequent sections.

24.6   Before you partition...

Before we apply pipeline partitioning to a session, we should know the following:

a.   Partition points: Where to add a partition and where not to. Understanding the effects of adding/deleting a partition point and its impact on the performance is vital.

b.   Partition types: When you add a partition point, you must specify the partition type at the point. Partition type defines how Integration Service (re)partitions the data.

c.   Partition key: What should be the data partitioned on? A table may have many columns. But we need to choose one/more columns on which we can apply the partitions. This selection should ideally lead to even distribution of data across all partitions.

d. Number of partitions: How many partitions are optimal for a given session? The answer to this question isn't simple. The selection of the partition key and the number of partitions is primarily driven by data and system resources. If you are selecting a transaction type as the partition key and the number of unique values in it are, say, 10. You can choose to have 10 partitions in your session. If you cannot spare so many resources at the time the session runs, you can probably choose to have 5 partitions for each processing rows belonging to two transaction types.

e. Session criticality and System resources: The amount of system resources that will be available at the time the session runs plays a vital role in deciding the number of partitions. Let us consider the example above. When we have rows that can be grouped in to 10 transaction types, we can choose to have 10 partitions – each processing one transaction type or we can have 5 partitions each processing 2 transaction types or even 2 partitions processing 5 transaction types each. The amount of system resources needed at the time of the session run is directly affected by the number of partitions you will have. But more the partitions, faster the session completes. If it is more critical to have the session complete faster, we may choose to have more partitions and, hence, leverage more system resources that are available. If it is less critical, we may choose to have it run for little longer and spare the system resources for other sessions running at the same time.

24.7 Database partitioning

24.7.1   Overview

Database partitioning can be used when you edit partition points at certain relational sources/targets. When database partitioning is used, PowerCenter Integration Service will query the database system tables to identify how the table is partitioned in the database. By configuring the same number of pipeline partitions, we can have integration service read data from each database partition into a corresponding pipeline partition. The most optimal usage of database partitioning technique is when source table, target table and the DI process are all partitioned in the same manner.

24.7.2   How to configure

Here are the steps to define database partitioning:

a. Go to workflow manager

b. Login to the repository

c. Open the folder →workflow in the workspace

d. Double click on the session to open session properties

e. In the Mapping tab, click on the Partitions sub tab (⬐)

f. In the partition map displayed, click on the source or target that you would like to partition

g. Click on the Edit Partition Point button (✐)

h. The Edit partition points dialog box appears

i. Click on the Add button (⬚) to add as many partitions as you have in the database

j. Select the partition type drop down as Database partitioning

k. Click OK to close the dialog box

l. Switch to the Transformations sub tab in the Mapping tab (⊞)

m. Select the source or target that you chose to partition

n.   On the right hand side, `Properties` section, `SQL Query` and `Source Filter` properties will show multiple values for each partition

o.   Override these values as needed

p.   Click `OK` to close the session properties

q.   Save the session and run the workflow

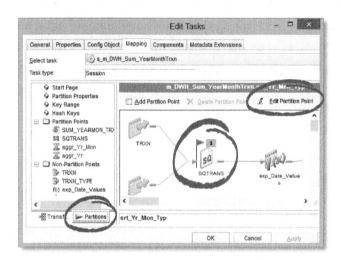

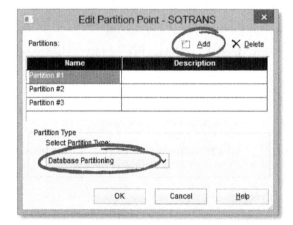

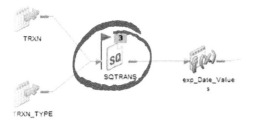

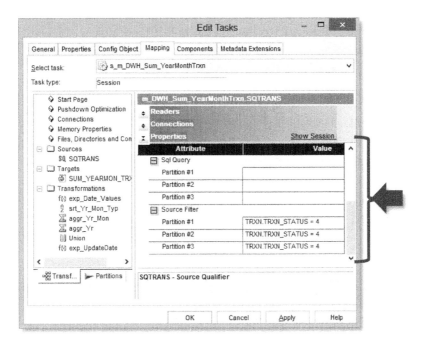

24.8 Round robin partitioning

24.8.1   Overview

When you have multiple partitions with varied data sizes, a partitioning point with round robin partitioning type can redistribute this data equally. Hence, this type of partitioning is to be used when there is no need to perform aggregations on the data. When aggregations need to be performed, it is important to group the rows properly in the corresponding partitions to be able to accurately calculate the summations. Since round robin partitioning equally distributes the rows across the partitions, a row is not always guaranteed to be in the same partition. Let's consider an example: We are reading data from a table containing 3 partitions. The data in these partitions is unevenly distributed. Thus, the time taken by the session is the time taken by the longest partition. Let's look at the number of blocks of data read by each partition.

Partition	Number of blocks read
Partition 1	5 blocks of data – approx. 50,000 rows
Partition 2	7 blocks of data – approx. 70,000 rows
Partition 3	9 blocks of data – approx. 90,000 rows

Now, if a round robin partitioning point is inserted at a transformation right after the source qualifier, the data is repartitioned such that all partitions have equal volumes of data.

The newly partitioned data is now distributed as follows:

Partition	Number of blocks read
Partition 1	7 blocks of data – approx. 70,000 rows
Partition 2	7 blocks of data – approx. 70,000 rows
Partition 3	7 blocks of data – approx. 70,000 rows

24.8.2   How to configure

Below are the steps to configure round robin partitioning:

a. Go to workflow manager
b. Login to the repository
c. Open the folder →workflow in the workspace
d. Double click the session to open session properties
e. In the `Mapping` tab, click on the `Partitions` sub tab (☞)
f. In the partition map displayed, click on the transformations that you would like to partition
g. Click on the `Add partition point`(⬚)
h. `Edit Partition Point` dialog box appears
i. If you have already applied partition on your source/target, those partitions will appear
j. Click `Add`(⬚) to add as many partitions as you need
k. Select partition type drop down as `Round Robin`
l. Click `OK` to close the dialog box
m. Click `OK` to close the session properties

n. Save the workflow and run

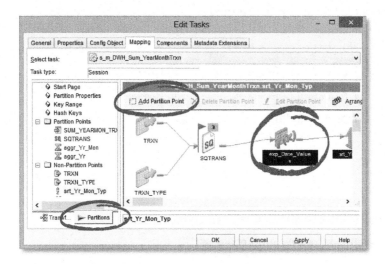

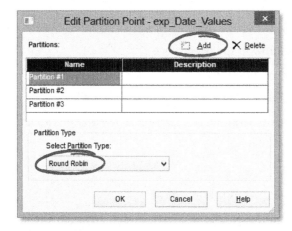

24.9 Key range partitioning

24.9.1   Overview

In key range partitioning, data is distributed on the range of values of selected port(s). For example, transactions data can be partitioned by amounts as follows:

Partition	Amount range
Partition 1	$1,000 or less
Partition 2	$1,000 - $10,000
Partition 3	$10,000 - $100,000
Partition 4	$100,000 and more

In round robin partitioning, Integration Service is responsible for creating close to equal data volumes across various partitions. In key range partitioning, this responsibility stays with the developer. The developer must analyze the data values in the column that is chosen for the partitioning and define partitions such that the data volumes are more or less equally distributed. Developers can use sophisticated tools such as Informatica Analyst to analyze and profile the data in these columns.

If key range partitioning is defined at the source qualifier, PowerCenter will generate where clauses for each partition to match the criteria defined. Developers can override the SQLs to define further filter conditions. If key range partitioning point is defined at the target, it should be aligned with database level partitioning (if applicable) for optimum performance.

24.9.2 How to configure

a. Go to workflow manager

b. Login to the repository

c. Open the folder →workflow in the workspace

d. Double click the session to open session properties

e. In the `Mapping` tab, click on the `Partitions` sub tab (▶)

f. In the partition map displayed, click on the transformations that you would like to partition

g. Click on the `Add partition point`(⬚)

    1. Click `Add`(⬚) to add as many partitions as needed

    2. Select the partition type as `Key Range` and click `OK` to close it

h. Edit Partition Key dialog box appears

    1. Select one or more columns on which you would like to perform key partition on and then click `Add >>`. The ports you selected will now show up in selected ports column

    2. Use arrows (⬆and ⬇) to control the order of the key ports

    3. Click `OK` to close the dialog box

i. The key range partitioning table is displayed just below the partition map

    1. Fill in the range value as appropriate

    2. You can leave the start range of the first partition and the end range of the last partition blank to indicate any minimum and any maximum values. For example, in the snapshot below, partition 1 will process any value less than or equal to 1,000 and the partition 3 will process any value greater than or equal to 10,000

j. Click `OK` to close the session properties

k. Save the workflow and run

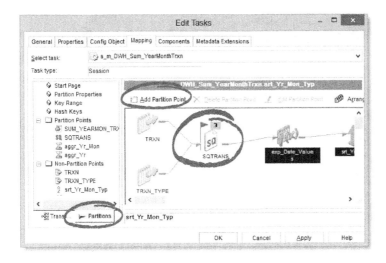

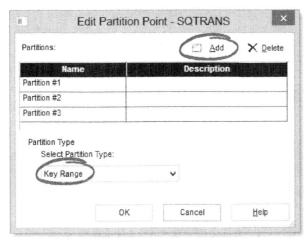

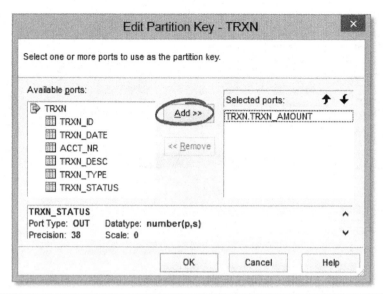

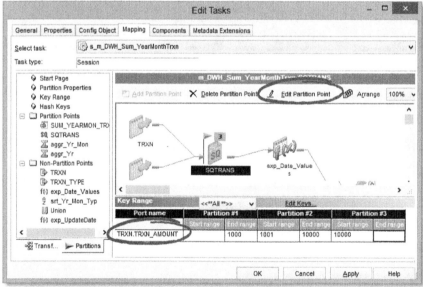

24.10 Pass through partitioning

24.10.1   Overview

Pass through partitioning is the simplest of all partitioning types available in PowerCenter. In a pass through partitioning, we simply create more pipeline stages by creating additional pipeline partitions and set them as pass through. When we create a pass through partition, PowerCenter does not redistribute the data. It simply retains the blocks in the partition as it is. However, by creating additional stage, we increase the parallelism, because we now break a long running thread into two smaller ones. Let us consider an example of processing two blocks using a mapping as shown below. We have two partition points, one at source and one at target. Let us look at what happens at runtime when this mapping executes.

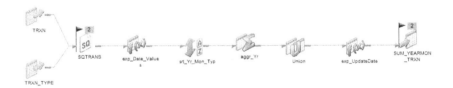

a. Block 1 (depicted in blue) is read by the reader process

b. Block 1 is then transformed by the transformer thread

c. While Block 1 is transformed by the transformer, reader goes back to reading Block 2 (depicted in orange) from the source

d. If the time taken by the transformer thread is longer than the time taken by reader to read block 2, block 2 will have to wait for its turn to be transformed. This waiting period is depicted with a dotted border

e. Block 1 is now passed onto writer to be written to the target

f. Block 2 is now processed by transformer thread and then passed on to the writer thread

g. The waiting period of block 2 for transformer thread can be reduced/eliminated by introducing another partitioning point/stage of type pass through partitioning in the transformations

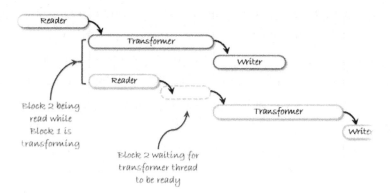

Now, to eliminate this waiting period of block 2, we introduce an additional pass through partitioning at the aggregator transformation. Now, when the session runs, the following happens at run time:

a. Block 1 (depicted in blue) is read by the reader process

b. Block 1 is then transformed by the transformer thread – unlike before, now the transformation happens till aggregation

c. While Block 1 is transformed by the transformer, reader goes back to reading Block 2 (depicted in orange) from the source

d. After transformation, Block 1 is handed over to another transformer thread 2 to continue rest of the transformation

e. Now, Block 2 that is already read by reader is ready to be transformed and will be picked up transformer thread 1

f. Once Block 1 is transformed by thread 2, it is passed over to writer thread

g. Block 2 is now handed over to transformer thread 2, while Block 1 is being written to target

h. Block 2 is then finally written to target

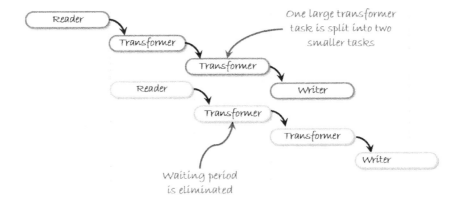

Pass through partitioning is very useful when transformations are complex and transformer thread is the bottleneck.

24.10.2   How to configure

Here are the steps to define database partitioning:

a. Go to workflow manager
b. Login to the repository
c. Open the folder → workflow in the workspace
d. Double click the session to open session properties
e. In the Mapping tab, click on the Partitions sub tab (➥)
f. In the partition map displayed, click on the transformation that you would like to partition
g. Click on the Add Partition Point button (✎)

    1. The Edit partition points dialog box appears

    2. Click on the Add button (⬚) to add as many partitions as you need

    3. Select the Pass through as the partition type in the drop down

    4. Click OK to close the dialog box

h. Click OK to close the session properties

i. Save the workflow and run it

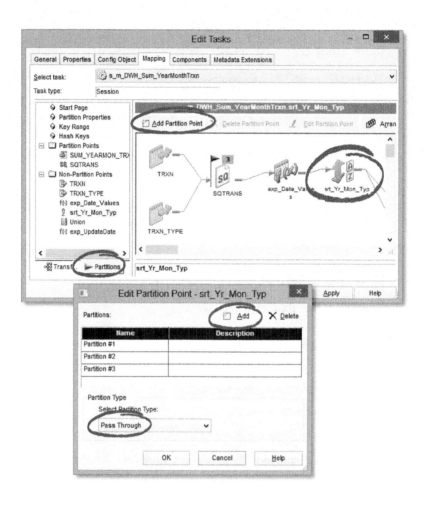

24.11 Hash key partitioning

24.11.1   Overview

When using partitioning, at times it makes sense to use different partitions at different partition points. However, when aggregation transformations such as aggregator, sort, and rank are used, it is important to distribute the rows such that each group's data is only within one partition. Failing to configure so, may lead to inconsistent and invalid computational results. This is where hash key partitioning is used. When we use hash key partitioning, PowerCenter will redistribute all the data such that data belonging to each group is within the same partition and is not across partitions. PowerCenter uses information such as sort keys, aggregator group by ports to determine how to reorganize the rows. Hash key partitioning has two variations: Hash Auto Keys and Hash User Keys. When using Hash Auto Keys partitioning, PowerCenter will automatically determine the ports on which the redistribution needs to happen. When using Hash User Keys partitioning, developer can define the columns that PowerCenter should use instead of automatically determining them.

 Typically Hash functions processes numerical data faster than character data.

24.11.2   How to configure

Here are the steps to define database partitioning:

a.   Go to workflow manager

b.   Login to the repository

c.   Open the folder → workflow in the workspace

d.   Double click the session to open session properties

e.   In the `Mapping` tab, click on the `Partitions` sub tab (☞)

f. In the partition map displayed, click on the transformation that you would like to partition

g. Click on the `Add Partition Point` button (✎)

    1. The `Edit partition points` dialog box appears

    2. Click on the `Add` button (⬚) to add as many partitions as you need

    3. In the select partition type drop down, select `Hash Key Auto (or User) Keys` partitioning

    4. Click `OK` to close the dialog box

h. Click `OK` to close the session properties

i. Save the workflow and run it

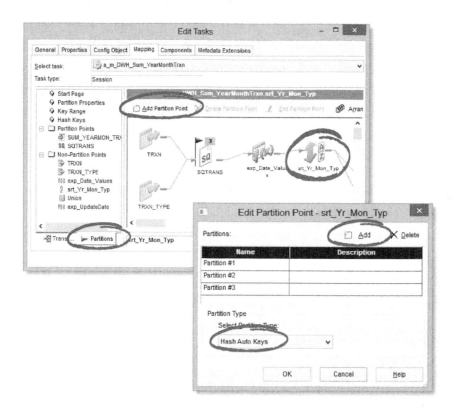

25

Pushdown optimization

Data Integration engines such as PowerCenter are optimized to perform transformations and process data at high performance rates. But there are always certain tasks that are best executed at the database level. Pushdown optimization feature of PowerCenter allows us to push such logic down to the source/target database. When the logic is pushed down to database, PowerCenter Integration Service generates SQLs that execute this logic within the database level. PowerCenter can push the logic to either source database or target database or both. It is important to note that during push down, PowerCenter attempts to push down as much logic as possible to database and the integration service executes the logic it cannot push down.

25.1 Source-side pushdown

In source-side pushdown, integration service will push as much transformation logic as possible to the source database. PowerCenter will analyze the mapping from source to target until it encounters a transformation whose logic cannot be pushed to the database. The logic that cannot be pushed to the database will be executed by the Integration Service. At run time, the integration service will generate a SELECT SQL that will include the logic of the transformations that are pushed down.

25.2   Target-side pushdown

In target-side pushdown, integration service will push as much transformation logic as possible to the target database. PowerCenter will analyze the mapping from target to source until it encounters a transformation whose logic cannot be pushed to the database. The logic that cannot be pushed to the database will be executed by the Integration Service. At run time, the integration service will generate INSERT / UPDATE / DELETE SQL that will include the logic of the transformations that are pushed down.

25.3   Full pushdown

In full pushdown, integration service will attempt to push as much logic to target database as possible. If it cannot push the entire logic to target database, it pushes as much transformation logic as possible to the target and then attempts to push the rest of the logic to the source database. Any logic that cannot be pushed to either source or target will be executed by the Integration Service itself.

25.4   How to configure pushdown

To configure pushdown optimization, execute the following steps:

   a.   Open workflow manager

b.   Login to the PowerCenter repository and open a PowerCenter folder→ workflow

c.   Open the properties of the session that you want to apply pushdown optimization.

d.   Go to the `Properties` tab and set the following properties

e.   If your mapping contains SQL Overrides in source qualifiers/lookups, check `Allow temporary view for pushdown`

f.   If your mapping contains sequence generator transformations, check `Allow temporary sequence for pushdown`

g.   Go to mapping tab and click `Pushdown optimization` on the left hand navigator

h.   Pushdown Optimization Viewer dialog box appears

i.   In the drop down labeled as `Pushdown option`, select `To Source` or `To Target` or `Full`

j.   In the mapping displayed, the transformations are numbered such as (**1**). Each of these numbers indicates groups such as a source side and target side pushdowns.

k.   In the bottom half of the dialog box, PowerCenter will display messages and SQLs generated

l.   Click `Close` to close the partitioning dialog box

m.   Click `OK` to close the session properties

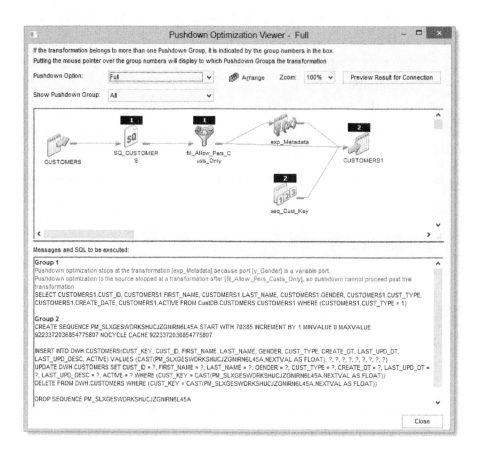

26

Reusability

PowerCenter has many levels of reusability built-in. To be able to understand the reusability levels in PowerCenter, we must look at all levels of code that can be created in PowerCenter repository. Take a look at the picture below:

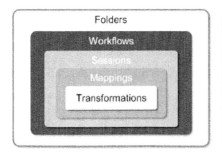 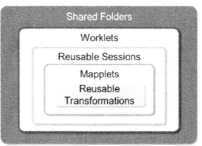

Transformations can be reusable or non-reusable. Transformations that are created directly within a mapping are, by default, non-reusable. Reusable transformations can be created in the transformation developer within the Designer tool. Reusable and non-reusable transformations can be used together in a mapping. Sometimes, however, there is a need to reuse more than one transformation. For example, we may want to build a reusable component that will validate the input data and return a validation result as its output. Such logic may require more than one transformation in it. This is exactly where Mapplets come into the picture. Mapplets, in simplest terms, are mappings with logical source and logical targets, known as mapplet input and mapplet output. A mapplet can be used within a mapping just like any other transformation – only difference being the mapplet itself is now comprised of a mini-mapping.

To be able to execute, a mapping is linked to a session. While each session can link to only one mapping, one mapping can link to any number of sessions. Imagine a transactions' mapping that processes millions of records. To be able to process this data faster, we might want to create multiple sessions – each session processing data for a different geography. In this case, there is only one mapping but many sessions. If we simply duplicate the sessions, the information in the session is duplicated causing overhead. So, we can create a reusable session (in Task Developer of Workflow Manager) and then reuse this session several times with different source filters.

A worklet is to workflow what a mapplet is to a mapping. A worklet is a mini-workflow containing an order of execution of one or more tasks. Such a worklet can be used one or more times in one or more workflows to repeat the execution of the logic.

A shared folder is very similar to a regular folder in a PowerCenter repository. The primary difference is that you can refer to any object present in a shared folder, from other non-shared folders. By doing so, a link is created between the shared and non-shared folders such that the shared object remains in the shared folder but a reference to it (called as a shortcut) is created in the main folder.

Reusable objects can be created in both shared and non-shared folders. Reusable objects within a non-shared folder can be shared only within that folder. Whereas, reusable objects within a shared folder can be referred to, from any folder within the repository.

26.1   Shared folders

Folders are created and managed in Repository Manager. To create a shared folder, your PowerCenter Administrator checks the Allow Shortcut checkbox in folder properties. It is also customary to prefix or suffix the word Shared in the folder name. For example, a shared folder created for Data Warehouse project might be named as DWH_Shared. A shared folder can also be recognized by its icon. A regular folder has a simple folder icon ( ), whereas a shared folder contains hand under the folder icon ( )– just like shared folders in windows.

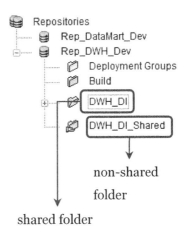

non-shared folder

shared folder

A regular folder can be converted into a shared folder anytime. But this step is irreversible.

 While deploying, shared folders must always be deployed before their corresponding regular folders so that the dependencies are deployed correctly.

26.2 Objects, instances and shortcuts

An object is any repository entity such as a transformation, mapping, mapplet, etc... When a reusable object is *used*, it creates what is called as an instance. An instance is a reference to an existing object with the ability to override some of its original properties. For example, when a reusable transformation is used within a mapping, that mapping only contains the instance of the reusable object and not the object itself. A shortcut is a special instance, where the object and its instance are in different folders. Typically, the object resides in a shared folder and the instance resides in a non-shared folder. A shortcut is usually represented with the icon (▣) along with its original object icon. When a shortcut is created, PowerCenter, by default, prefixes its name with `Shortcut_to_`. When a reusable object changes, all of its instances are automatically updated with the new values. Instances allow you to override some of their properties to be different from the original underlying object. In such case, when the instance is updated with a new value, a revert button (Revert) appears next to it. Revert button indicates that the instance has an overridden property different from its underlying object. Clicking the Revert button reverts the property value to the value defined in the reusable object. When an instance property is overridden, it no longer automatically updated when that property changes in the reusable transformation.

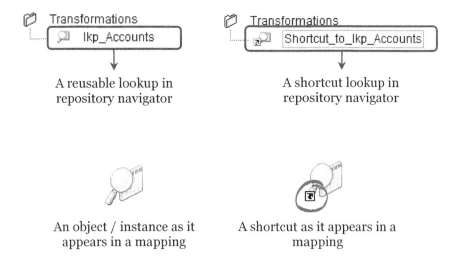

A reusable lookup in
repository navigator

A shortcut lookup in
repository navigator

An object / instance as it
appears in a mapping

A shortcut as it appears in a
mapping

26.3 Reusable transformations

Reusable transformations are created in Transformation Developer ( ) in Designer client tool. To switch to Transformation Developer, go to `Tools` menu →`Transformation Developer`. In the transformation developer, just create any valid transformation like you would to create it in a mapping. The following transformations are not allowed in the transformation developer

    a. Source

    b. Target

    c. Mapplet Input

    d. Mapplet Output

    e. Source Qualifiers (all types)

When a reusable transformation is created, its transformation type will show the keyword (Reusable) to indicate it is a reusable transformation. A reusable transformation appears in the Transformations section in the repository navigator. When a reusable transformation is dragged into a mapping, an instance is created. An instance always refers to the reusable objects to which it points. It derives its properties from the reusable object. Some of these properties may be overridden in the mapping. Properties that are overridden will show a revert button (Revert) next to them. Transformations created within a mapping can also be later promoted as reusable transformations. To do so, simply check the `Make Reusable` checkbox in the `Transformation` tab of the transformation properties.

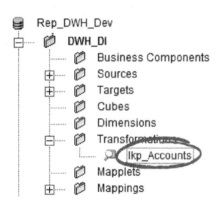

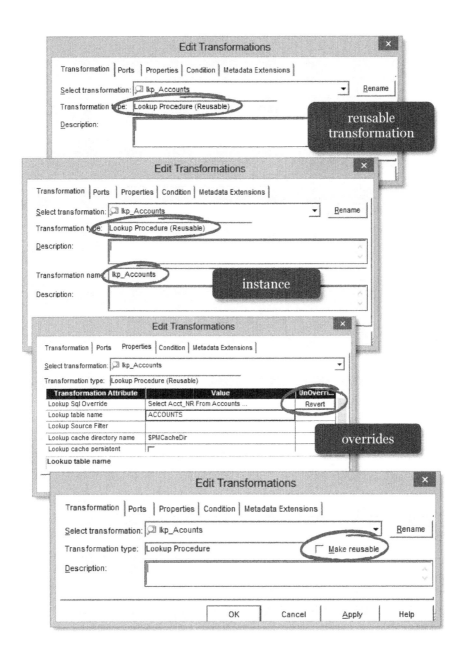

26.4 Mapplets

Mapplets are created in mapplet designer ( ) in the Designer client tool. A mapplet can be dubbed as a reusable mapplet. A mapplet is to a mapping what a function is to a program in a programming world. A mapplet typically has a mapplet input and mapplet output transformations as its source and target respectively. To create a mapplet, go to Mapplet Designer, Mapplets menu, Create. A mapplet contains one or more mapplet inputs and mapplet outputs. A mapplet cannot contain the following transformations:

  a. Normalizer
  b. Cobol Sources
  c. XML Sources
  d. XML Source Qualifiers
  e. Targets

A mapplet cannot contain other mapplets either. Once a mapplet is created, it can be used in any number of mappings. When a mapplet is used in a mapping, its inputs and outputs are represented as groups (like in router/union).

To create a mapplet, switch to the mapplet designer in the Designer tool and then go to the menu Mapplets → Create. A mapplet name dialog box appears. Provide a name to the mapplet and click OK. Mapplet is created. Add a mapplet input ( )

and mapplet output ( ) transformation for each source and target you expect the mapplet to have. To use the mapplet in a mapping, simply drag it from repository navigator on the left.

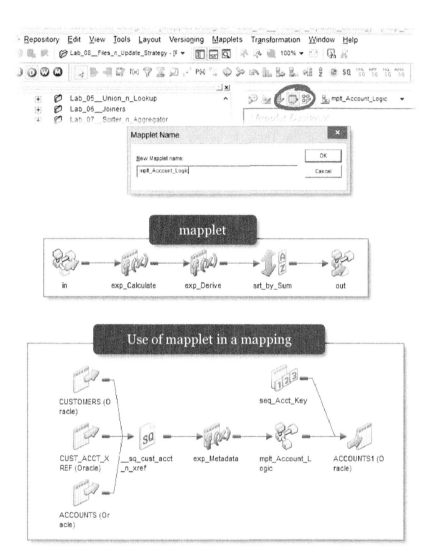

26.5 Reusable tasks

Tasks such as Session, Command and Email can be reusable or non-reusable. Reusable tasks are created in the Task Developer of the workflow manager (⊞). To go to task developer, go to `Tools` menu →`Task Developer`. By default, sessions created within a workflow are all non-reusable. For these tasks to be reusable, they have to be either created in the Task Developer or the existing tasks have to be converted into reusable by checking the `Make reusable` checkbox in the `General` tab of their properties. When a reusable session is used within a workflow, it creates an instance. The instance refers to the reusable object for all its properties. Some properties can be overridden in the instance. Properties overridden show the revert button (Revert) next to them. By clicking the revert button, the property value is reset to that of the original reusable object.

26.6 Worklets

Worklets are reusable workflow or mini-workflows. Worklets are to workflows what mapplets are to mappings. Worklets can be created and edited in the Worklet Designer (⊞) in the Workflow manager client tool. All principles in creating a workflow also apply to a worklet. A worklet can be embedded into a workflow just like any other task. However, like a mapplet, a workflow itself cannot be edited from within a workflow. It can only be edited in the Worklet Designer.

26.7 Session configuration

Session configuration is a template object that contains certain session properties that can be applied to several sessions within the repository. Session configuration primarily consists of logging, error handling, partitioning and session grid options along with several advanced properties. Several templates (simply known as session configurations) can be created. One of the most important use cases for session configuration objects is memory settings. Most of the sessions in a repository typically have the default memory settings. However, there may be certain sessions across different projects/folders that require additional memory for their processing. In such a case, instead of customizing the sessions individually, a new session configuration can be created with increased memory settings and this can be applied to the sessions that require additional memory.

27

Best practices

Although best Practices are some of the most important elements to be considered during design and development phases, they are ignored very often. It is a typical tendency of developers to develop first and apply the standards and best practices later. However, this practice must be discouraged for various reasons. First and foremost, once unit testing is complete, the code should not be changed – even to apply standards and best practices. Any change is code change. Secondly, there is usually no time left at the end of design/development (after unit testing is complete) to apply the standards/best practices as there is high pressure on moving the code to subsequent environments for quality testing. Finally, more often than not, developers maintaining a DI process are usually not the ones who developed it in the first place. Hence, it is extremely important to properly document the process both externally (in Word documents, PowerPoints, etc.) and internally (inside code by writing comments, using naming conventions, etc.). In this chapter, we discuss various kinds of best practices to be followed during design, development and testing phases of a Data Integration project.

27.1   Naming conventions

Naming conventions are the standard for naming various objects in repository so that is easy to recognize what they are and what they do. A list of different objects and how they should be named is given here.

27.1.1   Transformations

Source and Target:

Sources/Targets are by default named as their tables. Hence, their names need not be changed. In mappings, containing the same table name as source and target (either same table for updates or same table names in different databases), the source and target can be prefixed with src_ and tgt_ respectively to indicate their usage.

Source qualifier:

Source qualifier is named after source with a sq_ prefix. When you use a single source qualifier to fetch data from multiple sources list, the source names separate by a _n_ (a short form to represent the word and). If the source qualifier has customizations, i.e. properties such as SQL Override, Filter condition etc are configured, then prefix the transformation name with double underscores, example: __sq_Customers. If there is more than one type of source qualifier with a similarly named source, use the corresponding source type as the prefix. For example, if there is a mapping containing a relational source Customers and a MQ source also named customer, you can name them as rsq_Customers (relational source qualifier) and mqsq_Customer (MQ source qualifier).

Aggregator:

Aggregators are used to group data together. This must reflect in their names as well. When the group by contains more than one column, a short form notation can be used to denote the same.

Prefix	aggr_
Syntax	aggr_<GroupByClause>
Examples	→ aggr_Cust_ID
	→ aggr_Tranx_by_Date
	→ aggr_Custs_by_Region

In the first example above, the name suggests that the column name, with which we are grouping the data, is Customer ID. Second and third examples refer to both entity name (Transactions and Customers) as well as attribute names (Date and Region respectively). Instead of listing out all the column names, we simply named the essence of the column list. In the second example, date may physically be stored in more than field, but the naming convention suggests the logical representation of the same.

Custom:

Custom transformation is used to invoke external programs such as DLLs in windows and shared libraries in UNIX platforms.

Prefix	ct_
Syntax	ct_<Program_Module>
Examples	→ ct_Encrypt_BlowFish

In the example above, it is suggested that we are invoke a `BlowFish` encryption module in the external library called `Encryption`. In this example, the actual module name can be as simple as `encrypt.so` or something more complex like `enc_algs_10.15.1.3.so` but the intention is not to mention the actual complete module name but to hint the module name so that the developers can easily identify the module without having to open the transformation properties. In such scenarios, do not add the version number of the shared library or the DLL into the name of the custom transformation.

Data Masking:

Data masking transformation can be used to hide sensitive data by replacing with random data patterns. Masked data usually still complies to the same data validation rules as the original data. For example, a credit card number is replaced with another 16 digit number that still validates the credit card validation checks but is not a real card number and hence not assigned to any customer in the real world.

Prefix	`dm_`
Syntax	`dm_<entity | attribute_list>`
Examples	→ `dm_Customer`
	→ `dm_AcctNum`

In the first example above, it is suggested that we are masking the entire customer attribute in the same data masking transformation. In the second example, however, we are masking only the account number attribute from the table it is coming.

Expression:

Expressions should be named based on the purpose of the transformation instead of the steps that are being performed in it. For example, an expression may be used to trim all input fields before processing some logic. In this case, the expression should simply be named as `exp_Trim_All_Input`.

Prefix	`exp_`
Syntax	`exp_<core logic>`
Examples	→ `exp_Trim_Input`
	→ `exp_Pad_with_Spaces`
	→ `exp_ParseFullName_for_Names`
	→ `exp_PreProcess`

In the examples above, the names suggest that first expression is used to trim all input fields, the second one is used to pad extra spaces to fields, the third one is used to parse full name to derive first name, last name, etc. and the last expression suggests that is performing a preliminary validations or data parsing before core logic is applied.

Filter:

Filters should clearly indicate the data they allow to pass or the data they are allowed to discard.

Prefix	`fil_`
Syntax	`fil_<core logic>`

Examples

    → `fil_Past_Dates`

    → `fil_Allow_Active_Custs`

    → `fil_If_Debugging`

The three examples above represent three different naming conventions that are generally used for Filter transformations. These are simply the negative, positive and if cases. A negative naming convention indicates the data that is being discarded. The first example above is to be read as *Filter any Past Dates* suggesting that the filter will allow records with current date or future date. In the second example, positive data is suggested – meaning that the filter name is not representing what is being discarded but what is being allowed to pass. So, it should be read as *Filter Allows Active Customers* to pass. Sometimes, a filter transformation is used to determine whether or not data should be passed into a branch of a pipeline as shown in the snapshot below. In such cases the If naming convention of the filter is used. The If naming convention is used to indicate the condition on which records are allowed to pass and hence, is a positive naming convention.

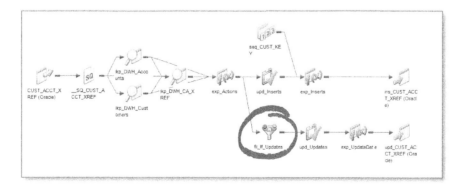

In the snapshot above, filter name `fil_If_Updates` is to be read as *If the records are marked for updates, allow them to pass.* The third example in the above list is used while building debug ready mappings, where a lot of debugging information is collected but is written to target only if the debug parameter is set to Y. This is controlled using a filter transformation named as such.

> For more information on debug ready mappings, please refer to Chapter 12 – Logging, Debugging and Exception Handling

Java:

Prefix	`java_`
Syntax	`java[e]_<logic	program>`
Examples	→ `java_Loop_Cust_Details`
	→ `javae_notifyDB`

The first example above suggests that the java logic has a loop inside it to iterate the customer details several times. The second example suggests that the java transformation is used to invoke an external java program (suggested by the extra e) named `notifyDB.class.` If the classpath or settings are customized within the java transformation, prefix it with two underscores (__).

> Use two underscores __ before the java transformation name to indicate a customized class path. Ex: `__javae_notifyDB`

Joiner:

Prefix	jnr_
Syntax	jnr_<master>_n_<detail>
Examples	→ jnr_Cust_n_Addr
	→ jnr_Acct_n_History
	→ jnr_Acct__n_History

The first example above suggests that the joiner is used to join customers with customer address table. In this example, customer is the master table and address is the detail table. The letter n is simply a short form notation of the word and. It is always customary to name master table first followed by detail table. In the second example, it is suggested that accounts is joined with history – with accounts being the master table again. The third example is a variation of the second example indicating that the joiner uses a master outer join denoted by an extra underscore before the 'n' (__n).

Use an extra _ before and/or after the letter n to denote an outer join. Hence ___n_ denotes master outer join, _n__ denotes detail outer join and ___n__ denotes a full outer join.

Lookup:

Prefix	lkp_
Syntax	lkp_[<system>_]<table | file>[_<attribute>]
Examples	→ lkp_DWH_Customers
	→ lkp_DWH_Custs_4_Cust_Key

The first example suggests that the lookup transformation is looking up on the Customers table in the DWH system. Lookup is generally used to fetch related data. Hence, mentioning the system (typically database) where the lookup table exists make the transformation more readable. In the second example, lookup is returning only one attribute. So, the attribute name is also mentioned in the lookup name. In this case, the Customer Key is returned from the Customers table of DWH.

Normalizer:

Normalizer is used as a source qualifier for COBOL sources or to transpose columns into rows.

Prefix	nrm_
Syntax	nrm_<source | transpose>
Examples	→ nrm_CUSTS
	→ nrm_Gen_Cust_Recs

In the first example, normalizer is used as a source qualifier for the COBOL source customers. In the second example, normalizer is used to transpose columns into rows for the customer entity. Hence it is named as *Generate Customer Records.*

Rank:

Rank is used to identify top/bottom 'n' rows. Hence the name should also reflect the same.

Prefix	rnk_
Syntax	rnk_<top | bottom | first | last>_<number>_<entity> [_by_<group>]
Examples	→ rnk_Top_5_Sales_by_Region → nrm_Gen_Cust_Recs

In the first example, normalizer is used as a source qualifier for the COBOL source customers. In the second example, normalizer is used to transpose columns into rows for the customer entity. Hence it is named as *Generate Customer Records.*

Router:

Router contains many groups of data and hence is difficult to name appropriately. When the groups are very few (for example 1 or 2) apart from the default group, it can be named based on the conditions. When there are many groups, router should be named based on the data it is routing rather than the conditions on which it is routing the data.

Prefix	rtr_
Syntax	rtr_<Entity>_by_<logic | condition>
Examples	→ rtr_Custs_by_Region → rtr_Accts_Ins_n_Update

In the first example, the name suggests that the router routes Customer data by region (typically state, city or other geographical attribute). In the second example, it is suggested that accounts information is routed by their row indicator (Insert or Update) and that there are only 2 groups in use (not counting the default); one routes the rows marked for inserts and another routes the rows marked for updates.

Sequence generator:

Prefix	`seq_`
Syntax	`seq_[entity_]<attribute this value is used for>`
Examples	→ `seq_Cust_ID` → `seq_DWH_Cust_Key`

The first example suggests that the value from sequence generator is used to populate *Customer ID* attribute. Similarly, the second example suggests that the value is used to populate *Customer Key* attribute in the *Data Warehouse*.

Sorter:

Prefix	`srt_`
Syntax	`srt_[entity_]<attribute or attribute group to sort on>`
Examples	→ `srt_City_n_State` → `seq_Acct_Date`

The first example suggests that the sorter sorts the data by city and then by state. The second example similarly suggests that the sorter sorts by the date attribute from the account entity. The notation of using an entity name before attribute name is very useful when the sorter receives data from more than one attribute.

SQL:

Prefix	`sql_`
Syntax	`sql_<operation>_<entity>_<attribute>[_logic]`
Examples	→ `sql_Del_Addr_Invalid`
	→ `sql_Upd_Acct_Stat_to_Pend`
	→ `sql_script_acct_reconcil`

The operation keyword represents the operation performed on the database by the SQL transformation such as `INSERT`, `UPDATE`, `DELETE`. Other generic operations can also be used such as `MERGE` and `SET`. If a script is invoked from this transformation, the keyword `SCRIPT` can also be used. In the first example above, we suggest that this transformation deletes all invalid addresses. The second one suggests that the account table's status field is set to pending. The third example simply suggests invoking a script that performs account reconciliation.

Stored Procedure:

Prefix	`sp_`
Syntax	`sp_<Procedure Name>`

Examples

→ `sp_acct_reconcil`

As indicated in the example above, the name suggests that the stored procedure to perform account reconciliation is executed.

Transaction control:

Transaction control is used to dynamically commit/rollback a transaction.

Prefix	`tc_`
Syntax	`tc_<commit|rollback>_[before|after_]<logic>`
Examples	→ `tc_Commit_on_PROC_Acct`
	→ `tc_Rollback_ERR_Accts`

The first example suggests that when a transaction with PROC status is received, a commit is issued. The second example suggests that if any error occurs during account processing, the transaction is rolled back.

Union:

Prefix	`un_`
Syntax	`un_<Entity>`
Examples	→ `un_Cust_Acct_XRef`

This is an example from one of the labs we had earlier where we union-ed customer and account cross reference information from the main table and the history table.

Update strategy:

Prefix	upd_
Syntax	upd_<operation>
Examples	→ upd_Mark_as_Inserts
	→ upd_Ins_r_Upds

The first example suggests that the update strategy marks all input records as inserts – usually used after a router that separates Inserts and Updates into multiple pipelines and the second one suggests that the update strategy marks the records either as Inserts or as Updates.

XML:

Prefix	xml_
Syntax	xml<p|g>_<entity_attribute>
Examples	→ xmlp_cust_addr
	→ xmlg_cust_addr_extract

The first example suggests that the XML Parser (indicated as xmlp) parses customer address XML content and the second example suggests that the address data is generated as XML (xmlg) and provided downstream as extract.

27.1.2　Workflow tasks

Sessions:

Prefix	`s_m_`
Syntax	`s_m_<mapping name>`
Examples	→ `s_m_CustDB_eAddr`
	→ `s_m_DWH_Init_Load_Accounts`

Assignment:

Prefix	`assign_`
Syntax	→ `assign_<value>_to_<parameter>`
	→ `assign_<description>`
Examples	→ `assign_N_to_DebugMode`
	→ `assign_Empty_All_Params`

Command:

Prefix	`cmd_`
Syntax	`cmd_<script name	activity>`
Examples	→ `cmd_start_tomcat`
	→ `cmd_DEL_All_Archived_Files`

Control:

Prefix	ctrl_
Syntax	ctrl_<action>_<object>
Examples	→ ctrl_Fail_WF
	→ ctrl_Fail_Parent

Event Raise:

Prefix	evtR_
Syntax	evtR_<event name>
Examples	→ evtR_InputFile
	→ evtR_CtrlTrigger

Event Wait:

Prefix	evtW_
Syntax	evtW_<event name>
Examples	→ evtW_InputFile
	→ evtW_CtrlTrigger

Timer:

Prefix	tmr_
Syntax	→ `tmr_<absolute time in 12 hr format><AM|PM>`
	→ `tmr_<time>_<secs|mins|hrs>_from_<here|start|parent>`
Examples	→ `tmr_0900PM`
	→ `tmr_01_mins_from_here`
	→ `tmr_12_mins_from_start`

27.1.3   Other repository objects

Mappings:

Prefix	m_
Syntax	`m_[ws_][app_]<service>[_logic]`
Examples	→ `m_CustDB_eAddr`
	→ `m_DWH_Init_Load_Accounts`

The first example suggests a mapping where `CustDB` is the application name and the `eAddress` is the service name. Similarly in the second example, `DWH` is the application name and Initial Load is the group of services, where Accounts is the service name. `ws_` prefix is attached for web service mappings

Mapplets use same guidelines as mappings with prefix `mplt_` instead of `m_`.

Worklets:

Prefix	`wklt_`
Syntax	`wklt_[App_]<Service	Function>`
Examples	→ `wklt_Dimension_Load`
	→ `wklt_DWH_Trxn_Load`

Worklets are named very similar to workflows. The application can be prefixed to represent the system/application to which the worklet belongs (`DWH` in this example). This is followed by the service name, which indicates the load of dimension tables and transaction tables accordingly in this case.

Workflows:

Prefix	`wf_`
Syntax	`wf_[App_]<Service	Function>[_Schedule]`
Examples	→ `wf_Dimension_Load_MTH`
	→ `wf_DWH_Trxn_Load_DLY`

As shown in the examples above, the workflows are scheduled to run monthly (MTH) or daily (DLY). The first example is a dimension load and the second one is a Data Warehouse transactions load.

27.1.4   General guidelines

While applying naming conventions, the following general guidelines can be applied regardless of the object:

a. Do not add schedule details (such as _DLY or _MTH) in the mapping / mapplet name. Mappings and mapplets cannot be scheduled and hence, it is not a good idea to name them by schedules. Additionally, the same mapping can be used by different workflows that run at different schedules.

b. Do not add database types (such as Oracle, SQL Server) in the mapping or session names. When a mapping is reading from or writing to databases, do not add the database type in their names. It is not uncommon for customers to migrate from one database vendor to another.

c. With the exception of the prefix and adjectives such as if, and or, always use lower case and name the transformation in Title Case. In title case, first letter of every word is capitalized. See the sample below.

d. Numbers can be used in place of words as long as the meaning is distorted. For example, instead of the words "to" and "for", the numbers 2 and 4 can be used respectively. See the sample below.

Rnk_Top_5_Sales_By_Region

→ rnk_Top_5_Sales_by_Region

sql_Upd_Acct_Stat_to_Pend

→ sql_Upd_Acct_Stat_2_Pend

e. Use common abbreviations, wherever possible. Some commonly used ones are:

Abbreviation	Word
Service	srvc
Application	app
Data warehouse	dwh
Data mart	dm
Customer	cust
Account	acct
Transaction	trxn
Partner	prtnr
Insert	ins
Update	upd
Delete	del
Reject	rej
Daily	dly
Monthly	mth
Quarterly	qrt
Yearly	yrl

27.2 Comments

Comments help users understand the purpose of the repository object. For objects such as mappings and workflows, it is very important as it helps understand the data flow or the process flow. Comments can also be used to describe any changes made to the objects and the reason behind those changes.

27.2.1   Mappings, sessions, workflows

While writing comments for mappings, sessions and workflows, utmost care must be taken as this is the first place where the developers look to understand an application that they did not develop. Hence writing user-friendly comments with enough details helps the developers maintain existing code without investing much time and effort. Inimtial comments (written first time the object is created) must explain in detail the entire logic of the mapping/workflow. If the object is a session, detailed information must be written about any custom configuration such as DTM buffer size, etc.

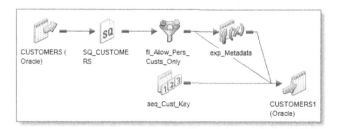

After initial comments, when updates are performed to the mapping, they must be recorded accordingly. Updates must be recorded in a format that is easily understandable by all users. One of the suggested formats is to have date time stamp, followed by user's initials and a note indicating the type of change. Add a separator (----- in the example) between every two updates. All updates must be recorded in reverse chronological order so that the latest update is available at the top and the initial comments are at the bottom. In versioned repositories, the comments should be recorded during check in and check out as well.

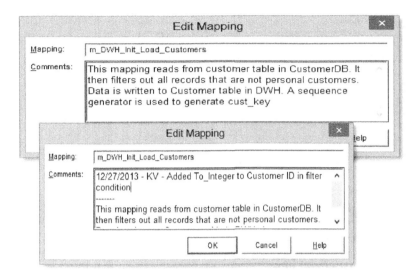

27.2.2   Transformations

Comments can be written in transformations to describe what logic is incorporated within. To write comments to a transformation, open its properties by double clicking on the transformation, going to the Transformation tab and editing the description field to write notes. All comments must be recorded in the reverse chronological order.

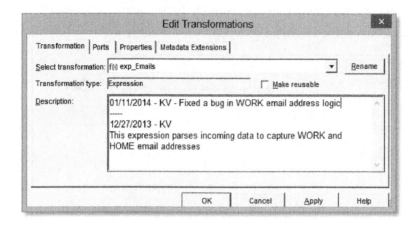

27.2.3   Expressions

Comments should be written within the expressions so that users can understand the logic clearly. Comments in expressions are lines that start with '--'. There can be any number of comment lines in an expression.

Comments in expressions

27.3   Readability

It is important for any programming code to be readable. DI processes are no exception. A mapping must be readable so that it is easy for the developers to understand and maintain it. Readability can be achieved by adapting several simple techniques as discussed in this chapter. Note that the techniques discussed in this chapter are only a starting point and do not form an exclusive list.

27.3.1   Split technique

When you have a complex expression logic, you should split it into reasonable amount of expression transformations to make the mapping more readable. The logic should be separated such that each of the separated logics can be regarded as a step in the overall data flow. Let us consider the example shown in the snapshots below. In this mapping, we originally have one expression processing logic for Customer IDs, Emails and Phones. While the fact that the expression may be processing data related to emails and phones is more visible, it is not clearly visible that the expression is also processing Customer ID information.

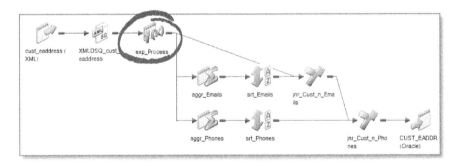

before applying *Split* technique

Now look at the same mapping after applying the split technique. We now see three expressions, all executing in parallel to each other. It is now clearly visible what each of these three expressions is performing.

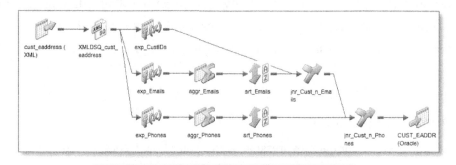

after applying *Split* technique

While split technique makes the mapping more readable, it also adds an advantage of performance. In the above example, all three expressions are executed in parallel, thus reducing the expression run time to one third. If the split technique is applied horizontally, i.e. if the expression is split into three expressions executing one after another sequentially, the performance improvement may not be so much, but still makes the mapping more user friendly.

27.3.2   Naming hints

Hints can be added in the names of repository objects, especially transformations and sessions to hint several customizations. These hints can be used in conjunction with comments in the objects to briefly describe any customization or usage of any non-typical options. One such example discussed in naming conventions is adding two underscores (__) before or after the name of the repository object. For example, adding two underscores before a joiner transformation can represent a master outer join.

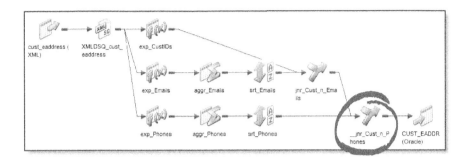

Usage of simple characters such as two consecutive underscores can be a powerful technique in increasing the readability of a mapping without affecting the mapping or the names of the objects. Let us take a look at how adding such hints to different objects in repository can increase the meaning of the transformation name.

Source qualifier:

Prefixed	Query override
	Ex: `__sq_Customers`
Suffixed	Query is not overridden. Other properties such as source filter, number of sorted ports, etc are changed
	Ex: `sq_Customers__`
Both	More customizations. See properties

Target:

Prefixed	Pre-SQL
	Ex: `__Customers`
Suffixed	Post-SQL
	Ex: `Customers__`
Both	More customizations. See properties

Aggregator:

Prefixed	Sorted input
	Ex: `__aggr_Emails`
Suffixed	
Both	More customizations. See properties

Joiner:

Prefixed	Sorted input
	Ex: `__jnr_Cust_n_Addr`
__ before_n_	Master outer join
	Ex: `jnr_Cust__n_Addr`
__ after_n_	Detail outer join
	Ex: `jnr_Cust_n__Addr`
__ before and after _n_	Full outer join
	Ex: `jnr_Cust__n__Addr`

Lookup:

Prefixed __	Lookup SQL override
	Ex: `__lkp_DWH_Customers`
Suffixed __	Lookup source filter
	Ex: `lkp_DWH_Customers__`
Suffixed _p_	Persistent cache
	Ex: `lkp_DWH_Customers_p_`
Suffixed _np_	Named persistent
	Ex: `lkp_DWH_Customers_np_`
Suffixed _d_	Dynamic cache
	Ex: `lkp_DWH_Customers_d_`
Suffixed _dp_	Dynamic and persistent
	Ex: `lkp_DWH_Customers_dp_`
Suffixed _dnp_	Dynamic and named persistent
	Ex: `lkp_DWH_Customers_dnp_`
Prefixed and suffixed with __	More customizations. See properties
	Ex: `__lkp_DWH_Customers__`

Rank:

Prefixed	Sorted input
	Ex: `__rnk_Top_5_Customers`
Suffixed	
Both	

Sequence Generator:

Prefixed	Using current value
	Ex: `__seq_DWH_Cust_Key`
Suffixed	Incrementing more than 1 or caching values
	Ex: `seq_DWH_Cust_Key__`
Both	

SQL:

Suffixed with _qs_	Query mode. Static connection
	Ex: `sql_Get_ID_qs_`
Suffixed with _qd_	Query mode. Dynamic connection
	Ex: `sql_Get_ID_qd_`
Suffixed with _ss_	Script mode. Static connection
	Ex: `sql_Get_ID_qs_`
Suffixed with _sd_	Script mode. Dynamic connection
	Ex: `sql_Get_ID_sd_`
Suffixed	Auto Commit enabled
	Ex: `sql_Get_ID__`
Both	More customizations. See properties

Transaction Control:

Prefixed	Commit/Rollback before
	Ex: `__tc_Commit`
Suffixed	Commit/Rollback after
	Ex: `tc_Commit__`
None	Complex logic. See properties

28

Process control

Process control is simply the ability to monitor and control the DI processes in both technical and non-technical (business) perspectives. Implementing a process control is the key element in being able to monitor DI processes, especially when the application constitutes of hundreds of DI processes. Workflow Monitor is the default monitoring application for all PowerCenter processes that can visually represent the currently running and already executed workflows/sessions. The information is visually represented but not easy to extract programmatically for reporting and other purposes. This information is also extremely helpful in determining restartability when errors occur. The only way to extract this information out of repository is to query repository tables/views. Hence, many applications build their own process control information to keep track of workflow/session execution. There is more than one way to implement such process control approach. Each of these approaches has its corresponding pros and cons. However, the focus of this chapter will be purely to discuss various features available in PowerCenter to build a process control rather than the rights and wrongs of all the approaches. To build a proper process control design, one must clearly understand how the entire DI application is monitored from a business perspective. Building a process control without a business perspective will result in simply building a system that logs session and workflow runs with no additional value. The business perspective helps build a process control design that not only logs the execution information of sessions and workflows, but also maintains this data in a way that can be reported easily without any complex reporting tools.

 The goal of this chapter is not to recommend a process control approach but to introduce several features/design patterns that help in building one.

28.1   When to start thinking about it ?

It is a common myth that Process Control is one of the last elements to think about during design and development phase. But this is a complete myth. Architects and developers should start thinking about process control in parallel to the rest of the system design. In fact, thinking about process control from the beginning helps design an application that is modular. A modular application is relatively more scalable and service oriented. When a module within a modular application is to be modified, its impact on other modules/services is minimal, thus reducing the cost associated with its maintenance, and increasing ROI.

28.2   Understanding process control

Before we begin discussing the technical implementation of process control, we must first understand what is being logged and why. An application must be looked in a non-technical perspective and proper checkpoints must be identified. Once checkpoints are identified, the processes between the checkpoints can be further divided into workflows for proper technical implementation. The checkpoints also help build restart-ability and recovery into the system. To understand this better, let us take a look at a sample case study.

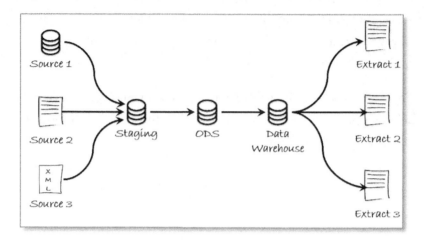

As shown in the above picture, the application has three sources: a database, a flat file and a XML file. All of this data is initially placed in corresponding Staging tables. Data is then cleansed and sent to Operational Data Store (ODS). Data from ODS is then sent through value-addition services, output of which is loaded to data warehouse. Data Warehouse provides extracts to downstream systems.

Now, say the entire data integration processes in this whole system run once a day. At a high level, the status of the application during the run can be summarized as:

Loading to Stage → Staged → Cleansed (loaded to ODS) → Valued Added (loaded to Data Warehouse) → Extracts Complete

The whole application may contain hundreds of workflows. However, at a high level business, users may be interested in only knowing the status as one of the above 6 steps, and not the status of each individual workflow. To achieve this, we require a system that can keep track of the workflows and session execution and send out alerts appropriately. This information can also be used to generate valuable reports such as "Which session has most failures?" or "Which session is the slowest of all?" This can also be used for status tracking. For example, completion of one or more workflows is determined as completion of a step (such as Staging) and beginning of another step (such as Cleansing).

28.3 Designing process control

To be able to provide proper status tracking, Process Control must be hierarchical. In the example mentioned above, let us say, each day we run all processes from staging to extracts and all these processes must complete within 24 hours so that they do not step on to next day's execution. Let us consider each of this as a "*Run*". In each run, we will perform all the steps from *Staging* to *Extracts* and there will be only one *Run* a day. In this example, we might design a process control with two relational tables: One to hold the master status and one to hold the detailed status. The master table might contain the following columns:

Run ID	A 12 digit unique ID for each run in the format: YYYYMMDDHH24MISS
Status	One of the possible values: INIT, STGD, CLNSD, DWH, EXTR, COMPL
Run_Start_Time	Time when run started
STGD_Compl_Time	Time when staging completed
CLNSD_Compl_Time	Time when cleansing completed
DWH_Compl_Time	Time when load to Data Warehouse completed
EXTR_Compl_Time	Time when extracts completed from DWH
Run_Compl_Time	Time when the run is considered complete

When a Run begins, we create a new entry into this master table with a new Run ID. Run ID is simply the date/timestamp of the second when the run started. When the run starts, workflows that read data from sources and load it to staging, will kick off. During this time, the Run status will be set to INIT (Initialized) and Run_Start_Time is set. Once the entire data load is complete, the status is changed to STGD (Staged) and STGD_Compl_Time is set. Now, the workflows that read staged data and perform cleansing are executed. This data loads the cleansed data to ODS. Once the data is loaded to ODS, Run status is set to CLNSD and the CLNSD_Compl_Time is set. Data then goes through value addition services and the final set of data is loaded to Data Warehouse. The status is then set to DWH and DWH_Compl_Time is set. Post Data Warehouse load, BI jobs can execute in parallel to extract jobs. When all extracts are completed, status is set to EXTR and EXTR_Compl_Time is set. This marks the completion of all DI jobs. However, there may be some maintenance tasks left over such as rebuilding indexes, re-enabling constraints etc. Once all the maintenance is complete, run is considered complete and the status is set to COMPL and Run_Compl_Time is updated.

By implementing these elaborate status updates, it is easy to track the entire run at a high level. This not only helps monitor different steps of the run in a way that makes sense to business users, but also provides valuable information such as "How long does it take to stage data?". Over time, we can trend and generate reports such as the one shown below. The session/workflow execution time can be easily translated into data that can be analysed and reported at a simpler level. The overwhelming session run information is aggregated and reported at a level that anyone can understand. This information is not only useful for the business users, but is also useful for architects and other technical folks for analysing the system performance and accordingly investing time and effort to improvise.

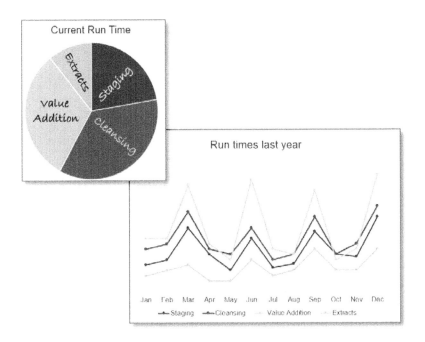

Now let us consider the detail table that supplements the information we added to the master table above. A detail table typically contains information at the most fundamental level – a mapping. Each mapping will be built to log its start time and end time (we will see how, later). All this information is captured along with the Run ID mentioned above so that it is tied back to a specific Run ID. The structure of a typical detail table is as follows:

Run ID	A 12 digit unique ID for each run in the format: YYYYMMDDHH24MISS. The Run ID in this table is a foreign key to the master table
Category	Category of the workflows. One of the possible values: STG, ODS, DWH, EXTR. This value is derived from the name of the workflow itself
Workflow	Name of the workflow

Mapping	Name of the mapping
Start_Time	Time when the mapping started
End_Time	Time when the mapping ended

Information in this table is useful in trending the details of execution of the workflows and sessions.

28.4 Implementation

Now that we understand the concept in theory, let us take a look at how to implement it. To do so, we should be able to achieve the following:

    a.   Create a Run ID at the beginning of the process
    b.   Use the Run ID in subsequent sessions, mappings
    c.   For every mapping, log the start time and end time
    d.   Update the Run Status

28.4.1   Creating the Run ID

The simplest way to create a Run ID is to add an INSERT statement in Pre-SQL in the first session of the first workflow. To make things more dynamic, this SQL Statement can be stored in a table or file and a mapping can be built to execute this dynamically using a SQL transformation. Such a mapping can be later used to execute SQL queries in other scenarios as well.

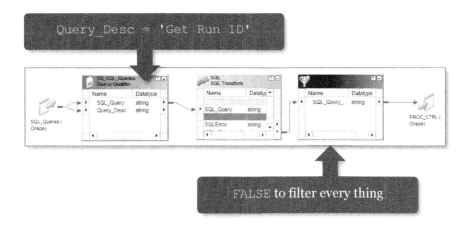

28.4.2   Using the Run ID in source qualifier

There are two ways of identifying the latest Run ID and using it in subsequent mappings. The first one is to simply read the process control master table in every source qualifier along with the corresponding source(s). So, if a Source qualifier has a query as below:

```
SELECT
        CUST_KEY, CUST_ID, FIRST_NAME
FROM
        CUSTOMER
```

It will now be modified as below:

```
SELECT
        (SELECT MAX(RUN_ID) FROM PROC_CTRL_MSTR) AS
RUN_ID,
        CUST_KEY, CUST_ID, FIRST_NAME
```

```
FROM

    CUSTOMER
```

This will fetch Run ID into every mapping. However, this process is tedious and also has several drawbacks. Some of them are:

→ To be able to get the Run ID, every source qualifier must be customized whether or not the mapping needs it

→ The process is very inefficient when there are complex joins of complex queries in the source qualifier

28.4.3   Using the Run ID through workflow variables

Another way of using a Run ID is to query the process control master table once for each workflow and then pass it on to other sessions through workflow/mapping parameters. To achieve this, the following is performed:

a. We create a mapping that reads Process Control Master (PROC_CTRL_MSTR) table and assigns the Run ID to a mapping parameter.

b. This session is created as the first session in a workflow. This workflow will also have a parameter to temporarily hold the Run ID.

c. This mapping parameter is then assigned to workflow parameter in the `Post Session on Success Variable Assignment` in the `Components` tab of the session properties.

d. In the subsequent sessions, the workflow parameter is assigned to the mapping parameter in the `Pre Session Variable Assignment` in the `Components` tab of the session properties.

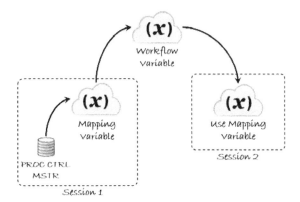

First, we create the mapping that reads the process control master table and gets the latest Run ID and assigns it to a mapping parameter. A Simple SQL Statement as below can be used to do so:

```
SELECT Max(Run_ID) as Run_ID FROM PROC_CTRL_MSTR
```

The mapping then assigns this value to a mapping parameter. To do so, an expression type mapping parameter is created within that mapping. The Run ID read from the Process Control Master table is assigned to the mapping parameter.

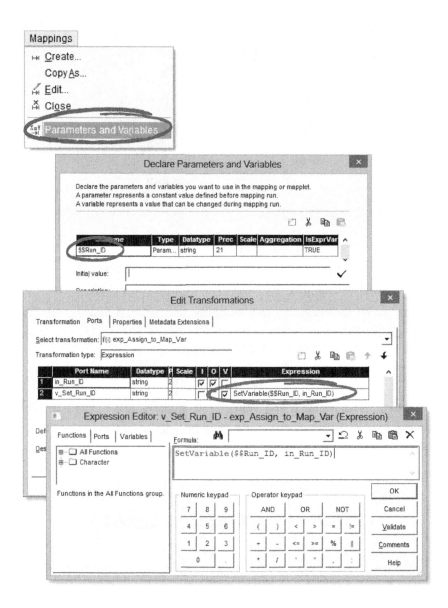

The `SetVariable` function can be used only once in a mapping. Hence, it is important to ensure that there is only one record that flows through the expression transformation. Once the value is assigned to the mapping parameter, this parameter needs to be passed over to workflow variables. So, create a workflow and a session for this mapping.

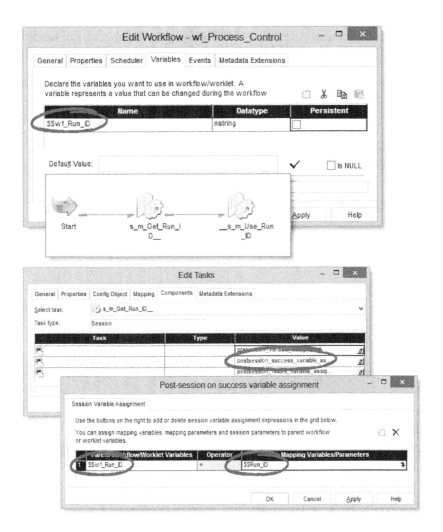

In the session properties, go to `Components` tab → `Post Session On Success Variable Assignment`. Then select the workflow parameter that receives the value and the mapping parameter that feeds into it. Once this session completes its execution, the mapping parameter value is now stored in the workflow parameter.

This workflow parameter can be passed on to subsequent session through `Pre Session Variable Assignment`. To do so, open the subsequent session properties, go to `Components` tab →`Pre Session Variable Assignment` and then select the mapping parameter that receives the value and the workflow parameter that feeds into it. It is important to note that every mapping that receives the value from the workflow variable must have a mapping parameter to hold the value.

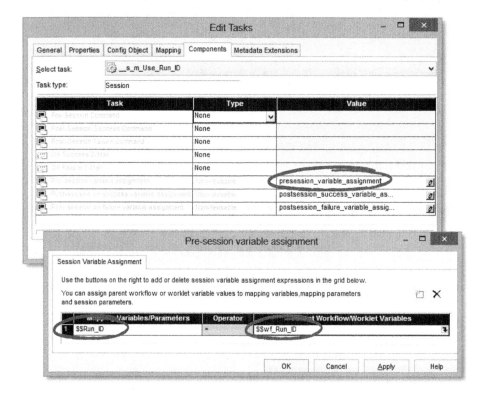

28.5 ProActive Monitoring

ProActive Monitoring for PowerCenter® (simply known as PMPC) is a product from Informatica®that allows you to monitor and proactively respond to different kinds of events in Informatica PowerCenter. ProActive Monitoring has many inbuilt rules to respond to workflows/sessions that are running late, sessions having source or target rejections, sessions or workflows that failed etc. ProActive Monitoring is capable of identifying events as and when they are happening. For example, an alert can be sent if a session is running 25% slower than its recent average. Unlike other monitoring tools, this alert is sent out while the session is still running. This gives a chance for maintenance group to fix and analyse the issue and act accordingly in time.

ProActive Monitoring has several services to fetch workflow, session run time information including start times, end times, etc. A new rule can be built in ProActive Monitoring to log information into Process Control tables whenever a workflow / session completes. The advantages of this approach are as follows:

a. Modular – The core DI logic is separated from Process Control logic

b. Scalable – ProActive Monitoring runs on RulePoint® framework which makes it scalable for enterprise level usage

c. Near real time – ProActive Monitoring's default services operate at near real time, hence the latency to log information in to process control tables is close to zero

d. Proactive – ProActive Monitoring can identify events and alert the users as and when the events are happening. While such logic can be custom built into the DI logic, it requires extensive time and effort

ProActive Monitoring for PowerCenter® is an independent product from Informatica and is not bundled with PowerCenter. Please contact your Informatica Administrator to find out if you are licensed for it.

29

Performance

Relative to programs developed in programming languages such as JAVA, DI processes developed in PowerCenter are naturally high performing. This performance comes from the architecture and framework that PowerCenter is built on. Performance of a DI process (just like any other program) depends a lot of on how it is developed. At times a DI process itself may be highly performing but in the grand scale of things, it may not be able to meet the performance requirement. Hence, when it comes to tuning the performance, we should follow both top-down approach as well as bottom-up approach.

29.1 Top-down or bottom-up?

In a top-down approach, we look at the entire architecture of the application and tune it at each level – the lowest being a single session. In a bottom-up approach, we start with improvising one session at a time and work our way up. While each of these approaches has its corresponding pros and cons, the best way to tune a DI application is to start with top-down and implement bottom-up. The combination of both the approaches provides fast and reliable results. To understand this in detail, let us look at the DWH application we discussed earlier.

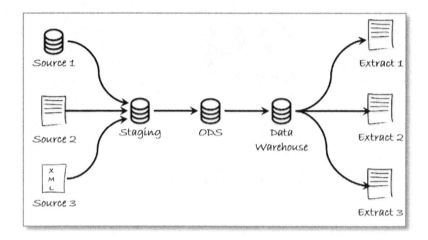

As a quick recap, in the application above, we have several sources that feed data into our staging environment, which then feeds into the Operational Data Store and then eventually the data loads into the Data Warehouse. At a later point in time, several extracts are provided from the Data Warehouse to downstream applications. Now applying to-down approach, we first identify what is the total time taken for end-to-end loads and what is the time taken for each step. Each step may contain several workflows, but we won't get into that detail yet. Let us look at the timings provided in the picture below.

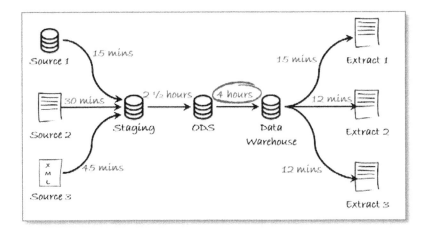

The total time taken from the point we receive source files to complete extracts is 7 ½ hours. This is calculated as follows:

a. Source to staging: 45 mins (longest of the 3 parallel jobs)

b. Staging to ODS: 2 ½ hours

c. ODS to Data Warehouse: 4 hours

d. Data Warehouse extracts: 15 mins (longest of the 3 parallel jobs)

Of all these steps, the longest running step is the ODS to Data Warehouse. Tuning this step will have the greatest impact on the end-to-end time. So, in a top-down approach, this will logically be the first step to look into.

Similarly, in a bottom up approach, we pick up the top 5 (for example) longest running workflows and analyze them to tune them to cause the maximum impact on the time taken end-to-end. So, let us say for example, the longest running workflow is the workflow that loads source 3 data into staging (highlighted in the picture in circled red), which is approximately 45 minutes. There are 5 different workflows that run between ODS to Data Warehouse and each of them are individually within 45 minutes. In this example, the longest running workflow between ODS to Data Warehouse is say, 15 minutes – almost 3 times slower than the longest running workflow.

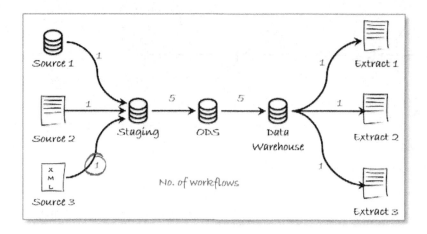

So, what do we choose? The result of top-down analysis or the result of bottom-up analysis? The best approach is to choose both. Remember that these are all possible candidates that we should look into before we make a decision. So, as a result of top-down analysis (5 workflows) and bottom-up analysis (1 workflow), we get a total of 6 candidates. We now have to consider all the 6 workflows to determine how well these can be tuned. Now, imagine, after thorough analysis, we are able to cut down the time taken by each of these 6 workflows by half, then we will be able to cut down the total time to approximately 5 hours.

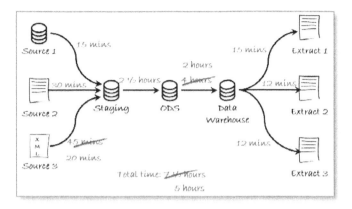

29.2   Can this mapping be tuned?

So far, we have identified a list of candidates that can be tuned purely based on the time they take. But how do we know if there is really any scope of improvement in these workflows/mappings? This is a very tricky question to answer. As a general principle, almost every process has some scope of improvement. But the real question is what do we gain by such improvement? We have to balance the time taken to tune the mapping/workflow and the time we gain. Within a workflow, we always start with the longest running session. We tune the mapping until it is optimized and then move on to the next longest running session. Once all the mappings within a workflow are tuned, the workflow run time is automatically optimized. The only exception to this approach is when we have several other tasks in the workflow that are not sessions. We will cover this scenario later. For now, we will focus on tuning the mappings.

To understand how to tune a mapping, we need to understand what is actually happening inside the mapping. Where is most of the time spent in the mapping? Let us take a look at an example.

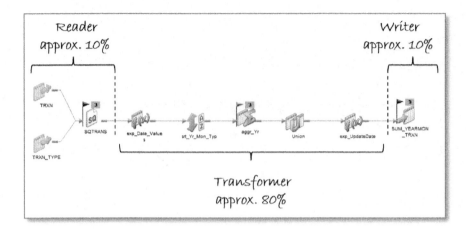

In a well-built mapping, most of the time is spent in transforming the data with minimal amount of time being spent to read the data from the source and to write to the target. When that is not the case, the mapping can be tuned to perform better.

In well-built mappings, the time DTM takes to perform transformations is more or less directly proportional to the number of active transformations. Hence, the more active the transformation is in a mapping, the longer it takes to execute. When DTM spends most of its time at one or more transformations instead of evenly spreading out, those transformations are blocking the data. Such mappings can also be tuned.

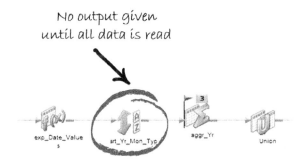

29.3 Bottleneck identification

A bottleneck is any object that is taking a longer time to run than it should. In a DI application, bottlenecks are easily identified by the time they take to complete their tasks. As we drill down, however, the bottleneck identification becomes more complex. For example, previously we have determined (with sample values) that the bottlenecks in our DWH system are workflows that run from ODS to DWH or the workflow that processes source 3 data into staging. Once we identify this and drill down, so that we can pinpoint the mappings, how do we know whether the bottleneck is the read or transform or write? The answer is simple: look in the session log. While we can't discuss the entire session log contents here, let us take a look at some of the important messages in session log that can help us identify bottlenecks:

Code	Message
RR_4049	SQL Query issued to database : (Thu Dec 12 07:16:45 2013)
RR_4050	First row returned from database to reader : (Thu Dec 12 07:16:46 2013)
WRT_8167	Start loading table [CUSTOMERS] at: Thu Dec 12 07:16:45 2013
BLKR_16008	Reader run completed

Code	Message
WRT_8168	End loading table [CUSTOMERS] at: Thu Dec 12 07:16:54 2013
WRT_8006	Writer run completed

Identification of a bottleneck can be easily performed by grabbing some quick estimates from the session log. For example, the time difference between `RR_4049 – SQL Query issued to database` and `RR_4050 – First row returned from database to reader` is us how long the source query ran in the database before a row is returned. This is a quick way of identifying the problem with the source query. It is important not to jump to conclusions while determining bottlenecks as things are not always what they seem. Sometimes, a bottleneck elsewhere may cause a ripple effect and slow down other processes. Let us consider a scenario of a writer bottleneck. When writer is too slow and takes longer to write each block of data, DTM and Reader will finish their current processing and will be waiting for the writer to start consuming blocks processed by DTM. Until writer consumes DTM's processed blocks, DTM cannot process Reader's processed blocks. Hence, at this point, both Reader and DTM are simply waiting for the Writer.

29.4 Identifying source bottlenecks

A source bottleneck exists when we spend more time reading the data than transforming it. When the read time contributes to the maximum percentage of the overall session runtime, a source bottleneck exists. Session log provides detailed information on when a query is issued to the database, when a first row is returned and when the reader finishes its reading. This information may not always be sufficient to determine a source bottleneck. A source bottleneck can be clearly identified when all that the mapping does is source data. To identify a source bottleneck, place a filter transformation immediately after the source qualifier and set its filter expressions as FALSE to filter out all rows. When this mapping runs, it will read all rows from the source (depending on the source qualifier configuration) and then filter them all in the memory. So, the time the mapping takes to execute is simply the Reader time. This approach works for any type of the source – relational, flat file, xml or any other type.

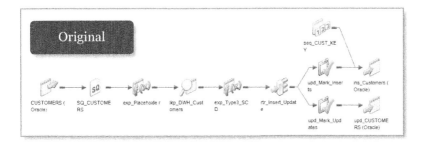

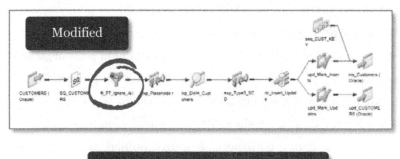

Identifying source bottlenecks

29.5 Resolving source bottlenecks

A source bottleneck usually means we are spending much more time trying to read from the data source(s) than transforming it. While working with relational sources, this usually means the SQL query we are using to run on the source database is not optimized. There may be several reasons why. Some of the most commonly found issues are:

- a. Incomplete or Invalid relationships
- b. Improper or no use of indexes
- c. Complex joins
- d. Tables are simply too big

29.5.1   Incomplete/invalid relationships

When we import table definitions into PowerCenter, PowerCenter uses the information available in its repository to generate default queries. When we import the table definitions, PowerCenter will try to analyse the tables and import any relationships associated with it. If the database user that we are using to import the table definitions does not have enough permission, PowerCenter may not be able to import the relationships (Primary Key, Foreign Key) into the Designer. If we have not properly or completely imported the table definitions and their relationships, the default query PowerCenter generates may not be optimized. This is especially true when we are joining several tables using source qualifier transformation. If the relationships are not properly imported, the query generated by PowerCenter may very well cause a Cartesian product.

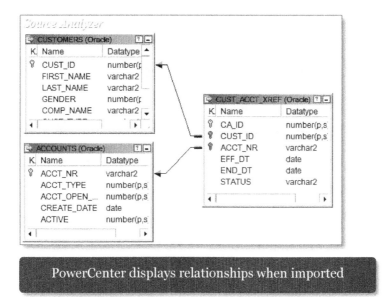

PowerCenter displays relationships when imported

29.5.2   Improper or no use of indexes

PowerCenter is not index-aware. It means that when PowerCenter builds queries to read source data, it does not take any indexes into account. It will primarily build a select statement (with joins if more than one table is involved) and run it against the database. You must look at the execution plan of the SQL to determine if appropriate indexes are being used. If the database is not executing the query as per your expectations, you can force it to use indexes by adding a hint. You add a hint in PowerCenter mapping's source qualifier by customizing the SQL query. You can use the generate SQL button to generate a default query and then add a hint to use an index.

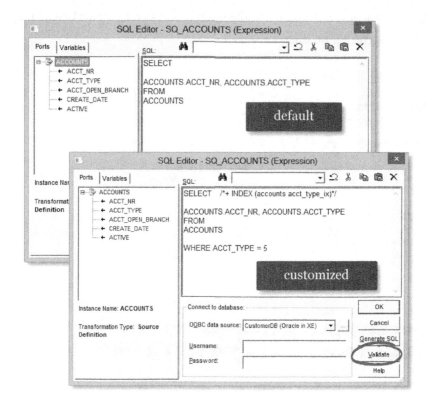

29.5.3   Complex joins

Similarly, when you have complex join, you can add hints such as USE_HASH (to force a hash join) in the same way we defined an index join. For more details on the hints, consult your database manual.

29.5.4   Tables that are too big

One of the most common source bottlenecks is too much data. When the source tables contain too much data, extracting it in a timely fashion is usually a challenge. Since the data is stored in tables that are external to the PowerCenter, we can use indexes and hints to force database to take a quicker path to retrieve the data. The overall read time can be optimized by increasing the Reader's efficiency in handling the data that is retrieved faster from the database. If the reader process and database are not operating at an approximately equal rate of data transfer, then we still have a read bottleneck. Let us look at these scenarios in detail:

If the database is not optimized to fetch data at a faster rate, then the reader process would wait for the database to provide more blocks. At this time, we see very busy system resources on the database but with little business on the PowerCenter side, simply because reader is waiting on the database. Unless reader can provide more blocks, DTM cannot transform them and Writer cannot write them. So the entire session goes into an inactive state.

If the source query and the database are tuned to fetch data at the most optimal rate, but the DTM and writer process are slow, this causes a bottleneck because reader cannot process the data as fast as the database can provide. When the first few blocks of data are retrieved from the database, they are processed by Reader, DTM and Writer. While DTM and Writer are processing their blocks, Reader goes back to source database to fetch more blocks. At this point, reader is fetching slower than the database can provide, which causes the database connection to be open longer and we see one or more inactive connections at the database level as they are simply waiting on the reader to come back to read more blocks.

Both of the above scenarios are bottlenecks and must be resolved. This can be performed in a couple of ways:

Partitioning:

Data can be partitioned preferably at both the database level and at the PowerCenter level. When the data is partitioned and we use pipeline partitioning in PowerCenter, we invoke several reader threads – one for each partition. Each of these partitions will fire a query on the database. Each query will retrieve a subset of the data. Each pipeline partition will process this subset of the data and load them to the target(s). Since each reader is associated with a database process that is only retrieving subset of data, the data is retrieved faster and consumed faster. Note that however, in this approach, we increase the number of connections made to the source database.

Early Filtering:

If data is being filtered in the mapping, it is recommended to move the filter in to the source, where possible. By placing the filter in the source database, we read less data in to PowerCenter mapping. When filters are applied at the source database level, care must be taken to use indexed fields. If the filtering is applied on non-indexed fields, full table scans may occur causing the mapping to run further slow. Analyse your execution plan to find out whether source filter is really improving the performance.

29.6 Identifying target bottlenecks

A target bottleneck exists when the session spends most of its runtime writing the transformed data to the target. Identifying target bottlenecks is very similar to identifying the source bottleneck. We calculate the difference in time of running the session "as-is" – in its original state and running the session without writing anything to the target. The difference in time will be the time the writer took. To ensure that the session doesn't write anything, we can place a filter transformation right before the target. If more than one target is present, we can place filters individually for each target to calculate the individual writer timings.

The filter before target approach can be used for any kind of target – relational or not. The idea here is to run the mapping like the original with only exception being that we don't write data to target. For some types of targets, the same effect can be achieved differently as well. In the example shown above, instead of creating a filter transformation in the mapping, we can also add an update override in the target transformation such as $1 = 2$. This will cause a where clause to be generated for the update as WHERE $1 = 2$. Since 1 and 2 are never equal, this update will never execute. Another way to identify a target bottleneck is also to write to a flat file instead of the relational target. Flat file reads and flat file writes take negligible amount of time. This can be changed either in the mapping or in the session properties. In the session properties, select target, on the right hand side, change Relational writer to Flat File writer.

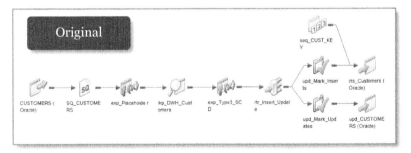

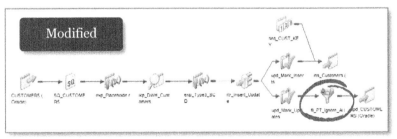

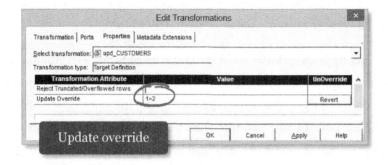

29.7 Resolving target bottlenecks

A target bottleneck usually means that we are spending too much time trying to write the data into the target. In PowerCenter, time taken to write to a flat file is negligible. So, typically a target bottleneck occurs in relational databases when we try to update/delete rows. Inserts are, as a rule of thumb, much faster than updates and deletes. However, inserts can also be very slow when the volume of data we are inserting is way too high.

29.7.1   BULK loads and indexes

When we have huge volumes of data that needs to be inserted, using conventional approach is very slow. In a conventional approach, we set the row status as INSERT either at session level or within the mapping. When we run such a session, PowerCenter issues INSERT statements to the database for each row. If there are one or more indexes on the table, the indexes will be updated as we commit the data. When we are loading huge volumes of data, we may notice that in the end-to-end run, the database spends more time updating the indexes than inserting the rows. This usually happens when the table we are loading has a lot of data and we are adding more. So, it is a good idea to temporarily disable all the indexes, load the data and then re-enable them so that the indexes are updated only once – after the load is complete. This can be performed using the Pre-SQL and Post-SQL. A disable index statement can be added in the Pre-SQL of the session and a re-enable index statement can be added in the Post-SQL. In such a method, we can also change the Target Load Type to BULK so that PowerCenter is aware that it can do a bulk load instead of individual INSERTs.

 In some databases, you MUST disable the indexes to perform a BULK load; otherwise, the session will fail

29.7.2   Updates

Updates traditionally are very slow in the relational databases. When we have to perform a large number of updates, especially in change detection processes, they consume a lot of time. Unfortunately, improving update performance is not as easy as with inserts. One of the possible methods to achieve faster updates is to temporarily store all the records that need to be updated in a staging table and then perform a database level update statement. Let us look at this approach in detail.

a.   Create a staging table that will temporarily hold all records that need to be updated

b.   Empty the staging table before the PowerCenter session runs (either manually or by placing a truncate query in the Pre-SQL) of the session

c.   Modify the PowerCenter session, such that it inserts records into staging table instead of main table. Since the staging table is emptied for every run and we are performing only inserts, the process is much faster

d.   Now run a SQL statement to update the data in the main table, directly reading from the staging table

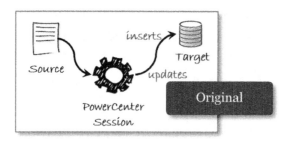

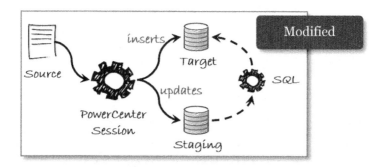

The staging table will have exactly the same format as the main target table – only the main target table will be persistent, whereas the contents of the staging table

will be deleted after the end of every run or at the beginning of the next run. The PowerCenter session will be modified to have two targets. All records that need to be inserted will directly go in to the main target table and the updates will be inserted into the staging table. Once the PowerCenter session execution is complete, the records in the main target table will be updated from the staging table contents. Sample syntax of such Correlated Update query is provided here. Please consult your database manual for a complete and accurate syntax.

```
UPDATE TgtTable Tgt SET (col1, col2) =

(SELECT Stg.col1, Stg.col2 FROM StgTable Stg

 WHERE Tgt.id = Stg.id

)

 WHERE EXISTS

(SELECT 1 FROM StgTable Stg WHERE Tgt.id = Stg.id )
```

29.8 Identifying transformation bottlenecks

Identifying the transformation bottlenecks is the most difficult part in identifying the bottlenecks. Before we attempt to identify a transformation bottleneck and resolve it, we must have already identified and eliminated source and target bottlenecks. When a mapping is running slower than it should and source and target are not the bottlenecks, then the mapping has transformation bottleneck. However, the key lies in finding out which transformation(s) are the bottleneck(s). To understand this, first we must understand the root cause of a transformation bottleneck. If all the transformations are built-in and optimized by Informatica, why will there still be a transformation bottleneck? Transformation bottlenecks do not occur because certain transformations are used. They occur when certain transformations are used in certain way for a given data flow. In practice, there are some usual suspects. Active transformations tend to take a longer time to process the data they receive than the passive transformations. To understand this, let us consider a mapping with Source→Source qualifier→Expression→Target. When this mapping runs, once the reader reads a block of data and passes it over to expression, expression transformation has everything it needs and hence will continue performing its calculations and pass the transformed data to the target. Now, if a sorter is added in this mapping after the source qualifier, the mapping will be Source →Source qualifier →Sorter →Expression →Target. When this mapping is executed, reader reads a block of data and passes it on to the sorter. Sorter receives the data and sorts it. Sorter, however, does not, by default, send the block data out to expression. This is an important differentiator, since the data in the two blocks may overlap when sorted. This forces the sorter to *not* output any data until all the input is read in, thus, slowing down the mapping.

Now, if we add an aggregator transformation right after the sorter, aggregator will also need all the input data before it can group the data together. However, since we sorted the data before it, it can flush out a group as soon as it is created. In sorted data, once a group is identified, it is guaranteed that there are no more records in the rest of the data that belong to this group. Hence the aggregator in this case will not be a transformation bottleneck, whereas the sorter will be. Analysing transformation bottlenecks is not as easy as other bottlenecks. Though, in this section, we look at some ways of identifying obvious bottlenecks.

29.8.1   Collect performance data

We can gather performance statistics every time a session runs. Performance statistics provide additional information about each transformation in the mapping. Performance statistics, when enabled, create an additional file in the same location as session log. This file contains information related to a number of records flowing in and out of each transformation. These counts are also very helpful when transformations such as filters, routers and aggregators are used. These counts help us map the data flow by looking at where the data is getting filtered / aggregated and by how much. When we choose to collect performance data, we can also optionally store the performance data in the repository for later reference. To turn on performance data collection, go to `Session Properties` → `Properties` **tab** → `Performance` **section** → **check the** `Collect Performance data.` **Check the** `Write Performance data to Repository` to store this information in the PowerCenter repository for later reference.

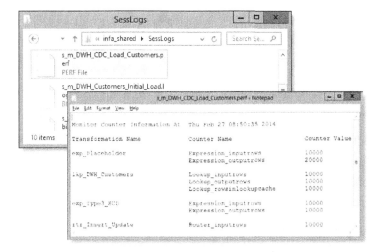

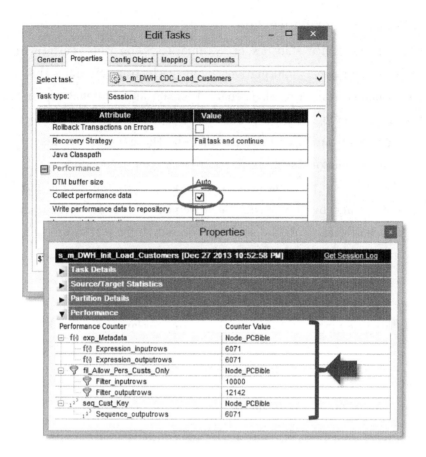

29.8.2   Session logs

When we collect performance data, session logs contain additional information about the transformation. One such example is shown below. The session log snapshot below show the transformation `exp_Metadata` receives `6071` records from `fil_Allow_Personal_Custs_Only` and sends `6071` records to the `CUSTOMERS` table with 0 dropped rows. If there are any transformation errors, the dropped rows will reflect accordingly.

TT_11034   [seq_Cust_Key]: Input - 0
TT_11038   Output - 6071,   Dropped - 0
TT_11031   Transformation [exp_Metadata]:
TT_11114   [exp_Metadata]: Input Group Index = [0], Input Row Count [6071]
TT_11034   [fil_Allow_Pers_Custs_Only]: Input - 6071
TT_11115   [exp_Metadata]: Output Group Index = [0]
TT_11037   [CUSTOMERS1]: Output - 6071,   Dropped - 0

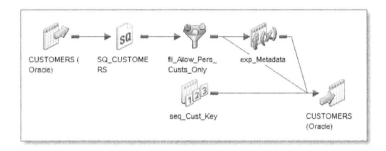

29.8.3   Transformation errors

Transformation errors slow down the mapping. When a transformation error occurs, PowerCenter needs to capture the error rejection reason, write to session log, skip the row and then move onto the next row in the block. This causes overhead on the PowerCenter Integration Service. While the overhead for a single row is almost negligible, when the transformation errors happen in thousands and millions, it adds up.

29.8.4   Implicit conversions

When data types mismatch, PowerCenter will attempt an intrinsic data conversion. For example, if a string variable is being assigned a numeric value, PowerCenter will automatically convert the number to string. This is known as implicit conversion. For implicit conversion to happen, data types must be compatible. For example, a numeric value can be implicitly converted to a string, but an intrinsic conversion for a numeric value to date will fail. When such a conversion is needed, it is always recommended to explicitly use a conversion function such as TO_CHAR.

29.9 Resolving transformation bottlenecks

While resolving a transformation bottleneck, a different approach is to be applied for every kind of bottleneck. In this section, we will look at some of the most commonly applied resolutions.

29.9.1 Sorted input

Transformations such as aggregators and joiners rely on the order of the data. By pre-sorting the data that flows into these transformations, their performance can be boosted. When the data flowing into an aggregator is already sorted, it becomes easy for the aggregator to group the data together. Additionally, when the input data is sorted, aggregator can send out the groups that it has processed instead of waiting till all the data is processed. This does not affect data integrity because the data is already sorted, which guarantees that the data for the current group does not appear after the group is complete. However, active transformations such as aggregators and joiners do not have a way to automatically identify if the data is pre-sorted. We need to let these transformations know that the input is already sorted. To do so, we check the Sorted Input property in the transformation properties.

29.9.2 Transformation scope

Transformation scope defines the extent of a transformation. All passive transformations such as expressions have the default transformation scope as Row. Passive transformations do not perform cross row operations and hence are limited in their scope. By default, all active transformations have the transformation scope as `All Input`. This means that the active transformation needs all the input before it will generate an output row. This is true for any active transformation that is not customized. As we have discussed earlier, transformations such as sorters and aggregators need all the input before they can generate an output row. In some scenarios such as sorted input, an active transformation may not have to wait for all the input but can process blocks of data. In these scenarios, active transformations can be configured to have their scope limited to `Transaction`. When the transformation scope is set to `Transaction`, the active transformation will flush any data that is completely processed every time it receives a commit signal from the Integration Service. For example, an aggregator that receives sorted input can flush all the groups it has formed so far when a commit signal is received. Since the input data is already sorted, all the groups, except the current one, can be sent out to subsequent transformation. While this is more of a functional feature rather than performance, this has direct impact on performance. As depicted in the picture below, when transformation scope is set to Transaction, the subsequent transformation (writer in this example) starts as soon as the aggregator processes 1st block of data. Though the total duration of the writer in this case is longer, the overall runtime is drastically reduced as the writer is performing most of its writing in parallel to the aggregator.

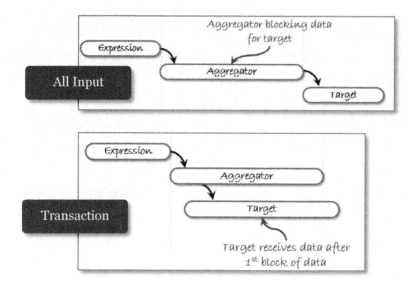

29.9.3   Incremental aggregation

When aggregators are used to perform aggregations on huge volumes of data, it takes a lot of time. In data warehousing scenarios, the aggregations calculated in every day's delta often needs to be accumulated to form monthly/quarterly aggregations. In such scenarios, incremental aggregation can be used to eliminate the need to recalculate the aggregations. When incremental aggregation is turned on, the session preserves the aggregator's cache so that it can be used as a base for the subsequent session runs. This eliminates the need to reprocess all the rows again and again.

29.9.4   Controlled data flow

A key aspect in improving the performance of a mapping is not to process data that is not needed. Consider a mapping where a lot of sorting and aggregations happen followed by a filtering logic. If the filter is eliminating approximately 25% of the data, then the sorter and aggregator are unnecessarily processing 25% additional data. This can be avoided by filtering the data as much as possible towards the beginning of the mapping rather than towards the end of it. It is also not uncommon to split the filter into two, such that a filter is placed at the beginning of the mapping to filter as much as possible and then have the filter at its original location to filter any computed data after aggregations.

29.10 Caches

29.10.1   Joiner caches

When joiner transformations are used, PowerCenter Integration Service caches the master data and then joins the detailed data as it comes in. Hence, several techniques can be used to improve the join performance.

Sorted Input for Master:

When the master data flowing into the joiner is sorted and the joiner's `Sorted Input` is checked, joiner will be able to cache the master data faster and would also be able to build the index at high speed.

Smaller dataset for Master:

Since the entire master data is cached, select the smaller of joiner's two data sets as a master to improve the performance. Huge joiner caches can lead to memory overspill and hence paging. If PowerCenter cannot fit all the data in the cache in memory, it overflows to disk. A disk operation is of higher cost in terms of time and hence should be avoided by all means.

29.10.2 Lookup caches

Lookup loads the entire result set of the lookup query into a cache. Cache is then indexed. Hence, lookup cache has performance overhead if not tuned properly. Following techniques can be used to improve the performance of lookup caches.

Cache columns:

Cache size can be huge if a lot of unwanted data is loaded into the cache. Hence, avoid reading all the data into the cache, unless needed. Select only the columns that are needed to lookup and return into the lookup cache. If two columns are participating in the lookup condition and only one column needs to be returned back, modify the lookup query to select only 3 columns.

Cache rows:

Similar to the number of columns, number of rows that are read into a lookup transformation must also be controlled. Avoid reading all the records in a given data set into the lookup, unless need be. Lookup's condition can be used to filter out any rows that do not have to be loaded into the cache.

Row order:

To be able to read lookup data in an optimal way, override the default ORDER BY clause generated by PowerCenter Integration Service with a set of columns that are indexed at the database level. This improves the query read performance while building the lookup caches.

Concurrent caches:

"`Additional Concurrent Pipelines for Lookup Cache Creation`" is a session property (`Config Object` tab) that can be used to control the number of parallel lookup caches that can be built. With Auto setting, PowerCenter will build all lookup caches in parallel.

Prebuilding caches:

By default, PowerCenter Integration service starts building a lookup cache, when the lookup receives its first input row. This behaviour can be modified with the session property "`Pre-build lookup cache`" in `Config Object` tab. If this property is set to "`Always allowed`", PowerCenter will start building lookup caches in the session initialization itself. If you have several unconnected lookup transformations, delaying the cache building may give a slight performance boost during session initialization.

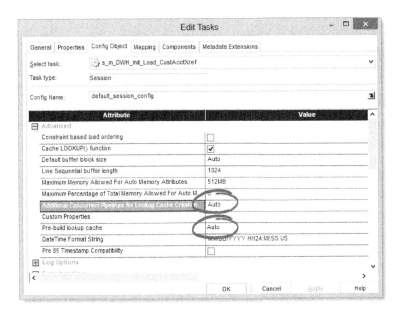

29.11 Scalability

29.11.1   GRID computing

A Session runs as a process in the operating System. When a workflow has multiple parallel sessions, PowerCenter invokes multiple processes on the same host machine by default. If the host machine has enough resources, PowerCenter can scale vertically to utilize those resources. If the resources required by the sessions are not available on the host machine, PowerCenter allows us to scale horizontally using the enterprise GRID functionality. When a workflow is executed on a GRID, PowerCenter Integration Service will automatically load balance the sessions across all the hosts upon which the integration service is running. PowerCenter can be configured to either distribute the sessions in a round robin fashion or by resource availability on the nodes. Either way, PowerCenter can have a workflow automatically scale across different nodes to best utilize the system resources. PowerCenter's Session on Grid functionality allows us to configure a session to be executed across several nodes.

29.11.2   Pushdown optimization

Pushdown optimization is the ability to "push" logic to source/target database(s). Performing complex calculations, at times, can cause transformation bottlenecks. Sometimes, performing these calculations/aggregations in the database engine may make more sense. Best example is when we need sorted input into aggregators and joiners. In such a case, we can push down the sorting logic to underlying database, where it can be optimally performed. Database engine can leverage indexes on the table to sort the data as needed. Hence use push down optimization as necessary to push appropriate logic to database and improve transformation performance.

29.11.3   Pipeline partitioning

When processing huge volumes of data using a single partition/thread is not efficient, we use Pipeline partitioning. Pipeline partitioning can be used on logical groups of data. Semi static fields such as state code, day of the month, etc are used to partition the data. Once partitioned, data can be processed in parallel by different pipelines of the same session. Use pipeline partitioning when rows are not important and data can be logically grouped into partitions. For optimal performance, align PowerCenter partitioning with source/target database partitions.

29.12 Memory

With regards to memory, PowerCenter allows us to customize the memory settings at session level. Two most important parameters in this regard are: DTM buffer size and buffer block size.

29.12.1   DTM buffer size

DTM buffer size is the total amount of memory PowerCenter allocates to DTM. Increasing DTM buffer size causes PowerCenter to create more buffer blocks and vice versa. Increasing DTM buffer size provides only initial performance boost as PowerCenter can create more blocks of data. Once all blocks are read, DTM buffer size will have minimal impact on the session performance.

29.12.2   Buffer block size

Buffer block size plays a vital role in performance tuning of a session. A block is made of a set of rows. Default buffer block size is 512MB. PowerCenter will read and write data in terms of blocks. To improve the session performance, configure the buffer block size to be a factor of the row size. A row size can be calculated by adding up the maximum lengths of data for each column in a row. For example, if a row contains 3 string fields of length 10, 20 and 30 characters, the total row size is

60 characters. Having a buffer block size as a multiple of 60 improves the session performance. When different transformations/sources/ targets use different lengths for the same port, choose the largest column size.

29.12.3 Auto memory settings

The default buffer block size is set to Auto. At session level, we can configure the default values for the auto setting using the session property "Maximum memory allowed for Auto memory attributes". This option has a default value of 512MB. Configure this option to specify a default value for all transformations with "auto" memory setting. We can specify the memory in different units such as KB, MB or GB by suffixing these reserved words. If none of the reserved words are specified, PowerCenter will treat the values as bytes. Here are some examples. Note that there is no space between number and the suffix:

Usage	Meaning
512	512 bytes
512KB	512 Kilo bytes
512MB	512 Mega bytes
2GB	20 Giga bytes

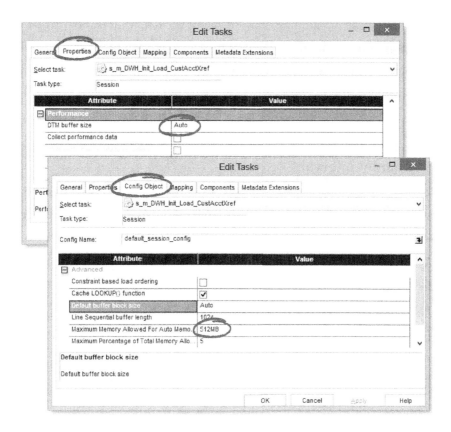

29.13 Other techniques

There are many other miscellaneous techniques that can be used to improve the performance of a workflow/session.

29.13.1   Source based commit

When transformation bottlenecks are present, source based commit is helpful in momentarily boosting the performance. When source based commit is setup, PowerCenter issues a commit signal after every 10K rows (default commit interval) are read. When a commit signal is issued, all active transformations with transformation scope as "Transaction", flush out the data that is ready so far. In a mapping, where a lot of data is read and some data is written to the target, source based commit helps flush the data out of the buffers more often and hence clear up buffers for upcoming data.

29.13.2   Commit interval

Commit interval is the frequency at which PowerCenter issues a commit signal. The default value is 10K rows. It is important to understand that PowerCenter does not exactly commit at the interval specified but uses it in conjunction with the block size to determine the optimum commit point. Commit interval can be decreased to increase the frequency of commits. This is used in scenarios where the amount of memory available for database buffers is limited and data needs to be committed frequently.

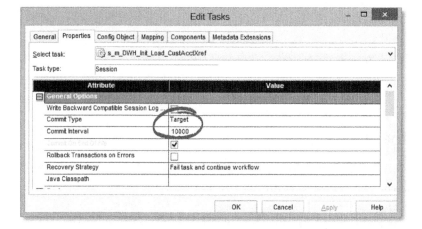

30

Internationalization, Unicode data

As part of enterprise data integration, it is important to process global data. Global data typically represents data in multiple languages. PowerCenter can process data in many languages. A code page defines the character set for a given language. UTF-8 and UTF-16 are some examples of such code pages. They can represent any character defined in the Unicode character set. UTF stands for UCS (Universal Character Set) Transformation Format. PowerCenter is a Unicode application. However, to access Unicode data using PowerCenter, we must accurately set the PowerCenter's data movement mode and the host's locale settings. The actual settings depend on the type of data we intend to process. While the Unicode standard constitutes several character sets, PowerCenter uses UCS-2 internally. PowerCenter converts all input data into UCS-2 format, processes them and converts them back to target character set before writing. This conversion is intrinsic and is completely transparent to the developers or administrators.

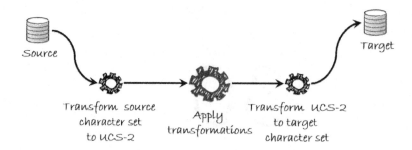

30.1 PowerCenter repository service

When PowerCenter repository service is created, administrator selects the code page in which the repository is to be created. This selection is based on the kind of metadata that you would like to store within the repository. When PowerCenter repository is created in a code page, repository allows its metadata to contain compatible characters. This metadata includes object names, comments, metadata extensions, etc. For example, a repository service created in UTF-8 encoding of Unicode can contain simplified Chinese characters as shown in the picture below.

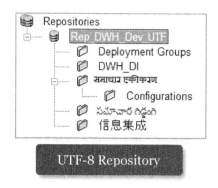

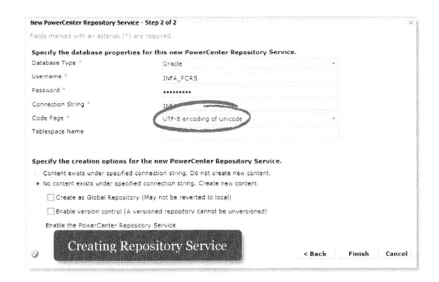

30.2 PowerCenter integration service

When a PowerCenter Integration service is created, administrator selects the data movement mode to be ASCII / Unicode and also selects the code page in which integration service will process the data. A Unicode Integration Service can process data in any compatible code page including UTF-8. An Integration Service can only process code pages supported by the underlying node's operating system. Windows, UNIX and Linux operating systems (and their variations) have different code page support.

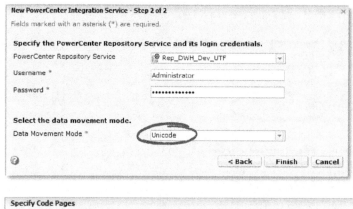

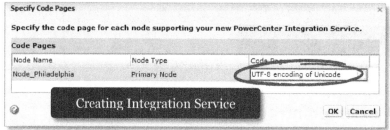

 For a complete list of supported code pages, please refer to your operating system's manual and the PowerCenter manual

30.3 Working with database code pages

While reading from or writing to a relational database, database code page settings and the database client code page settings have to be taken into consideration. Before a mapping is built and executed, the following steps must be executed:

a. Configure database client on the PowerCenter Integration Service nodes to be same code page as their corresponding databases.

b. Create relational connections in Workflow Manager and specify the corresponding database code page. This will be discussed in detail later.

c. Configure all nodes that integration service runs on to have a compatible code page.

d. Have a Unicode integration service that has code page compatible with source/target databases

30.3.1   Relational connections

Before configuring relational connections in PowerCenter, developers must know the underlying database settings. Connections created in the workflow manager are merely letting PowerCenter know what to expect when it communicates with the corresponding database.

 Please contact your database administrator to find out the code page of your database

Once you have the code page details from your DBA, the same settings can be applied for the source/target relational connections in the workflow manager. To open the relational connections, open the workflow manager and go to `Connections`→`Relational`. Relational Connection Browser appears. For a new connection, click `New…` and then select the database type. If a connection already exists, select the connection and click `Edit…` Snapshots for some of the databases are shown here.

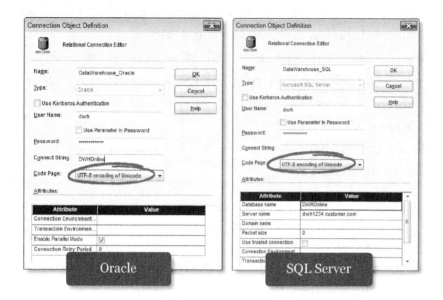

30.4 Working with flat files

Though theoretically more simpler, the biggest challenge with processing flat files containing multi-byte characters is the lack of knowledge of the exact code page in which the file was created. Unlike relational tables, flat files do not have any metadata, hence it is almost impossible to accurately recognize the code page in which a file is created after it was created. The only authentic way of identifying a file's code page is to know the code page in which the source system created it. Once the code page for the file is determined, this code page must be specified within the PowerCenter so that PowerCenter can interpret the file accurately. When importing the flat file, we can let PowerCenter Designer know the code page of the source file so that the flat file definition is created accordingly. Code page of a flat file definition can also be changed at a later stage. Once the definition is imported, switch to the `Source Analyzer`, edit the source by double clicking on it, go to the Table tab →Advanced button and update the code page as shown in the snapshots.

Once a mapping is built and a session, workflow is created, code page settings can also be overridden at the session level. To configure the code page at the session level, edit the session properties, go to Mapping tab → select the source / target file → in the Properties pane, click Set File Properties. Flat File Source (Target) dialog box will be displayed. Select the file you wish to change and then click Advanced... The File properties dialog box is then displayed. Select a codepage and then click OK to close the dialog box. Code page defined in the session properties overrides all other settings.

Code page of a flat file can be dynamically set using a workflow variable. Define the workflow variable in the session properties

PART 5

DATA INTEGRATION USING INFORMATICA DEVELOPER

31

The new platform

Informatica's DQ platform is the next generation framework that hosts Data Quality, Data Services and other products of Informatica. In this chapter, we look at an introduction to the DQ platform and some basic operations in it. Unlike PowerCenter that has many thick clients, DQ platform has a single thick client – Informatica Developer → tool. Developer can be used to develop mappings and execute them. Conceptually, DQ platform is similar to PowerCenter. DQ platform contains Model Repository Service (similar to PowerCenter repository service) that interacts with Developer client and stores all DQ objects in the repository (database tables). Model Repository is also organized into folders. These folders can contain Physical Data Objects (similar to table definitions in PowerCenter), transformations, mapplets and mappings. All these objects are conceptually similar to PowerCenter. All mappings developed in Informatica Developer are executed using Data Integration Service (runtime engine similar to PowerCenter Integration Service). Unlike PowerCenter, mapping execution can be directly monitored in the Developer itself. It is also possible to view data preview in the developer itself without having to build the complete mapping. In this chapter, we will understand the basics of the Developer tool.

31.1   First time configuration

To use developer, we must first register the domain and the model repository we wish to use by performing the following steps:

a.   Open the Developer tool

b.   Go to `File` menu →`Connect to Repository`

c.   `Connect to repository` dialog box appears

d.   Click `Configure Domains...`

e.   `Preferences` dialog box appears

f.   In the add domains section, click `Add...`

g.   `New Domain` dialog box appears

h.   Provide the domain name, host name and port number

i.   Use `Test Connection` to test the details and click `Finish`

j.   The domain name is now added in the `Preferences` dialog box. Click `OK` to close

k.   You are now back in the `Connect to repository` dialog box. Click `Browse...`

l.   Expand the domain name and select the model repository service and click `OK`

m.   The domain name and repository name are now displayed in the 'connect to repository' dialog box. Click `Next`

n.   Provide username and password and click `Finish`

o.   The repository is now added to the `Object Explorer`

p.   In future, to connect to the model repository, Right click the repository name in the `Object Explorer` and click `Connect`

q.   Type in your username and password and click `Connect`

31.2 Adding a project

Projects are created within a repository to organize code. Projects can contain folders. The following steps need to be performed to add a project in the developer tool.

a. To add a project in the Developer, right click on the model repository in the Object Explorer and click Connect.

    1. Provide your username and password and click connect

b. Once connected, right click the model repository and select New→Project

c. New project dialog box appears

    1. Provide a new project name and click Next

    2. Select the users and provide them appropriate permissions on the project and click Finish

d. Project appears in the Object Explorer

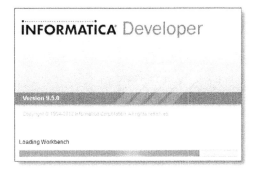

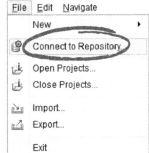

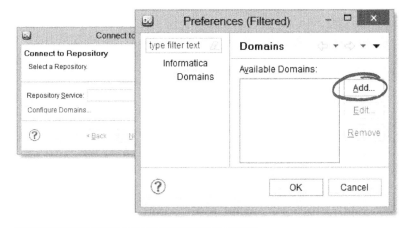

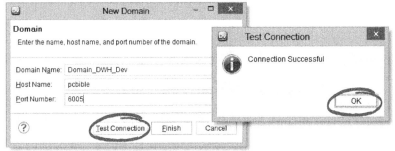

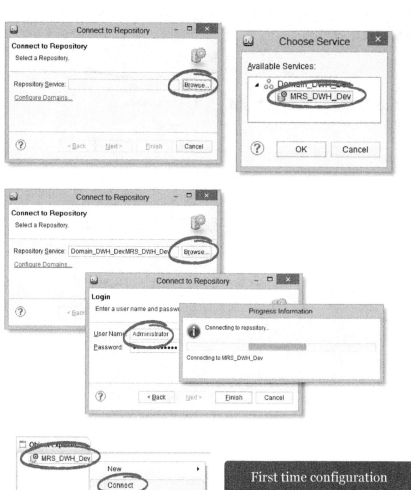

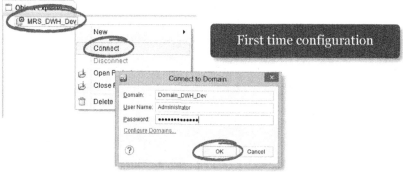

First time configuration

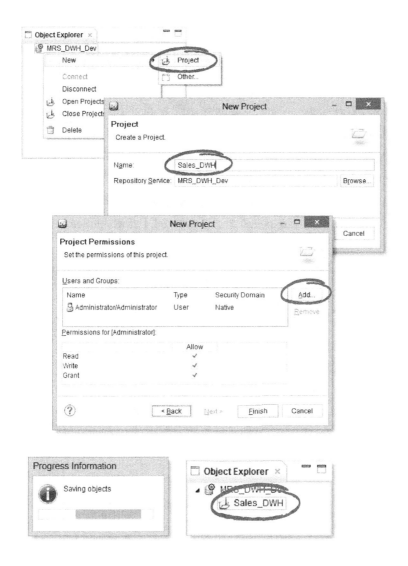

Project Setup

31.3   Developer UI

Developer tool is built on Eclipse framework. Let us take a look at the Developer UI and understand various components. Below are some of the main components:

a.   Workspace: Workspace is the primary work area within Developer tool. This is where we develop mappings, edit the physical data objects, etc.

b.   Object Explorer: Object explorer contains a list of all the objects in the model repository in a hierarchical fashion.

c.   Connection Explorer: Contains a list of (usually a subset of) connections in the domain. A connection needs to be created before tables and other objects are created in the Developer workspace.

d.   Properties Pane: When an object is selected in the workspace, properties pane shows various properties of that object. Properties pane contains several vertical tabs to switch between categories of the properties.

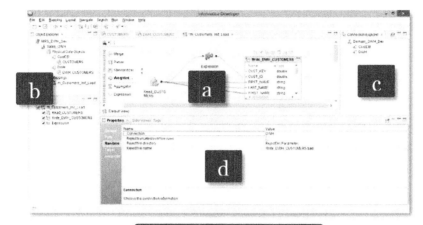

Developer UI

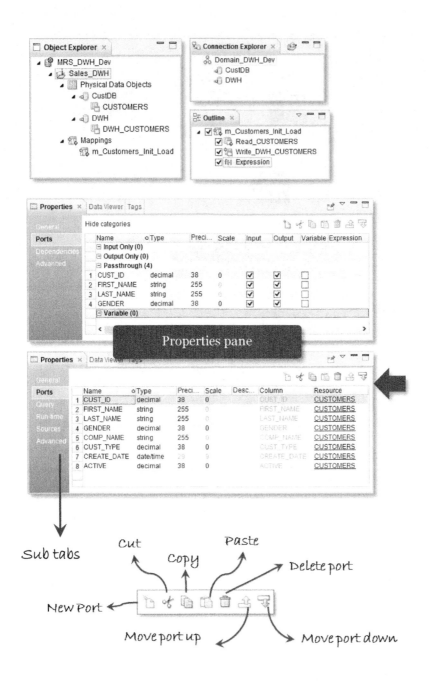

Sub tabs in a tab

Workspace tabs

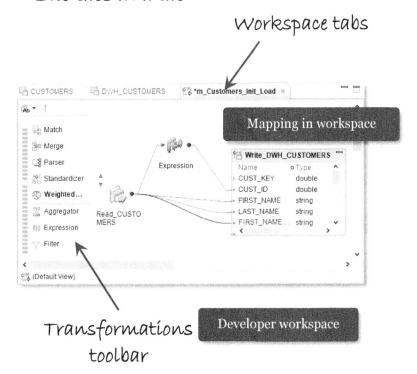

Transformations
toolbar

32

Building jobs in Informatica Developer

Creating a mapping and executing it in new platform is conceptually the same as PowerCenter, though the user interface varies quite a bit. In this chapter, we look at all the steps required to create a mapping and successfully execute it in the new platform.

32.1 Connections

Connections can be created in PowerCenter Administrator web console that can be used in the Developer tool. Follow the steps given below to create a connection in the administrator:

a. Go to `Administrator` console

b. Go to `Domains` tab →`Connections` sub tab

c. Right click the domain name →`New`→`Connection`

d. Select the connection database type (such as `Oracle`)

e. Provide username, password, connection string details and click `Finish`

f. Connection is created

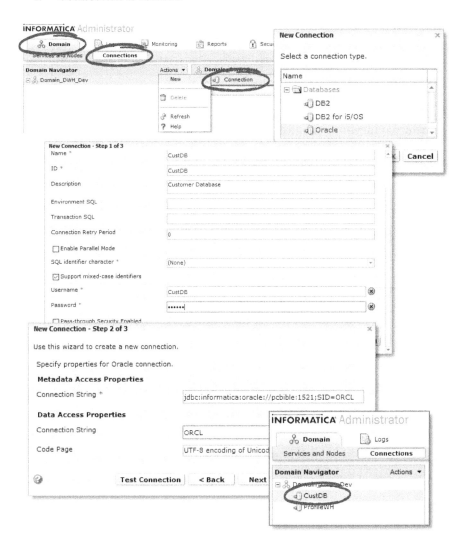

32.2 Physical data objects

Just like in PowerCenter, to begin developing a mapping, we need to import the source and target definitions first. These are known as Physical Data Objects (PDOs).

a. Connect to the Model Repository

b. Open the project where you would like to create a mapping

c. Ensure connections are already created

d. Add the connections in the developer tool

    1. In the `Connection Explorer`, right click → Click `Select Connections`

    2. `Select Connections` dialog box appears

    3. In the available connections, expand the domain and select a connection and click ">"

    4. Connection will be added to selected connections. Click `OK` to close the dialog

    5. Connection will appear in the `Connection Explorer`

e. Create a new physical data object for source

    1. Right click on the project/folder and click `New`→`Data Object`

    2. New Wizard appears

    3. Select `Physical Data Object`→`Relational Data Object`

    4. Select a connection, where this object (table) exists

    5. Select `Create data object from existing resource` and click `Browse…`

    6. Select the table you want the object to be associated with

    7. Click `Finish` to save the physical data object

f. Create a new physical data object for target

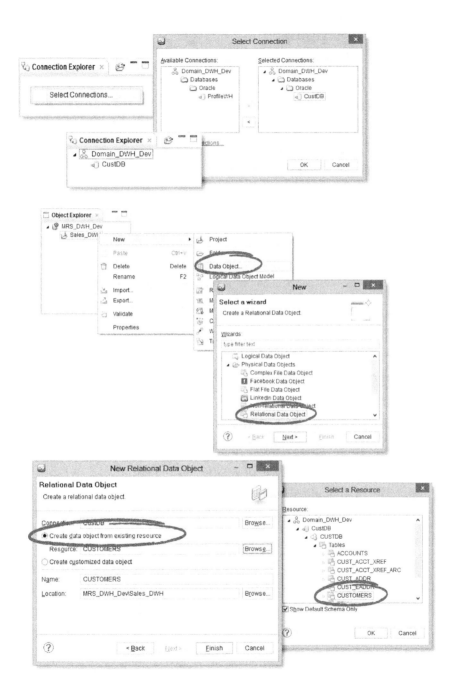

32.3 Creating a mapping

Before a mapping is created, ensure that you have setup connections and have imported the physical data objects into model repository. To create a mapping, follow these steps:

a. Connect to model repository

b. Open the project where you want to create the mapping

c. Create a mapping

    1. Right click on the project/folder and click New→Mapping

    2. Provide a name to the mapping and click Finish

d. Drag the source and target

    1. Drag the source from the object explorer into the mapping

    2. Add to mapping dialog box appears

    3. Select Read→As Independent data object(s)

    4. Click OK to close the dialog

    5. The PDO is added with Read_ prefix in the name

e. Drag the target

    1. Drag the target from the object explorer into the mapping

    2. Add to mapping dialog box appears

    3. Select Write and click OK to close the dialog

    4. The PDO is added with Write_ prefix in the name

f. Connect the ports from the source to the target

g. Save the mapping

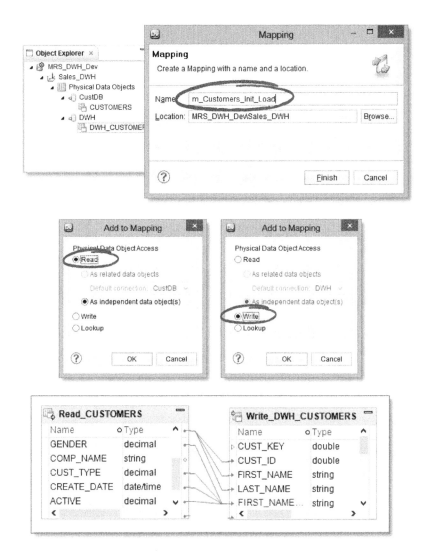

32.4 Mapping execution

Once the mapping is saved, right click on the workspace and click Run Mapping. If you are running a mapping for the first time in this domain, you will be prompted to set a default Data Integration Service. Click OK. In the Data Integration Services dialog box, select a data integration service and click Set as Default and click OK to close. Mapping will run.

Appendix

Informatica's Global Customer Support

Informatica's my support portal can be used to contact Informatica Global Customer Support (GCS) when help is needed. Informatica Support contact details are available at Informatica's website

 To contact support, you will need your project number. Please contact your Informatica Administrator to know your project number

Informatica's my support portal offers great tools to support the Informatica developer community. The following are the activities that you can perform in my support portal:

a.   Raise support tickets and contact Informatica's Global Customer Support

b.   Search knowledgebase for resolutions of any issues you might be facing

c.   Read How-to Libraries for knowledge of performing advanced tasks

d.   Interact with Informatica Developer/Administrator community via discussions

e.   Access product documents

f.   Download Hot-Fixes and important updates

g.   Access Velocity – Informatica's standards

In this appendix, we will look at performing some of these activities. The below snapshot shows how to access knowledgebase and to enter online support.

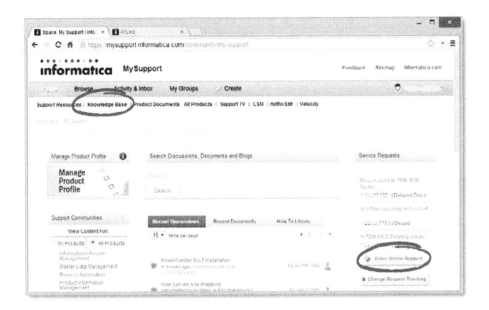

Click the `Enter Online Support` button to enter ATLAS application. To be able to raise a support ticket (known as service requests), your login must be associated with a project. Every service request is associated with a project. ATLAS home screen will show you a quick overview of all your recent support activities. You can see one or more projects your profile is associated with, any currently open service requests or create a new service request. If you have SR# (Service Request number), you can perform a quick search with the option given on the right. You can create two types of SRs:

    a.   Technical SR → Raise any technical questions to the support

b. Admin SR → Raised by administrators to manage online support access and to change the primary contact of the project

c. Shipping SR → Request new software downloads, upgrade licenses

Before creating any SR, make sure that you have selected the correct project first. You can select a project by clicking on the project name in the `Select Project` section. To create a technical SR, simply click the Create Technical SR in the Project Quick Links.

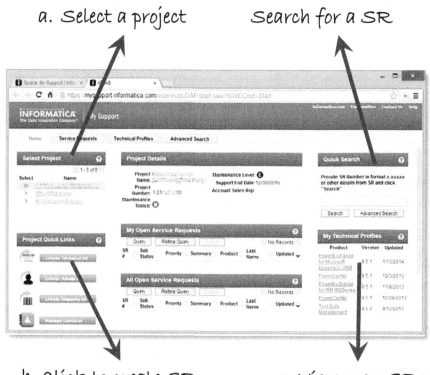

Creating a technical SR

Let us take a look at how to create a technical SR. Below are the steps to create a brand new technical SR:

a. Select a project and click on Create Technical SR

b. Enter Technical Service Request Details screen will appear

    1. Select a product and version

    2. Select a Hotfix if your environment is using one. If your environment is running on PowerCenter Advanced Edition 9.5.1 Hotfix 1, you should select PowerCenter AE 9.5.1 in Product Version and Hotfix 1 in Hotfix. If your environment does not have any hotfix, leave this blank

    3. If your issue is in non-production, select Development/QA as Environment. Otherwise, select Production

    4. Select a priority

        a. P1 – Dev / Prod down

        b. P2 – Dev / Prod Severe impact

        c. P3 – Dev / Prod minor impact

    5. Select a problem type. If the list does not cover your problem, select other

    6. In summary, briefly describe your problem. Do NOT over describe the problem in summary. That is what Description is for.

    7. If you are referring to an error code from session log or service logs, type it in the error code field

    8. Describe your problem in as much detail as possible in the description

    9. If the search knowledgebase is checked, knowledgebase will open in a popup window so that you can search for any known issues/resolutions

c. Click next after filling all the details. Review all the details and click next

d. Once SR is submitted, make sure you attach any documents necessary. Some of the documents that you should consider submitting to Support are:

1. Session Logs, Workflow logs
2. Mapping exports and Workflow exports from Repository Manager
3. For data issues - sample / test data
4. Infrastructure details such as Operating System, version, Nodes, GRID information, etc
5. Service logs provided by your Informatica administrator
6. Core dump files
7. Any error codes you might have received from your database engines/web services

 Do not share any sensitive data / information with support without prior consent within your organization and Informatica

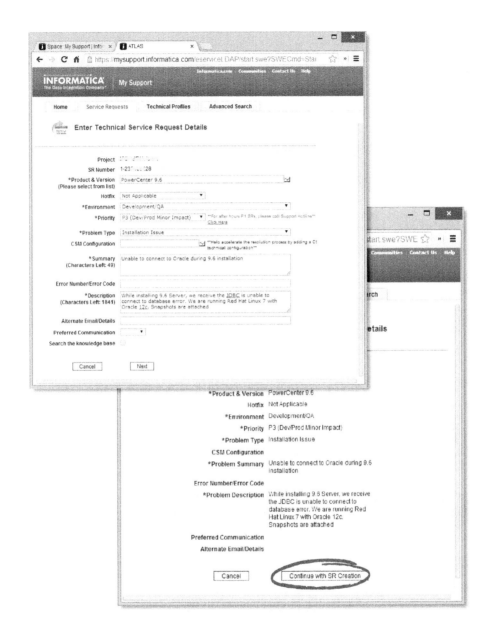

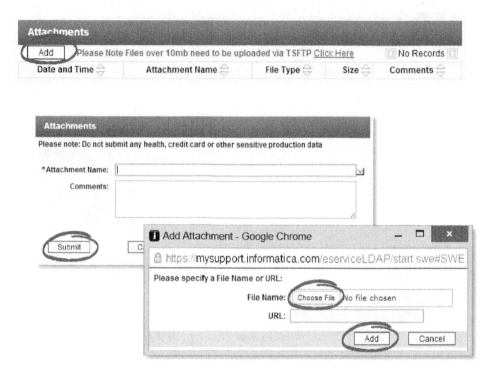

 You will receive an email from support@Informatica.com with the SR number in the subject line when the SR is created or updated by support. You can add your updates by simply responding to the email thread. Do NOT edit the subject line

Support Knowledgebase

Support knowledgebase consists of hundreds of articles that discuss several problems and their resolutions. Support knowledgebase can be accessed by clicking the Knowledgebase link in the support resources on the 'my support' portal. Once the knowledgebase portal is loaded, you can search by the error descriptions, error codes or by knowledgebase ID, if you are aware of that.

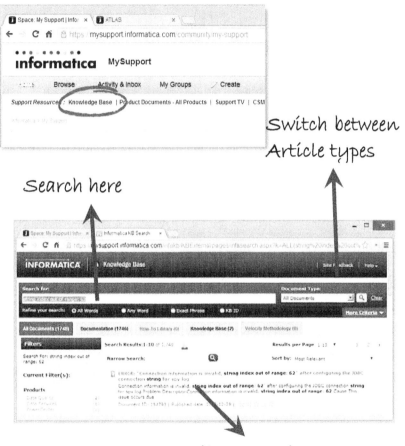

Velocity Methodology

Velocity is Informatica's official governance and best practices methodology. Velocity hosts a wide variety of best practices for all Informatica technologies including PowerCenter. You can find enterprise strategies, life cycles, naming conventions, standards and much more for PowerCenter, B2B, ILM and many other Informatica products. Velocity can be accessed from the 'my support' portal. Within the velocity, you can browse the articles by:

    a.   Enterprise strategies

    b.   Enterprise competencies

    c.   Project types

    d.   Methodologies

Velocity can also be accessed using the famous velocity wheel. The velocity wheel is clickable. Click on the enterprise strategy or competency or the product suite itself. Velocity methodologies discuss various phases of a project life cycle. Velocity recommended lifecycle consists of the following phases:

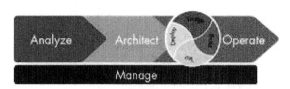

Source: Informatica

Best practices, sample deliverables and templates can also be accessed from the methodology page.

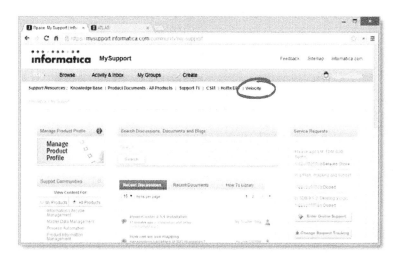

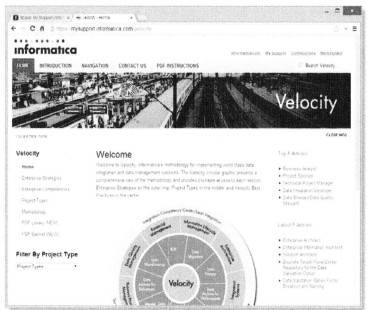

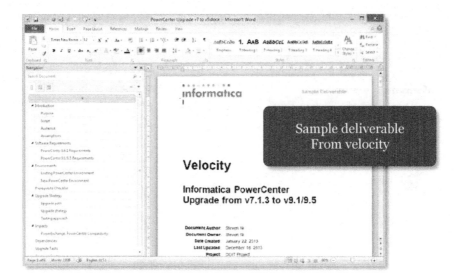

CPSIA information can be obtained at www.ICGtesting.com
Printed in the USA
LVOW03s2315230315

431685LV00005B/33/P